THE GOVE___E_____   ___ __ _____ /ALES

This book is dedicated to all the students, staff, academics, officials, politicians, journalists and administrators that study and try to make sense of the world of Welsh Government and Politics.

THE GOVERNMENT AND POLITICS OF WALES

Russell Deacon, Alison Denton and Robert Southall

EDINBURGH
University Press

Edinburgh University Press is one of the leading university presses in the UK. We publish academic books and journals in our selected subject areas across the humanities and social sciences, combining cutting-edge scholarship with high editorial and production values to produce academic works of lasting importance. For more information visit our website: edinburghuniversitypress.com

Edinburgh University Press Ltd
The Tun – Holyrood Road, 12(2f) Jackson's Entry, Edinburgh EH8 8PJ

Typeset in Humanist by
Servis Filmsetting Ltd, Stockport, Cheshire and
printed and bound in Great Britain by
CPI Group (UK) Ltd, Croydon CR0 4YY

A CIP record for this book is available from the British Library

ISBN 978 0 7486 9973 5 (hardback)
ISBN 978 0 7486 9974 2 (webready PDF)
ISBN 978 0 7486 9975 9 (paperback)
ISBN 978 0 7486 9976 6 (epub)

Online material: https://edinburghuniversitypress.com/book-the-government-and-politics-of-wales.html

Contents

Boxes, Tables and Figure

Tables

Figure

Introduction

For those seeking to understand more about the government and politics of Wales, it is not always that easy a task. If you have looked, you may have struggled to find any material that gives you a comprehensive explanation as to how politics and government work in Wales. It was with this very factor in mind that we set about compiling this text. This book should therefore help you start to understand a lot more about how the modern-day government and politics of Wales functions.

Although the lifespan of the Welsh Assembly now spreads across three decades, there has never been a substantial book that covers the mechanisms and concepts of the modern-day government and politics of Wales. We believe this is the first. It is clearly not the first book to examine Welsh politics or Welsh government, but it is the first to do so in a systematic fashion that covers a wide spectrum of 'Welsh' institutions.

The book starts by reflecting back on the historical journey that Wales has travelled and how this has shaped the governance of the present-day Welsh nation. Across the chapters the key events or personalities that shape Welsh politics and government are noted. It is true that many of the aspects of government and politics in Wales remain similar to and are still influenced by the government and parliament in Westminster or Brussels and Strasbourg. There are, however, growing differences in the way that politics and governance operates in Wales. It is these differences therefore that remain at the heart of this text.

One of the substantial problems a student of Welsh government and politics has is that the system is constantly evolving towards a parliamentary model of governance. This is similar to that in Scotland and Westminster. It may well be that within a short time the Welsh Assembly itself also becomes known as the Welsh Parliament. After all, in already meets in the Senedd (Parliament) building in Cardiff Bay for its plenary sessions. This constant political evolution therefore means that some sections of the text may need updating. So the reader should also ensure that they update themselves with events occurring at the Welsh Assembly and in the Welsh Government.

As authors we have made every effort to ensure that the information we have provided is accurate, and we are grateful in this respect to the Assembly staff, academics, journalists, lobbyists, pressure groups and Welsh politicians who have helped us in gaining this information. Where we may have not got it fully right we would be grateful if people could let us know, so that future editions of the text are even more accurate.

There is, of course, a huge caveat to this text. Welsh politics, like British politics, is entering a period of uncertainty. Brexit and the rapid evolution of the Welsh Assembly itself, means that Welsh politics certainly does not stand still. Bearing this in mind, however, readers should note that this book will provide you with the basics of understanding the distinctiveness and similarities of Welsh and British politics. Like all good students of politics, however, you must ensure that you keep abreast of the developments in Welsh politics by watching and reading the news and exploring the appropriate websites and academic publications and studies. This study does not cover elections after 2016.

Russell Deacon
Alison Denton
Rob Southall

Online material to support this book, in particular related to the case studies and end of chapter questions, can be found at https://edinbur ghuniversitypress.com/book-the-government-and-politics-of-wales.html

Acknowledgements

The authors would like to thank the many people from the Welsh Assembly, Welsh Government and various other bodies and political parties that have helped to provide the information for this book. We would also like to thank Edinburgh University Press for their support in publishing this text and the WJEC Government and Politics subject officer Rachel Dodge for her encouragement in producing this text, as well as Lyn Flight for her copy-editing work.

1

The Evolution of Welsh Devolution

Russell Deacon

Overview

Of the four nation-states that make up the United Kingdom and Northern
Ireland, Wales was the last to have a legislature (a law-making body) that
could create its own laws (primary powers). Known as a distinct nation
for almost two millennia, its closeness to England economically and
politically created a British and Welsh political nervousness that led
to a very slow level of devolution. This first chapter therefore examines the long evolution of Welsh devolution. The story travels from the
Acts of Union under Henry VIII in the fifteenth century to the eventual
establishment of a Welsh Assembly at the end of the twentieth century.
This chapter also explores the relevance of three other factors in the
development of Wales, namely: the monarchy; the Welsh language;

and individuals in the shape three of Wales' political giants that also influenced the United Kingdom's national political scene.

- What were the key political events that shaped Welsh national political distinctiveness prior to the establishment of the Welsh Office in 1964?
- How and why did Welsh political devolution continue to develop from the arrival of the Welsh Secretary in 1964 to the appointment of the Assembly's First Minister in 1999?
- What made the the Labour Party, the dominant political party in Wales, go from being mainly against to being almost wholly for political devolution?
- How Welsh devolution compares with that of Scotland and Northern Ireland?
- The role and nature of the monarchy in Wales, including that of the Prince of Wales.

With the end of the Cold War in 1989 Europe suddenly had a dozen or so newly independent countries. All of these had sudden requirements for new constitutions, new or invigorated national parliaments and voting systems. A decade later it was Wales' turn to have a have new legislature, voting system and the transfer of political sovereignty from one nation to another. This, however, was an evolution of power rather than a revolution transferring new powers to Wales. Therefore, from the outset we should be aware that political change in Wales often occurs over the course of generations, rather than suddenly. So although Wales is an old nation, much older than many other nations, its political progression can be charted over the centuries not just over the decades.

The history of political development in Wales

In 1998, the former Welsh Secretary, Ron Davies, declared of the forthcoming referendum on the Welsh Assembly that 'devolution was a process and not an event'.[1] So it was to prove in practice. When the Welsh Assembly came into being in 1999 therefore, it was also, as we have noted, the culmination of not just one event but almost 150 years of gradual evolution of political devolution. By then, it had been almost half a millennium since Welsh politics had formally been combined with English politics through the Acts of Union, and a century and a quarter had passed since the first Act of Parliament that specifically applied to Wales: the Sunday Closing (Wales) Act 1881. Yet these were just two of the many events in a long, slow period of political evolution that resulted in Welsh political devolution.

Welsh political evolution, 1536–1964

There have been historical accounts of the Welsh and their neighbours interacting almost as long as there has been recorded history in the British Isles. The various tribes of Wales, for instance, were well known during the Roman period, and afterwards during the reign of the Anglo-Saxons the country that we know today had started to look more like its modern-day counterpart. During the reign of Alfred the Great, there had been an intertwining between Welsh and English politics. This occurred as minor Welsh princes sought protection from the Welsh king Rhodri the Great (Mawr),[2] through protective alliances with the Wessex king Alfred the Great. Yet, as these ninth-century events indicated, Wales was never united as one nation, instead, it formed a series of a smaller kingdoms united by the Welsh language, shared Christianity, some common customs and sometimes against a common foe, whether this be the Vikings or the Norman kings. Bit by bit, however, the native Welsh princes faded from history and the decline of the last notable Welsh prince, Owain Glyn Dwr, in 1415 marked a period in which ironically the Welsh Tudor dynasty created a crown that by the end of their reign would see following monarchs rule over all the nations of the British Isles.

With the defeat of Glyn Dwr in the fifteenth century, the whole of Wales was drawn closely into England's sphere. At first this was in a quasi colonial manner, but after the so-called Acts of Union (1536–42) under Henry VIII, Welsh subjects became 'equal' to their counterparts in England. This, however, was on an 'English dominance' basis. For the next five centuries it would mean that English laws, language and customs would be regarded as superior to any the Welsh had before. The Welsh language, although not officially outlawed was not officially encouraged and was kept alive mainly by the mountainous geographical nature of Wales which limited the influx of English migration. Only in 1942 did the Welsh Courts Act recognise the official use of Welsh for the first time since the Acts of Union. Wales had become a series of fifteen county shires similar in structure and nature to those of England.

Until the mid-nineteenth century, therefore, Wales was mostly a geographical expression, reminding people of a distinctive past but not so much a distinctive present. In this it was similar to those kingdoms that had existed during Anglo-Saxon period, such as Mercia and Wessex, historical names on a map. Yet this was all to change in the mid-nineteenth century. As the electoral franchise widened in Wales, so the Liberal Party, the party of the middle and working classes, toppled the Tory dominance of the majority of Welsh parliamentary constituencies.[3] With this political rise came a new brand of Welsh nationalism. Non-conformist religiously, this nationalism was determined to make Wales distinctive by disestablishing the Church of England from Wales, and also shaping Wales into a nation-state in its own right.

The powerful new Welsh Liberal nationalism led, amongst others, by Tom Ellis and David Lloyd George, sought to create a political and social movement that would equal that occurring in Ireland. *Cyrmu Fydd* (Young Wales) was promoted as the answer to a new Liberal call for strong Welsh nationhood and greater political clout in Westminster. Yet the geographical nature of Wales and poor communications meant that there was often little in common between neighbouring counties, let alone between north and south Wales. Journey times in Wales could take many days, and often Ireland or England represented quicker alternatives as centres of administration, trade or legal recourse rather than travelling within Wales itself. Thus, the mainly English-speaking south of Wales felt little in common with the mainly Welsh-speaking north, and therefore they rejected *Cymru Fydd* fearing that the north would dominate the south. Around a century later, these same arguments would help to defeat the St David's Day devolution referendum of March 1979. The Welsh Liberal Nationalists failed to establish *Cymru Fydd* or to gain home rule (a Welsh parliament), but they did manage to establish a number of Welsh institutions (see Table 1.1) and gain disestablishment of the Church in 1920. This started the process of making Wales distinct from England.

It was under the Welsh Liberal Prime Minister, David Lloyd George, that Welsh influence was felt most strongly at Westminster. Prime Minister between 1916 and 1922, Lloyd George, although born in Manchester, was in every other sense Welsh and proud of displaying that fact. After 1922, however, as both he and his fellow Welsh Liberals

Table 1.1 Key events on the road to a Welsh Assembly, 1536–1964

Year and event(s)[a]	
1536–42	Acts of Union between Wales and England were carried out by Henry VIII.
1540s–1860s	Anglicisation of Welsh life, especially among middle and ruling classes.
1830	Abolition of the Court of Great Sessions, the last major Welsh institution left over from the Acts of Union.
1868	Start of fifty years of Welsh political nationalism as a major force in British public life, mainly under the Welsh Liberals.
1886	*Cymru Fydd* (Young Wales) movement started, which sought to promote Welsh devolution.
1889	Welsh Intermediate Education Act acknowledged Wales as a separate administrative region for the first time.
1892	The National Institutions (Wales) Bill 1892, which proposed the creation of a Secretary of State for Wales, was defeated.
1892	Foundation of the University of Wales, whose graduates later went on to campaign for, then create and run, the Welsh Office.
1896	Central Welsh Education Board (CEB) was set up to administer the 1889 Education Act. The first all-Wales public administration body.
1897	Foundation of Welsh Liberal Council, the first Welsh focus within a political party.
1906–21	Golden Era of Welsh Liberal administrative devolution. The period marked devolution of the administration of education, health, agriculture and fisheries to Wales.
1920	Disestablishment of the Church in Wales.
1921	Private Members Bill seeking to introduce a Welsh Secretary failed.
1925	Foundation of *Plaid Genedlaethol Cymru* (later known as *Plaid Cymru*),whose initial aims were to promote increased Welsh devolution.
1938	Pro-Welsh Secretary delegation led by Morgan Jones, Labour MP for Caerphilly, was informed by Neville Chamberlain that he would not allow a Welsh Secretary/Office to be established. He gave the grounds of 'expense, the existing devolved administrative structure being adequate and the lack of a significant distinction existing between Welsh and English public administration'.
1939	Ministry of Health in Wales, headquarters, was built in Cathays Park, Cardiff. The building was later to become the Welsh Office headquarters.
1942	Welsh Courts Act gave official status to the Welsh language on a limited basis for the first time since the Acts of Union.
1943	Prime Minister Winston Churchill rejected further calls by Welsh MPs for a Welsh Secretary.
1944	Welsh Question Time established in the House of Commons.

(Continued)

Table 1.1 (Continued)

Year and event(s)[a]

1945	Devolutionist Welsh Labour Party candidates call for an economic planning authority and a Welsh Secretary via political pamphlet *Llais Llabur* (Voice of Labour).
1945–51	Labour Party remained split on the issue of a Welsh Secretary/Office, with Aneurin Bevan leading the anti- and James Griffiths the pro-groups.
1951	An independent Advisory Council for Wales and Monmouthshire (Welsh Council) established to advise the government on Welsh affairs.
1951	The Conservatives added the remit of Minister for Welsh Affairs to the Home Secretary's portfolio (David Maxwell Fyfe at the time).
1951	The Liberals (the most pro-devolutionary party) are reduced from five to three seats and are no longer the second party of Wales at Westminster. This goes to the Conservatives.
1956	S. O. Davies, Labour MP for Merthyr Tydfil, put forward a Private Member's Bill for a Welsh parliament. The Welsh Labour Party opposed it and the Bill failed.
1959	Labour published *Forward with Labour: Labour's Policy for Wales*, which gave a firm commitment to a Welsh Secretary/Office
1961	The Conservatives established a Welsh Grand Committee (consisting of all Welsh MPs) in order to placate the growing demands for a Welsh Secretary/Office.
1964	The Labour Party repeated the promise of a Welsh Secretary/Office in their general election manifesto, *Signposts for a New Wales*, and win the subsequent general election by a small margin
1964	James Griffiths became Welsh Secretary at the age of seventy-four. Goronwy Daniel joined the Welsh Office from Fuel and Power to become the Welsh Office's first Permanent Under Secretary.
1965	The flooding of the Welsh-speaking village of Capel Celyn for a reservoir for Liverpool, despite the objections of thirty-five out of thirty-six Welsh MPs, raises awareness of the weakness of the political process in Wales and inspires moves towards devolution amongst a number of politicians in all parties.

[a] See Kenneth Morgan, *Rebirth of a Nation: Wales 1880–1980*, Oxford University Press, 1980, p. 45.

stars faded politically, it was the Labour Party that came to dominate Welsh politics. Over the coming century they have held the majority of Welsh MPs, Assembly Members (AMs) and, frequently, Welsh council-lors and European MEPs. It was they that would therefore mainly shape the future direction of the Welsh nation. Yet the Labour Party in Wales was not one that supported what it regarded as the 'narrow' Welsh nationalism of the Welsh Liberals. Instead, it supported an internation-alism linked to the ideology of socialism across the world, rather than developing institutions in just one part of it. Nationalism was regarded either as a dangerous form of extremism or as part of a nineteenth-century romanticism with little part to play in the modern world of the twentieth century. Although this attitude was not true of all Welsh Labour MPs, it was true of most of them, including the most prominent.

Yet whilst for the first half of the twentieth century Labour was reluctant to stimulate Welsh nation pretensions, the most unionist of the British political parties, the Conservatives, were not. In 1905, the Conservative government made Cardiff Wales' first city; another Conservative government would make it the capital city fifty years later. In doing so, they were acting politically in order to gain some of the soft nationalist support for themselves. They started a process of pro-Welsh actions in 1905, which they would repeat again and again if they felt there was a political advantage in doing so. The Labour government under Clement Attlee (1945–51) in contrast had failed to introduce a Welsh Secretary or Welsh Office to match that of Scotland. When they won office in 1951, however, it was the Conservatives who added the remit of Minister for Welsh Affairs to the then Home Secretary's portfolio (David Maxwell Fyfe). The minority party in Wales seemed to have become more Welsh than the majority party. Within the Labour Party this impression helped to galvanise the hand of the pro-devolutionary deputy leader of the party, Jim Griffith (MP for Llanelli). Griffith was able to overcome internal Labour Party opposition and ensure that when they were in power at Westminster once more Labour would introduce a new departmental office for Wales and a cabinet secretary to go with it. Therefore, with their victory in 1964, it was Jim Griffith who became the new Welsh Secretary and was able to help ensure that both the new position and office became a permanent rather than a temporary institution.[4]

The road to the Welsh Assembly: Welsh political devolution, 1964–99

Earlier we noted that the Welsh Liberals' desire for and ability to deliver extensive political devolution was halted when the Labour Party came to political ascendancy in Wales. Eventually, the Labour Party warmed to executive and administrative devolution in the 1960s, but it would be almost half a century before all of types of devolution occurred in Wales. The party's ideological commitment to international socialism and its rejection and then fear of Welsh nationalism after the rise of Plaid

Cymru in the 1960s, meant that it was still mainly opposed further political devolution. This meant the rejection of a potential Welsh Assembly,
first, as a policy ideal and, then, when it was forced onto the political
agenda in late 1970s, with many in the Labour Party in Wales enthusias-
tically supporting a No vote at the ballot box. These prominent No campaigners included notable future Labour Party leader Neil Kinnock and
former Welsh Secretary and future House of Commons Speaker George
Thomas. After the Labour government's 1 March 1979 (St David's Day)
referendum had ended in a dismal failure for the pro-devolutionists, the
prospect of a Welsh Assembly had to rest for a generation.

While the Welsh Liberal Democrats and Plaid Cymru were always
pro-political devolution, neither party formed part of a Westminster
government nor looked likely to do so in the late twentieth century.
Therefore, Welsh political devolution would have to come either from
the Conservatives, who under Margaret Thatcher and then John Major
remained pro-unionist and wholly opposed, or from the Labour Party.
After 1992, under the pro-devolutionist Scottish Labour leader John
Smith, the Labour Party across the United Kingdom committed itself to
a Scottish Parliament and Welsh Assembly. In Scotland, commitment to
a Scottish Parliament outside of the Conservative Party was almost uni-
versal, and the other political parties, aside from the Scottish National
Party (SNP), worked together on achieving this political objective almost
as soon as the Conservatives were back in power in 1979. In Wales,
however, the Labour Party only worked weakly with the other political
parties. It spent most of the period between 1992 and 1997, through the
then Shadow Welsh Secretary Ron Davies, seeking to ensure that there
would be much wider support for a Welsh Assembly than in 1979. The
effect of this lack of cross-party cooperation, however, meant a much
weaker type of political devolution than that proposed for Scotland or
Northern Ireland. This resulted initially therefore in no tax-raising or
primary law-making powers, as in Scotland.

Why did Labour change its mind on devolution?

In 1979, as we have already noted, many prominent figures in the
Labour Party in Wales and many of its elected members and activists
were hostile to devolution. Yet in 1997 the vast majority within the
party supported the Yes campaign. Why was this? The Labour Party had
changed its mind over devolution due to three central reasons:

1. Loss of the Welsh voice at Westminster. There had been four successive Conservative election victories between 1979 and 1992. This meant that despite always electing a Labour majority at elections Wales had Conservative government and a Conservative Welsh secretary of state. Initially, these secretaries had been Welsh or on the' left' or 'wet' side of the Conservative Party, who entered into a more consensual form of politics with much of the Welsh Labour establishment. In May 1993, however, the pro-Thatcherite, Eurosceptic MP for Wokingham, John Redwood, became Welsh Secretary. Redwood's actions during his period in office and the fact that he knew nothing of Wales or Welsh politics prior to his appointment, reminded the Labour Party in Wales of the problems of not having a government of its own. It acted as a handy reminder for why devolution might by a useful counter to Westminster Tory governments.

2. The 'us too argument' that became more prominent among Labour Party members in Wales when they were aware that devolution would be implemented almost certainly within a short space of time in Scotland after any Labour victory.

3. Some individuals in the Labour Party also made a considerable difference. Labour leader John Smith put devolution back onto his party's mainstream policy agenda. Tony Blair, Smith's successor, sought to entrench any new Welsh Assembly through a referendum and, most importantly, ensured that the referendum was held in the immediate aftermath of the Labour Party's 1997 landslide victory. The same election had also removed all anti-devolutionary Conservative parliamentary opposition from Wales, ensuring that all forty Welsh MPs supported pro-devolutionary policies. The most important political figure within Wales, however, was Ron Davies, both as Shadow and actual Welsh Secretary. It was Davies who shaped the future Welsh Assembly so that it both gained the support of Labour and the other pro-devolutionary political parties. It was Davies who ensured that all sides in the Labour Party were on-board for the referendum and that any dissenting voices were 'kept quiet' during the referendum campaign.

Moving over to a Welsh Assembly

From the arrival of the first Labour Welsh Secretary in 1964 until the successful Assembly referendum in 1997 each Welsh Secretary, almost without exception, sought to expand the role and function of the Welsh Office and that of the office holder. As we shall see in Chapter 3, the Welsh secretaries were often the most junior members of the Cabinet, but they were also ambitious and it was this ambition that helped to build up the Welsh Office into a Civil Service department that was in turn capable of servicing the new Welsh Assembly. This political ambition laid the groundwork for distinctive Welsh policy. It ranged from establishing a national educational curriculum for Wales (*Curriculum Cymreig*[5]) to ensuring that Wales went from a system of two-tier local government to one of unitary authorities.

The process of Wales being recognised as a nation-state

In the United Kingdom we have an uncodified constitution. This means that our constitution is not contained in one single document. For those countries with a codified constitution, the nature of the state's component parts, their roles and functions are normally clearly defined. This is not the case in the United Kingdom. It is not easy therefore to categorise all the constitutional sources that refer to or define the nature of the Welsh nation within the United Kingdom. This means that we must seek guidance from the various Acts of Parliament or other historical events in order define Wales as a nation-state. Many of these Acts, events, conventions and other constitutional sources that define Wales as a nation-state with ever growing powers of political sovereignty are noted in Tables 1.1 and 1.2.

Thus, we can say from the British constitution that through statute or convention the Westminster Parliament and Whitehall recognise Wales as a nation-state separate from England for many aspects of governance and legislation. Consequently, by these constitutional measures alone, Wales can be seen as a nation-state, with a number of elements of its own political sovereignty. This means, therefore, that it is not just a region of a larger state, despite the fact that it is frequently still defined as such in both UK and international documents and publications. It is recognised at a nation internationally, for instance, in sport such as football, rugby and the Commonwealth Games, with the same status as any other sovereign nation. Although unlike other sovereign nations, it does not have its own legal sovereignty, which means it cannot sign treaties or engage in other international obligations without going through the UK government. Although both the Welsh Secretary and First Minister

Table 1.2 Important events on the road to a Welsh Assembly, 1964–99[a]

1964–79	A succession of Welsh Secretaries brought in new responsibilities; created new public bodies, ranging from the Welsh Development Agency to the Wales Tourist Board; then established an annual Welsh block grant from Westminster to fund the duties of the Welsh Office in 1979. At the same time, the Barnett formula was established in order to determine any additional expenditure to Wales on top of this Welsh block grant
1979	St David's Day referendum for a Welsh Assembly was defeated by five to one.
1979	The Welsh Affairs Select Committee was established, in part to fill the void left by the failure to establish a Welsh Assembly
1983	The General Election manifestos of the Welsh Liberal/SDP Alliance and Plaid Cymru made it clear that both political parties still supported the idea of a Welsh parliament.
1979–87	Labour ignored the issue of political devolution for Wales in manifestos. In 1987 they lost the General Election, which caused them to re-examine the concept of a Welsh Assembly.
May 1987	Future prominent Labour figures Jon Owen Jones and Rhodri Morgan were elected as Labour MPs. Rhodri Morgan became a member and Jon Owen Jones the Chairman of the Campaign for a Welsh Assembly. Their drive pushed the issue of a Welsh Assembly further up the Labour Party agenda.
Oct. 1987	A working group was appointed by the Labour Party to look at the future of local government in Wales. When it reported back in 1989, it recommended the establishment of a Welsh Assembly.
1992	In their General Election manifestos the Labour Party, Plaid Cymru and the Liberal Democrats all stated they would establish a Welsh Assembly/ parliament.
1994	The Wales Labour Party established an internal Constitutional Policy Commission, which produced a series of reports over the following years, endorsed by their party conference, detailing how the Welsh Assembly would be run.
1996	Ron Davies, Shadow Welsh Secretary, announced that the new assembly would be elected by a proportional representation electoral (PR) system, and would be introduced only after a referendum.
March 1997	Ron Davies, the Labour 'leader' in Wales, and Alex Carlile, the Welsh Liberal Democrat leader, signed a joint declaration committing both parties to campaign for a yes vote in any referendum.
May 1997	The Labour Party won the General Election. In July, they published a White Paper, *A Voice for Wales*, which detailed the nature of the new assembly.
Sept. 1997	The Welsh Assembly referendum was held on 18 September. Half the Welsh counties voted No, but the numerical superiority of the other eleven allowed a narrow majority for Yes. The final vote was 50.3 per cent Yes and 49.7 per cent No, with just over half of the Welsh electorate voting.

(Continued)

Table 1.2 (Continued)

July 1998	The Government of Wales Act gained Royal Assent. The only major difference between the Act and the White Paper, *A Voice for Wales*, was that the assembly would now be run on a cabinet system instead of the previous model designed on local government committees.
May 1999	The first elections to the Assembly were held. Labour gained twenty-eight seats, Plaid Cymru seventeen, the Conservatives nine and Liberal Democrats six. Alun Michael became the First Secretary and Lord Dyfydd Elis Thomas its Presiding Officer.

[a] See Russell Deacon, *Devolution in the United Kingdom*, Edinburgh University Press, 2012; Leighton Andrews. *Wales Says Yes*, Seren, 1999.

can sign treaties on Wales' behalf with the consent of the Foreign and Commonwealth Office.

The principality that isn't

Yet, because Wales is part of the United Kingdom with its legal system and much of its political sovereignty still resting in another capital and another nation, that is, London, England, there continues to be some confusion over Wales' own status as a nation-state. Historically, Wales has been defined as a 'principality', but this is not actually the case. Although it is true that on and off there has been a prince/princess of Wales since the sixteenth century, Wales itself is not actually recognised as a principality internationally. This is because under international law a principality is a sovereign state, whose ruling monarch is a prince or a princess with an executive role in its administration. Neither the current nor previous princes/princesses of Wales have had any role in administrative control over Wales. This means that the term 'principality' has become archaic in constitutional terms.[6] Whereas it is true that a Principality of Wales did exist at times between 1216 and 1542, its area and nature were significantly different to that of modern Wales. Therefore, it may well be that the only part of Wales recognised internationally as a principality is the rugby stadium of that name in the centre of Cardiff.

Thus, it would appear that Wales is not a principality, but it is a nation-state without its own legal sovereignty. Just like the other three nation-states in the United Kingdom, ultimate legal sovereignty remains in London rather than their own capitals. Part of the uncodified British constitution is the convention that a previous Westminster Parliament/government cannot bind is successor legally. This means, therefore, that although Wales has been seen as a separate nation across much of its history it remains within the power of Westminster to end this at any stage or to redefine the very nature of Wales. Without a codified constitution therefore the nature of the Welsh nation-state will always remain in limbo, dependent on the desire of the current Westminster Parliament to continue its existence.

The comparison between devolution in Scotland and Northern Ireland and the reasons for the slower Welsh development

Devolution arrived in the United Kingdom and Northern Ireland at the end of last millennium. It was in Wales, however, that there was both the least support and the experience of dealing with devolution as an administrative and political concept. Until 1972, Northern Ireland had its own law-making parliament, known as Stormont after its geographical location. In Scotland, there had been a parliament until the Act of Union with England and Wales in 1707, after which it dissolved itself and united to form the Parliament of Great Britain. However, because Scottish law and many of its own institutions continued in existence, it made the state culturally and politically distinctive from the rest of the United Kingdom. When offered the chance of establishing a new legislature in 1979, the Scottish people voted in favour of doing so, but not by the required electoral threshold imposed in order to bring the legislature into being. After the failure to establish a legislature a political cross-party National Convention in Scotland was established. This gained widespread support for a Scottish parliament to be established as soon as a Labour government was returned to power. None of this historic legacy or cross-party enthusiasm for political devolution existed in Wales. In Scotland, the September 1997 referendum on whether to have a parliament was endorsed by almost three in four Scottish voters. The Welsh Assembly referendum, in contrast, only passed by a narrow majority of a few thousand votes. It seemed that there was still much reluctance to embrace a new Welsh legislature across much of Wales.

The reluctance to move forward on continued Welsh devolution continued within significant elements of both Labour and Conservative party members, local government and Westminster MPs, even following devolution. As a consequence, this reluctance slowed down sill further the evolution of Welsh devolution. The overall result of this was therefore that while Scottish devolution continued to evolve at considerable speed, even after four terms the powers of the Welsh Assembly had still not equalled those of the Scottish Parliament in 1999 let alone that parliament's subsequent evolution of powers.[7] So what were the principal reasons for this reluctance? They appear to be:

1. The 'conservative' and unionist nature of the dominant political parties in Wales, that is, both Labour and Conservative, meant that there was resistance to enhanced devolution in order that it did not reduce the power of Westminster.
2. The weaker strength of the strongly pro-devolutionary parties in Wales, Plaid Cymru and the Welsh Liberal Democrats, compared with their counterparts in Scotland. the SNP and Scottish Liberal Democrats. This is particularly notable with respect to the role that Scottish Liberal Democrats played in the former Westminster coalition government (including holding the Cabinet Scottish Secretary post), the dramatic rise of the SNP from 2011 onwards and the demise of other political parties in Scotland.
3. The weaker Welsh economy, which ties it more closely into the need to be supported by the English economy than does the economy of Scotland. Welsh politicians therefore lack the self-confidence of their Scottish counterparts in pushing forward with further devolution.
4. The lack of a widespread civic society and media in Wales, which is not comparable with that of the other nations of the United Kingdom. This means that there is not the same civil driving force to support further devolution among the wider public in Wales.

While political evolution in Wales has been gradual, other elements of the British state have also slowly sought to adapt. In this respect there are still some other elements of the constitutional set-up that differ for Wales. With the monarchy, for instance, there are still no royal palaces in Wales, as there are in the other three UK nations. The role of monarchy itself is long-established in Wales and is spread throughout the nation, but at the same time it is evolving in order to deal with the new political structures (see Box 1.1).

Box 1.1 The monarchy in Wales

It is Clarence House, London, that is the official residence of the Prince of Wales and the Duchess of Cornwall, not a building in the Welsh capital

Cardiff. In fact, for nearly five centuries the royal family had no Welsh base at all. This changed in April 2007, when the Prince of Wales bought a private residence in Llwynywermod, near the village of Myddfai, Llandovery, Carmarthenshire. This is now used as a base for the Prince's Welsh tours and is the only royal residence in Wales.

As Welsh devolution has progressed, the interaction between the monarchy and Wales has by necessity increased. It has gone beyond the ceremonial and into the constitutional/political arena. Welsh politicians now have an increasing interaction with the monarchy on a regular basis. Welsh government ministers, for instance, are now officially appointed by the Crown. Welsh legislation in turn is given royal assent in order to become law.

The visits of monarchy to Wales are comparatively rare, but they also have a network of royal deputies to undertake their royal role for them on a more regular basis. These are known as lord lieutenants and are royal rather than political appointments. In Wales, as elsewhere in the United Kingdom, these lord lieutenants act as the personal representative of the monarch across Welsh counties in an unpaid capacity. Although they wear the same ceremonial dress as their counterparts elsewhere in the United Kingdom, their uniforms are distinguished by the addition of Prince-of-Wales feathers. Originally, they were responsible for organising the county's militia, ready for times of war or civil disturbance. Today, however, their role is mainly ceremonial and the monarch normally appoints a military officer, nobleman, businessperson or other prominent person in the county to the post. Their royal duties include arranging royal visits and escorting the royal visitors, presenting medals and awards on behalf of the sovereign and even advising on the Honours nominations themselves. They in turn can appoint deputies.

Lord lieutenants are also supported by another royal appointment, that of high sheriffs.[8] They play a close role in supporting the systems of law and order and dealing with the visits of high court judges. Their appointment is through a nomination process determined through the Presiding Judge of the Circuit and the Privy Council

In 1996, Welsh local government went from a system of eight county counties to twenty-two new ones. The lord lieutenants, however, remained appointed to the eight, now extinct, 'preserved counties', as do the high sheriffs, for instance, Gwynedd and South Glamorgan.

In a nation that is not overtly royalist in nature and whose politicians often display an undercurrent of republicanism, the royal structures within Wales are as strong as anywhere else in the United Kingdom. As political sovereignty continues to develop in Wales, so it is likely that the royal presence will also increase at all levels to compensate for these changes.

Wales' historic legacy at Westminster: the extent and nature of senior Welsh political figures/leaders at Westminster across the twentieth century

A lot of this book concentrates upon politicians who have become prominent in the Welsh Assembly. Yes, Wales has had other political leaders that have been prominent on the national and international stage, and it is often forgotten that three Prime Ministers in the twentieth century held Welsh constituencies: David Lloyd George, Ramsay MacDonald and James Callaghan. We should also, therefore, perhaps spend a little time reminding ourselves that as Welsh politicians are also elected to the Westminster Parliament they have also had an impact on national politics which goes beyond the most obvious holders of the post of Welsh Secretary and their role in the Cabinet. From the perspective of being a Welsh politician, rather than a politician elected in Wales, David Lloyd George, Aneurin Bevan and Neil Kinnock are arguably the most prominent Welsh politicians of the twentieth century, and therefore have some more detailed biographies in Boxes 1.2–1.4. Aside from these, however, what was the impact of other Welsh politicians at Westminster? In respect of measuring success we need to note that there are four posts that have traditionally been regarded as the most senior in the UK government. These are the Prime Minister, Foreign Secretary, Chancellor of the Exchequer and Home Secretary. Prior to 1908, there had been some politicians with Welsh constituencies who had held the posts of Chancellor and Home Secretary, but this year marks the rise of David Lloyd George onto the political stage and the of the two subsequent Welsh constituency MPs who would follow in his footsteps as Prime Minister.

Welsh politicians have held these prominent four posts some fourteen times (Table 1.3). We need to note, however, that some of these MPs held more than one post over time. Labour's James Callaghan holds the record, having held all four posts. This, therefore, means in reality that only eight 'Welsh' MPs held these top posts over seventy-one years, only five of which, however, also held Welsh constituencies. So although

Table 1.3 The four senior government posts held by a Welsh MP or prominent Welsh-born politician, 1908–79[a]

Post/Welsh MPs	Labour	Conservative	Liberal
Prime Minister	2[b]	0	1
Foreign Secretary	2	0	0
Chancellor of the Exchequer	2	1	2
Home Secretary	3	1	1

[a] Does not include Welsh Conservatives, Geoffrey Howe, Foreign Secretary and Chancellor of the Exchequer, or Michael Howard, Home Secretary, who did not represent Welsh constituencies. Equally, Michael Heseltine, although Deputy Prime Minister, did not hold any of the four top offices of state or a Welsh seat.
[b] Ramsay MacDonald was later expelled from the Labour Party while Prime Minister, but this was not during his tenure as the MP for Aberafon.

five 'Welsh' MPs were Home Secretary, three of these, Merlyn Rees, Roy Jenkins and Gwilym Lloyd-George, all held their constituency seats outside Wales during their tenure in office.[9]

Of the parts of Wales that have proved to be the most fruitful in terms of producing national politicians, it is southeast Wales that comes to prominence. Monmouthshire is perhaps the Welsh county with the greatest record in producing Westminster cabinet members. As well as McKenna, Aneurin Bevan and Neil Kinnock, Labour Chancellor and Home Secretary Roy Jenkins were also born in the same constituency. It was this same seat that would also elect the Conservative MP Peter Thorneycroft (Monmouth MP 1945–66). He remains the most successful member of his party elected from Wales, and is also one of the most prominent in the world of business. The Eton-educated Chancellor of the Exchequer was also the long-serving president of the Board of Trade (Business Secretary) between 1951 and 1957, and became Margaret Thatcher's chief aide as chairman of the Conservative Party from 1975 to 1981.

> **Box 1.2 David Lloyd George, 1st Earl Lloyd-George of Dwyfor, 1863–1945**
>
> Although he was born in Manchester of Welsh parents, David Lloyd George was brought up in Llanystumdwy on the Llŷn Peninsula in North Wales by his Welsh-speaking mother and uncle, Lloyd, his father having died when he was a young child. By the turn of the twentieth century, the Lloyd George, the MP for Caernarfon Boroughs, had become one of the dominant Welsh Nationalist Radicals in the Liberal Party in Wales, promoting hopes of Welsh

home rule (a Welsh parliament) and political independence not seen since the Middle Ages. In the event, Lloyd George concentrated his efforts and talents instead on establishing the welfare state: old age pension and the start of the National Health Service, constitutional change to reduce the power of the House of Lords, and tax reforms that would underpin the welfare state. Through his posts as Chancellor of the Exchequer, Minister of Munitions and then Prime Minister, Lloyd George was instrumental in winning the First World War and dealing with the immediate postwar consequences, including the Treaty of Versailles, the establishment of new nations in the Middle East, including Palestine, and home rule and the partition of Ireland.

Lloyd George was also a controversial figure throughout his lifetime and beyond due to his personal life, accumulation of personal wealth through dubious means and forming a coalition with the Conservatives that split the Liberal Party in two. Nevertheless, he remains one of the most well-known and admired Welsh politicians not only in the United Kingdom, but across the world today.

Aside from the four prominent posts, it is also worth noting that Labour MP George Thomas, later Viscount Tonypandy, was also the Speaker of the House of Commons between 1976 and 1983 during the turbulent period of the end of James Callaghan's government and the first term of Margaret Thatcher's Conservative Party. Female Welsh MPs have been less noteworthy in highly prominent posts, however. No Welsh female constituency MP or peer has served above the level of Minister of State. The Liberal MP, Megan Lloyd George, did become deputy leader of the Liberal Party and a number of Labour MPs became Ministers of State. These ranged from Eirene White, a minister at the Foreign Office in 1966, to Baroness Kinnock, Minister of State in the same department in 2010. The failure to climb to the final rung on government ladder, however, for females has not been helped by:

1. the lack of female MPs in Wales until relatively recently, meaning that there were simply not that many women to be available for such posts in the first place;
2. the reluctance of various governments to nominate any Welsh MPs for top posts, let alone women;
3. the failure of the Conservatives to elect female Welsh constituency MPs and, therefore, to have none to nominate when they were in power; and

4. the dominance of Welsh politics by the Labour Party, meaning that only during Labour governments are most Welsh MPs likely to stand a chance of getting a government post.

For a party that has dominated Welsh politics for almost a century and produced two Prime Ministers with parliamentary Welsh seats (Ramsay MacDonald and James Callaghan) during the twentieth century, there were also some notable national figures that did not quite reach the most senior positions in the UK government (Boxes 1.3 and 1.4).

Box 1.3 Aneurin 'Nye' Bevan, 1897–1960

Aneurin Bevin was born in Tredegar, Ebbw Vale, the son of a coal miner, who became a champion of social rights and socialism. He did poorly at school, but was able to become head of the local miners lodge by the age of nineteen. It was there that he established himself as a renowned orator and 'troublemaker'. Bevan then spent periods studying at the Central Labour College in London, and then seeking employment during the economic slump of the 1920s. In 1928, his political career kicked off when he was elected to Monmouthshire County Council and the following year was elected as the MP for Ebbw Vale.

During the 1930s, Bevan strongly advocated the socialist cause both inside and outside Parliament, in the process becoming a political foe of Winston Churchill but nevertheless supporting him as Prime Minister over Neville Chamberlain. During the 1930s, Bevan remained actively anti-fascist to the extent that his activities and campaigns got him expelled from the Labour Party for a time. Bevan believed that the Second World War would lead to a better society for the working class in the United Kingdom, and after Labour's 1945 General Election landslide became a key figure in achieving this aim. Labour Prime Minister Clement Attlee appointed Aneurin Bevan as Minister of Health, with a remit that also covered housing in 1945. It was Bevan that undertook the immense task of creating a National Health Service, which came into existence in 1948. This is still seen as one of the greatest social welfare achievements of all time. Bevan remained a controversial figure, national campaigner on issues relating to peace and war, ideologue and socialist political icon of both his time and today. Aneurin Bevan remains a central iconic Welsh Labour political figure more than half a century after his death with a think tank, health board, hospital and many other public buildings and streets bearing his name.

Box 1.4 Neil Kinnock, Baron Kinnock, 1942–

Like Aneurin Bevan, Neil Kinnock was also born in Tredegar, Ebbw Vale. Kinnock graduated from Cardiff University and was a tutor in the Workers' Education Association before becoming the MP for Bedwellty (later Islwyn) in 1970. A fierce opponent of Welsh devolution in 1979, he became Shadow Education Secretary under fellow Welsh MP, James Callaghan's leadership of the Labour Party in 1979. It was during this period that he established himself as 'left winger' and fierce critic of Conservative Prime Minister Margaret Thatcher. Following their defeat in the 1983 General Election, Kinnock took over the leadership of the Labour Party from another Welsh MP for the neighbouring parliamentary seat of Ebbw Vale, Michael Foot.

Over the next decade Kinnock set about modernising the Labour Party and tackling the Militant Socialists both within and outside his party, which had prevented the Labour Party from moving to the centre and to a position that made it more electable. Although Labour never won office under his leadership, he is credited with rebuilding the party so that it was able to gain office under Tony Blair in 1997.

In 1995 Kinnock resigned from Westminster in order to become a European Commissioner, and in 2005 he was ennobled to become a member of the House of Lords. Kinnock helped to establish a political family, with his wife Glenys becoming a Welsh Labour MEP and then as Baroness Kinnock serving as a minister under Prime Minister Gordon Brown; his son Stephen became the MP for Aberafon. Despite never having achieved a position in government in the UK, Neil Kinnock became one of the most prominent Welsh politicians of his era.

Despite this substantial historic record of numerous Welsh Westminster politicians holding senior posts across British history, there have been no recent examples for over a generation of Welsh politicians gaining the top posts. In the four decades since James Callaghan left 10 Downing Street in 1979 there have been no Welsh constituency MPs from any party to hold one of the four main offices of state. Although Neil Kinnock became the most prominent Welsh politician when he headed the Labour Party (1983–92) (Box 1.4), there has been no repeat of this since then.

Conclusion

In this chapter we have established that the current government and politics of Wales did not arrive suddenly. Just like the wider politics of the rest of the United Kingdom, it was established over many centuries. For almost all of the Welsh devolutionary timeline, it was the galvanising effect of politicians in Wales who had the vision to inspire and persuade others that devolution could succeed. At the same time, cautious unionist politicians in Wales and Westminster did much to stop or slow devolution down. This means that it still does not equal the scale or scope of devolution across other parts of the United Kingdom.

In Chapter 3 we will pick up again on those aspects of the historical journey concerning Welsh political evolution, although this time it will be specifically on the story of Wales and Westminster. The continuation of this story will make it even clearer that Wales continues to evolve politically, often in unexpected and contradictory ways.

Questions for discussion

1. To what extent is it true to say that the Welsh devolution has been an evolutionary rather than a revolutionary process?
2. Illustrate the key factors that made the Labour Party in Wales reverse its opposition to devolution.
3. To what extent is it true to define Wales internationally as a principality?

Case study: Welsh political leaders[10]

Reviewing the three case studies on David Lloyd George, Aneurin Bevan and Neil Kinnock (Boxes 1.2, 1.3 and,1.4) and the surrounding text address the following questions:

1. Define the leadership elements that all of the three leaders have in common. In your answer you should consider factors such as charisma, oratory and other leadership skills.
2. Choose a current figure in the Welsh government and compare their biography against that of the three in the case study. Note down any similarities and differences and indicate the possible reasons for this.

Welsh Politics, Ideology and Political Parties

Alison Denton and Russell Deacon

Chapter contents

Overview

The 1888 edition of the *Encyclopaedia Britannica* entry on 'Wales' reads, 'For Wales, See England'. Few could believe this to be the case today. Politics within Wales has always been slightly distinct from politics in the rest of the UK but, for largely historical reasons, Wales has struggled to have its national politics regarded as being on a par with that in Scotland or Northern Ireland. For many centuries Wales was viewed politically by the ruling class of the United Kingdom (which included many Welsh gentry) as an addendum to England, especially after the Acts of Union in the 1530s. It was not until the devolution referendum in 1997 that Wales finally re-established its own political institutions with some separation from Westminster. That is not to say, however, that Welsh politics failed to develop in the intervening years, as we saw in Chapter 1. On the contrary, developments such as the establishment of regular Eisteddfodau, the disestablishment of the Anglican Church in Wales, the founding of Plaid Cymru and the establishment of the Welsh Office showed the desire in Wales for a separateness, a recognition of the issues that make Wales distinct from the rest of the United Kingdom. The opportunity to fulfil that desire for separateness and to develop Welsh politics within the context of Wales, and separate to but also within the context of UK politics, came with the establishment of the National Assembly for Wales, following the devolution referendum result in 1997.

Politics in Wales has been dominated by the left, and can be is illustrated by considering that the last time the Conservative Party won a higher percentage of the vote in Wales than in England at a General Election was in 1859. Early on the Liberal Party dominated Welsh politics, winning a majority of seats and votes in Wales at every election from 1885 to 1910. This Liberal hegemony was broken by the rise of the Labour Party nationally after 1922. As a result, Wales has also seen prolonged Conservative Party weakness, and has experienced a dominant party political system for the last 150 years of either the Liberals or Labour parties. This distinctiveness and a number of others that today differentiate Wales politically from England, are covered in this chapter.

Key issues to be covered in this chapter

- What is the 'Three Wales Model' and is it still relevant today?
- How do you define the political parties in Wales with respect to the political spectrum?
- Have there ever been any Welsh political ideologists that have influenced political parties in Wales and elsewhere?
- Why does the political left dominate Welsh politics and what is its appeal?
- What explains the recent slide in support for Labour in Wales?
- Is the Welsh language still a political issue?
- What is the nature of nationalism and unionism in Wales?
- Why is Plaid Cymru technically an ethnoregionalist party and not a nationalist one?

- Who are the main political parties in Wales?
- What is an independent?
- How do the political parties elect their leaders?
- What are the leaders' roles?
- What is the nature of political party membership and the wider structures of the political parties?
- How do Welsh political parties create their manifestos and their policy?
- How does the newest political party in Wales, UKIP, operate?

The 'Three Wales Model'

Probably the most important specifically Welsh political science determinant of both voting habits and the political party split in Wales has been determined by what is referred to as the 'Three Wales Model'. The characteristics of Welsh identity and political structure have been the subject of debate for some decades. For most of the late twentieth century, Welsh identity and the political divisions underlying it were explained in terms of geography in this 'Three Wales Model' developed by Dr Denis Balsom in 1985.[1] This model produced the three politically distinctive geographical areas in Wales:

1. *Y Fro Gymraeg*: northwest and west-central Wales. This area has the highest percentage of first-language Welsh speakers and is strongly identified as 'Welsh'.
2. *Welsh Wales*: The south Wales valleys through to the west of the Gower Peninsula. This area has a very high percentage of people identifying as Welsh and the highest percentage of people born in Wales, but is not particularly strongly Welsh-speaking. It is overwhelmingly working class with a weak economic base.
3. *British Wales*; northeast Wales, the Marches and west-central Wales, Cardiff and the Vale of Glamorgan, and Pembrokeshire. This area has higher percentages of people born outside Wales, less dominant Welsh identification and lower numbers of Welsh-speakers than the other two areas. It has a greater predominance of middle-class voters.

This 'Three Wales Model' divide also seems consistently to define Wales politically – Plaid Cymru do well in Y Fro Gymraeg, whilst the south Wales valleys (Welsh Wales) are a Labour stronghold. British

Wales tends to vote Conservative or Liberal Democrat. The validity of this model appears to be confirmed by the devolution referendum result in 1997, with Y Fro Gymraeg and most of Welsh Wales voting Yes, while British Wales voted No. At first glance, therefore, it would seem that the Three Wales Model was accurate and capable of explaining the voting behaviour of different regions of Wales.[2]

Is the Three Wales Model still valid?

At each election the accuracy of the Three Wales Model is explored. Therefore, for instance, the validation of the Three Wales Model was questioned in the context of the 1997 Welsh Assembly referendum. The former head of the Institute of Welsh Affairs, John Osmond, pointed out that the greatest shift in opinion towards devolution occurred between 1979 and 1997 in English-speaking areas of Welsh Wales, and that more Yes votes were cast in some areas of British Wales than in areas of Welsh Wales in 1997. Overall, 39 per cent of the Yes votes were cast in the counties that ended up as more than 50 per cent No. The No counties of Conwy, Wrexham, Pembrokeshire and Powys had larger Yes votes than the Yes counties of Merthyr Tydfil, Blaenau Gwent, Anglesey and Ceredigion. Osmond concluded that the geographical area Three Wales Model was less significant than commentators had believed. He also shows that age was more of a factor than geographical area in 1997. People under forty-five when polled were more likely to vote Yes by a ratio of three to two, while those over forty-five when polled were more likely to vote No by a similar ratio. The result in the end was so close because younger people are less likely to turn out to vote.[3]

Analysis of elections since 1997 seems to suggest that the Three Wales Model, with its emphasis on social class, language and location, is inadequate in fully explaining contemporary politics and identity in Wales. Despite this fact, there is still a distinctiveness to Welsh politics: the Conservative Party and Liberal Democrats tend to underperform in Wales compared with the UK as a whole; Labour in turn has tended to dominate; Plaid Cymru offers a nationalist perspective that is popular with a significant section of the electorate in Wales; and the fortunes of other parties, such as UKIP, fluctuate. Recent research suggests the importance of valence issues (a political issue in which voters share a common interest, such as a successful NHS) in shaping the response of the Welsh electorate to parties and their leaders, and in this Wales has much in common with the rest of the United Kingdom. Welsh politics and identity are distinctive, but the reasons for this seem to lie in choice-based theories that also apply more generally across the United Kingdom,[4] rather than in any class, language or geographical explanation peculiar to Wales alone, as the Three Wales Model suggested. Therefore, Balsom's model could be said to be weaker, but still provides us with some indication of the distinctiveness of Welsh politics, albeit to a lesser degree than when it was formed in 1985.

The nature and extent of the political spectrum in Wales

When you wish to determine where a party sits politically you examine the political spectrum. The origins of this term date back to the era of the French Revolution, where in front of the Assembly's Speaker the aristocracy sat on the right of the speaker and the commoners on the left. From this seating derived both the terms and the ideology of the left and right wings in politics. Since then the spectrum has been defined so that the extreme left represents those types of ideology associated with Communism (collectivism, authoritarianism) and the extreme right with fascism and extreme nationalism (advocating individualism and/or authoritarianism). Ideologically, the further a party moves to the left, the more state intervention it endorses and anti-capitalist it becomes; the further to the right, the more pro-capitalist and anti-state it becomes.

In Wales there are no mainstream political parties either on the far right or left. The political parties therefore mainly fall around the centre/centre right and centre left. The Welsh Liberal Democrats are classified as being centre or slightly centre left; Labour, the Greens and Plaid Cymru are all on the left (all these parties also stress their socialist credentials). The Welsh Conservatives are on the right and UKIP further to the right. All the main Welsh political parties go back and forth either closer to the centre or further to the left or right, depending on both the members and leadership. None, however, have crossed from right to left or vice versa.

Devolution initially saw a generally leftward shift in the axis of Welsh politics, but then in 2016, with the breakthrough of UKIP, Welsh voters started supporting the parties on the right of the political spectrum to a greater degree. Another major result of devolution has been that the parties in Wales have found their own voice ideologically, and it is a voice that is often quite different to that of the same party on a UK-level. Welsh Labour, for instance, has consistently backed policies in Wales that are at time at variance with those of the UK Labour Party and in government in Westminster. Examples include Welsh Labour support for comprehensive education in Wales and its resistance to greater privatisation in the health service. Welsh Labour stands firmly on the left of the spectrum, and this has altered very little under successive Labour leaders in Wales. The Welsh Liberal Democrats also differed from the party in London on issues such as tuition fees for university students.

How is the political spectrum apparent in Wales?

To those studying or interacting with politics and political parties, the political spectrum acts as a handy shorthand to determine the ideology of a political party and its support base. Thus, when it comes to working together we can see that Plaid Cymru's position on the spectrum is similar to that of Welsh Labour. It is similar in that it is a party firmly of the left, albeit with very distinct differences in policy on issues such as nuclear power and independence for Wales. The similarities between the two parties allowed them to work in coalition between 2007 and 2011. They were not so close, however, that their differences did not later erupt into conflict and prevent the early election of a new First Minister by the Assembly immediately following the Assembly elections of 2016. Here Plaid Cymru leader Leanne Wood said that she could not see how her party could be in the business of propping up Labour in any way despite ideological closeness.[5]

The political spectrum in Wales is varied, from left to right. What is most noticeable, however, is the absence of any large, successful party of the centre. Since the early 1920s, the Welsh Liberals have been the third, fourth or even fifth party of Welsh politics, often just holding on by one seat. The success of their counterparts in Scotland, Northern Ireland or England has eluded the Welsh party to a large extent. In a crowded political field in recent years it has become increasingly difficult for them to be clear about their message and programme. The reduction of their AMs to just one in 2016 revealed the extent of the meltdown of liberalism in Wales, a phenomenon reflected in the rest of the United Kingdom. Their determination, however, to be the United Kingdom's most strident anti-Brexit party may make them much more ideologically distinct in the future.

The rise in support for the political right in Wales has been something of a surprise to those who observe Welsh politics. Wales has traditionally been regarded as a centre left nation ideologically, and as recently as 2005 there were no Conservative MPs in Wales. Yet since 2005 support for the right in Wales has increased electorally for both the Conservatives and UKIP. In the Brexit Referendum of 2016 Welsh electoral support increased to over 50 per cent to support the central political aim of Wales' most right-wing party, UKIP, leaving the EU. Traditionally, the Welsh were supporters of parties on the left of the political spectrum, and the recent rise in support for parties and policies on the right suggest that the Welsh electorate is also moving in this direction. We should also note that an important point in determining to which part of the political spectrum a party belongs is which political philosophies it follows. In this respect political parties mainly shape the philosophies of British or international political ideologists or politicians. They have, however, also produced some of their own, which have shaped political parties in Wales, the United Kingdom and the wider political world (Box 2.1).

Box 2.1 Welsh political ideologists

Although Wales has not produced volumes of Welsh political philosophers or theorists, it has produced some notable examples. This has had an impact on the political direction of parties both within and outside Wales. Some of the most central figures have been:

Richard Price, 1723–91: active in radical, republican and liberal causes such as the American Revolution.

Robert Owen, 1771–1858: social reformer and one of the founders of Utopian Socialism and the Cooperative movement.

Tom Ellis, 1859–99: helped to design and then push for a new Welsh type of political nationalism within the Liberals.

David Lloyd George, 1863–1945: British Liberal Prime Minister who developed social Liberalism and what was later known as Keynesian economics.

Saunders Lewis, 1893–1985: Welsh nationalist who helped found Plaid Cymru and also advocated a specific type of Welsh nationalism, linked at times to fascism.

Aneurin Bevan, 1897–1960: a political icon of the Labour Party, who advocated a form of Marxism popular until the 1960s (Bevanism).

Peter Thorneycroft, 1909–94: Conservative MP for Monmouth who was instrumental, through chairing the Tory Reform Committee, in moving

> Conservative ideology to successfully compete with the appeal of Labour in 1945, and later facilitated the arrival of Thatcherism in 1979.

The appeal and dominance of the left in Welsh politics

As we noted earlier, the Labour Party has dominated Welsh politics for a century and has led the Welsh Assembly government for all five terms. It first won the majority of parliamentary seats in Wales in the General Election of 1923, and has been the major partner, or the only party, in every Welsh government since devolution. Since 1918, Labour has come first in every Wales-wide election except one (the European Parliament elections of 2009).[6] Popular analysis has been that Wales is a 'Labour country'; the Conservatives have struggled to win many seats in General Elections or in the Assembly. However, recent elections have suggested that this tradition looks set to change, but there is still a need to assess why this appeal for a left of centre 'socialist party' has lasted for so long.

The enduring appeal of the left in Welsh politics may in fact be relatively easy to understand. The Labour-supporting tradition speaks to the history of industrial Wales, a land of 'coal mines, terraced houses, working-men's clubs, male voice choirs and the proud traditions of an industrial working class'.[7] Influential politicians of the Labour movement nationally were Welsh – Jim Griffiths, Roy Jenkins, Aneurin Bevan, Neil Kinnock – or represented Welsh constituencies – Keir Hardie, Ramsay MacDonald, Michael Foot, Jim Callaghan, Peter Hain. Wales benefited when there was a Labour government: the establishment of the Welsh Office and a Secretary of State for Wales in the 1960s, and support for devolution to Wales in the 1970s and 1990s. And Wales was deemed to have suffered under Conservative governments: the flooding of Capel Celyn and the Tryweryn Valley in the 1950s; the closure of the coal mines and the steel industry in the 1980s and 1990s. So you could be forgiven for assuming that this inherent party loyalty, born of tradition of suffering, endures.

Professor Richard Wyn Jones wrote shortly after the 2016 Assembly election results that: 'The Labour Party in Wales has continued its remarkable record as the UK's most successful electoral machine.'[8] It was also noted that closer analysis reveals some cracks in Labour's hegemony in Wales. Labour's share of the vote in Wales has been declining. The 2010 General Election saw Labour's vote share in Wales fall to 36.2 per cent – almost 20 per cent below the mark achieved in 1997 –

'Labour's Welsh citadel had not fallen yet, but the ramparts were visibly trembling'.[9] Despite this, Labour achieved its best share of the vote in Assembly elections the following year. However, the 2015 UK General Election saw Labour's vote share in Wales back to 2010 levels at 36.9 per cent, and the 2016 Assembly elections in Wales confirmed this trend. Here Labour's share of the constituency vote fell from 42 per cent in 2011 to 35 per cent in 2016, and regional list support from 36.9 per cent to 29 per cent. The reasons behind Labour domination of Welsh politics can be seen in Box 2.2.

Box 2.2 Why have Labour continued to dominate Welsh politics?

Labour have been the majority party in all five elections, this has not been the case for any other political party in any other legislature in the United Kingdom. There are a number of reasons for Labour's continued success. The foremost are:

- the electoral system is less proportional than elsewhere, relying on the First Past the Post electoral system (FPTP) for forty of the AMs (see Chapter 8);
- Labour has more stable support in Wales than anywhere else and has had so for nearly a century;
- class alignment is still strong, with support for Labour coming from a much larger worker class as a percentage of the population supporting them, particularly in the South Wales Valleys and large urban centres;
- the Conservatives, the other main party in the United Kingdom, have less support in Wales than in England;
- the other political parties are traditionally much weaker than the Labour Party in Wales in terms of organisational support, party membership and historic appeal;
- nationalism does not have the same strong appeal as it does in Scotland or Northern Ireland.

The political role of the Welsh language

"The lingua franca is English, but certainly when you are dealing with Welsh communities it is useful to be able to speak Welsh," said David Jones.[10]

He was aware, whilst in office as Welsh Secretary, that the Welsh language still retains a political importance. As we noted earlier, for many centuries it was indeed almost solely the presence of the Welsh language that helped to distinguish Wales from England. In the 1901 census, just under half of the population (49.9 per cent), or some 929,000 people, claimed to speak Welsh.[11] For the century following this census, however, the Welsh language was in decline, until it stabilised in the 1970s at around 20 per cent of the population. Although it is still spoken by over half a million people, some 81 per cent of the Welsh population are not able to speak Welsh. Today, the language is spoken most widely in the county of Gwynedd, with over half of the population (56 per cent) being Welsh-speakers, and is at its lowest in Blaenau Gwent, with only around one in eighteen of the population being Welsh-speakers (7.8 per cent).

The status of the Welsh language is a political hot potato in Wales. Every Welsh government has therefore committed itself to expanding the number of Welsh-speakers. Between 2001 and 2011, the target increase was 5 per cent, but in reality, its use actually fell by 2 per cent, causing further political anguish about the future of the language. Plaid Cymru remains most closely connected with the politics of the Welsh language as the party was actually founded mainly around the issues of protecting it and enhancing its status. It was aided by wider civil pressure outside the party and, from the 1960s onwards, by a series of civil protests by *Cymdeithas yr Iaith Gymraeg* (Welsh Language Society) together with pressure from other parties. This brought the issue of the Welsh language to the forefront of government policy in Wales.

The first piece of legislation to change the status of the Welsh language since the Acts of Union was brought forward by the Northern Wales National Liberal MP Henry Morris Jones during the Second World War.[12] Some twenty-two years before the foundation of the Welsh Office, the Welsh Courts Act 1942 permitted limited use of the Welsh language in courts for the first time. It would be another quarter of a century before the language was given wider status. In 1967, the Labour-run Welsh Office introduced a Welsh Language Act. This Act for the first time gave the Welsh language equal status to English in a number of public areas. Across the decades that followed support for the Welsh language became increasingly seen as a political rather than a cultural issue.

Initially, in both the Labour and Conservative parties there was a reluctance to support the Welsh language financially. For many Labour

Party activists the language was seen as a promotion of 'narrow-minded nationalism' and as a barrier to the wider goals of international socialism. This was fuelled by the rise of Plaid Cymru in the Welsh-speaking areas of Wales and the belief that if the Welsh language was supported and grown elsewhere it could only further support their cause electorally. As a result, there was little enthusiasm for supporting the promotion of the Welsh language among most Welsh Labour MPs.

Whereas the Conservatives in Wales were also suspicious of supporting the Welsh language in Anglicised areas, they did not have the same concerns about supporting it in those areas of South Wales in which they were not an electoral force. The Welsh Conservatives did, however, face a fierce Welsh-language battle of their own in the early 1980s. This was not in Wales but in England. This battle occurred when the new Conservative Welsh Secretary, Nicholas Edwards, sought to introduce the long-awaited Welsh-language TV channel, *Sianel Pedwar Cymru* – S4C (Wales Channel Four). Now the Conservative Party became divided between the pro-Welsh Conservative Party members, who supported S4C, and their powerful English colleagues, who did not. It was a bitter battle that also taught Welsh Conservatives to fight their corner harder in future. They also realised the political importance of supporting the Welsh language, and over the coming two decades poured millions of pounds into the promotion of the Welsh language.[13]

In education, in 1988, for instance, the Conservative-run Welsh Office, made Welsh a compulsory subject for all schoolchildren as part of the National Curriculum in Wales. Then, from 2000, the teaching of the Welsh language was made compulsory in all schools up to the age of sixteen.[14] In addition, under John Major's government in 1993, a second Welsh Language Act strengthened the position of Welsh in public life. It also established a Welsh Language Board (WLB) which was responsible for promoting the use of the language and ensuring that public bodies treated the Welsh and English languages equally. The WLB was later scrapped in 2011 as part of the Welsh Labour government's 'bonfire of the quangos'. It was replaced instead by a Welsh Language Commissioner, with broadly the same remit as the WLB (Box 2.3).

Box 2.3 The Welsh Language Commissioner: what do they do?

The former Chair of Cymdeithas yr Iaith Gymraeg, Labour Party member and former chair of the Welsh Language Board, Meri Huws, became the

First Welsh Language Commissioner. In her new role she enforces the duty of public bodies to provide for Welsh-language services and she has the power to investigate occasions where there are attempts to interfere with the freedom to speak Welsh. This had previously occurred on a number of occasions in North Wales where Welsh-speakers had been instructed by their employers not to speak Welsh at work. It is also her role to inform public bodies across Wales which services they are required to provide in Welsh and to what standard. This has the legal backup of fines and enforcement powers if these do not occur.

The development of and support for the Welsh language continues to evolve now in Wales, rather than through the legislative processes of Westminster. In November 2012, the National Assembly for Wales (Official Languages) Act 2012 received Royal Assent, and in so doing became the first Bill created in the Welsh Assembly to become law in Wales. This new Act reconfirmed the official status of the Welsh language and established the post of a Welsh Language Commissioner (Box 2.3). The Act also created a Welsh Language Partnership Council to advise government on its Welsh-language strategy.

Not everyone is happy with the policies made to promote the Welsh language, however. Public authorities and some businesses disagree with being required to bear the extra costs of translation work, and in those counties where only a small percentage of the population speak Welsh, there continues to be some resistance to having to learn Welsh at school. After their General Election defeat in 1997, the Conservatives also came out strongly against the compulsory elements of the Welsh-language legislation. Through their 1999 Welsh Assembly manifesto, for instance, they sought to make Welsh no longer compulsory in post-fourteen education. Yet, despite these protests, the existence of the Welsh language remains significant in Welsh public and private life.

However, despite this protection and support the Welsh language still remains an area of political concern with respect to its decline. S4C has suffered large cuts in its funding, by 25 per cent in 2011, with its funding reduced from £101 million in 2009 to £82.8 million in 2014/15.[15] In addition, in 2013, S4C became the responsibility of the BBC, losing its independent status and fixed grant from the Westminster government. This, in turn, has caused considerable concern among Welsh-language campaigners such as Cymdeithas yr Iaith Gymraeg, and Welsh politicians seeking to promote the use of the Welsh language. To the added frustration of both parties, broadcasting still remains a non-devolved issue, which means that politicians in Cardiff can do little directly to influence policy over S4C's future. This is something that Plaid Cymru has brought to the forefront politically, which in turn illustrates that ninety years after its founding the party still retains issues concerning the Welsh language at the heart of its own policy agenda.

The nature of nationalism and unionism in Wales

The dynamics that unified the United Kingdom and have held it together in union are of less relevance in the twenty-first century. Britain no longer has an empire, and is a much more culturally and ethnically diverse nation than ever. The viability of smaller nation-states is greater with better technology and communications, and with supranational organisations such as the European Union (EU) and NATO to which nations can belong, reaping the rewards of protection without losing sovereignty completely. Devolution has fuelled nationalism and demands for independence in Scotland, and in Wales Plaid Cymru was a coalition partner in government between 2007 and 2011 and cut a 'deal' with Welsh Labour to have influence over policy as the largest opposition party in 2016. Significant differences in policy and emphasis have emerged between the nations of the United Kingdom since devolution, and further powers have been ceded to them by Westminster bit by bit. There is an emerging tension between forces uniting the United Kingdom and forces disuniting it, causing the nations of the United Kingdom to differ from each other rather than be the same. The future of the union is a live political topic and devolution is a genie that will not go back into the bottle. This represents a particular problem for political parties in Wales to respond to. The position of Plaid Cymru on Welsh independence is a little unclear, but it is the only party in Wales calling for this. Other parties support unionism in various forms, and public opinion in Wales does not support a breakup of the union.[16] Devolution was in part conceived as a mechanism for preserving the union, not for breaking it up. Labour government minister Douglas Alexander said in 2007 that 'The great outcome of devolution is it allows people to demonstrate their identity within the United Kingdom and, at the same time, not break up the United Kingdom.[17]

Nevertheless, there are a number of reasons why devolution may still lead to the breakup of the union eventually. Welsh Labour has always seen the solution to the problems of the United Kingdom, including Wales, as lying in a strong Labour government at Westminster. Indeed, between 1945 and 2001 there were regular UK General Elections in which Labour gained more votes than the Conservatives in England.[18] The trend since 2005, however, has been for the Conservative Party to do well in England and for other parties to do well in Scotland and Wales, a situation that reinforces the differences and makes it harder for parties like Welsh Labour to maintain strong connections with the UK government in the interests of Wales within the union. With changes to the electoral system for UK elections, including the removal of some MPs from Wales and Scotland, there is a possibility that Labour will find it difficult to regain power in the United Kingdom in the short- to medium-term at least, further reinforcing the differences between Wales and England. Constitutionally, the future of the union should Scotland leave is far from certain. The benefits of the union to England are a matter of political debate and the future of the union would be very fragile if there were calls for England to leave it if Scotland did. The position in which Wales would find itself would be difficult then, given the lack of desire for independence and the reliance of Wales on central UK funding.

In Wales, with the exception of Plaid Cymru, all the political parties support the continuation of the union within the United Kingdom, although both Labour and the Liberal Democrats support this union on a federal basis rather than the existing political union. The dominance of the political parties supporting the union, the economic reliance on England, the failure of Plaid Cymru to appeal to more than a fifth of the electorate and the lack of support for independence have given Welsh nationalism, as a force for independence, limited appeal. Unlike in Scotland, the percentage of the Welsh population, under a variety of different scenarios, in favour of independence remains in most polls well under a fifth. This means the pro-union parties retain their dominance in Wales politically.

Why is Plaid Cymru technically an ethnoregionalist party and not a nationalist one?

Although Plaid Cymru had its origins as a traditional nationalist party supporting Welsh nationalism, and at times it senior members were close to European fascism, it has deviated into a different category of party.

Today, however, political scientists do not always refer to them directly as 'nationalist' parties. This label they reserve for those anti-immigrant parties or groups, normally on the far political right, such as the BNP and the English Defence League. Instead, Plaid Cymru is technically referred to as an 'ethnoregionalist' party. The same label is also given to the SNP, Plaid Cymru's sister party. This means that both parties represent a specific regional/national group within a larger nation-state, in this context the Welsh and the Scottish peoples in the United Kingdom. In the political world and in the media, however, they remain defined as nationalist parties, but we need to be aware that there is a clear distinction between nationalist and ethnoregionalist parties in their ideological backgrounds. Neither Plaid Cymru nor the SNP are anti-immigrant parties and tend to be left of centre on most policies. Having stated this, however, you will find that in most texts they are still commonly known by the label, 'nationalist party'.[19]

The Welsh political parties

Without the political parties in Wales, any distinctiveness in Welsh politics would be greatly reduced because the drive towards national distinctiveness would be far more limited. In this respect, the Welsh Liberals started to formulate a different Welsh structure and policies in the late nineteenth century.[20] Plaid Cymru did so from 1925,[21] and the other political parties much more recently in Wales. There are now five main political parties in Wales who have elected representatives to one of the three main legislatures in which Wales has representation: the Welsh Assembly (Assembly Members, AMs), the Westminster Parliament (Members of Parliament, MPs) and European Parliament (Members of the European Parliament, MEPs). These parties, all of whom have Wales or Welsh in their name, are:

- Plaid Cymru;
- Welsh Conservative Party;
- Welsh Labour Party (Wales Labour);
- Welsh Liberal Democrats;
- UKIP Wales.

UKIP has never had an MP elected in Wales and the Welsh Liberal Democrats have never had an MEP elected. Aside from these two parties, every other one of the five has had members elected in each of the three legislatures, as well as in local government. There are also some minor political parties in Wales, such as the Welsh Green Party, Welsh Communist Party and even the Abolish the Welsh Assembly Party. They, however, have not had sufficient electoral appeal to gain representation on a national level or even local authority representation. They are therefore not covered in this book.

Before political devolution in 1999 the two main parties in Wales – Labour and Conservatives – acted mainly as regional elements of the national party, with their headquarters in London.[22] Policy was determined on an ad hoc basis in Wales for some specifically Welsh areas, such as local government reform or the Welsh language. The vast bulk of the policy, however, was determined in London on an UK or English-Wales basis. For Plaid Cymru, it was solely in Wales and for the Welsh Liberal Democrats, who operate in a federal party system, there was autonomy on a wide range of Welsh policy areas.

Today, all the parties have widespread autonomy, which ranges from choosing their own leaders to developing their own political manifestos. The latter can contrast sharply with the party in Westminster. The Welsh Conservatives' desire to reintroduce grammar schools and the Welsh Labour Party's introduction of free prescription fees are just two of many examples of where Wales and London now differ on policy areas.

Independents

At a local authority level non-party-aligned councillors – called 'Independents' – are more successful. In a number of Welsh unitary authorities they have been elected in sufficient numbers to either act as the main opposition, form part of the council cabinet or control the council in their own right. Sometimes, they combine together and construct their own manifesto. If they do not, it can be difficult for voters to gauge where they stand on the political spectrum or what policies they will introduce whilst in office. At elections beyond those for councils, although Independents frequently stand they have only won where the candidate has previously been known for representing another political party, normally Labour. Members of Parliament and AMs may also become Independents, if they have the party whip withdrawn from them for a particular reason or chose to resign it. A number of both

Welsh MPs and AMs have gone along this route, and may either rejoin their party or continue as an Independent until the next election when they normally lose their seat through resignation or electoral defeat.

Electing the Welsh party leader

For the largest political party in Wales, Labour, the leadership electoral system has been more complex than the others in the past; a system known as the electoral college. In this respect Carwyn Jones was elected through the Labour Party's Welsh electoral college in 2009. It divided the electorate into three different sections: (1) elected members (Welsh Labour AMs, MPs and MEPs); (2) ordinary party members; and (3) affiliate sections (such as trade unions and the Co-operative Party). Each part had a third of the vote and the electoral system used was the Alternative Vote (AV) system. The system was criticised for putting too much power over the election result outside of the hands of ordinary party members. In 2014, the Collins Review of the way in which the Labour Party elected its leaders changed the system to what is known as One Member, One Vote (OMOV). Here every party member, whether they are an AM or just an ordinary party member, get an equal say on who should be the national Labour Party leader. In 2016, there was a contrast between the high level of support for Jeremy Corbyn from ordinary party members in Wales and the lack of support among the party's elected members. This highlighted the ideological gap there can be between a party's grassroots and its elected members.

All the other current Welsh political party leaders in the Welsh Assembly, with the exception of UKIP, were elected by their party's members using OMOV. Although the type of voting system varies, the electorate is still the wider party membership. Only Labour in 2009 and Plaid Cymru for all its leadership elections have had Welsh leadership elections with more than two candidates running at the same time. Plaid Cymru are also the only party to have had contested leadership contests for every leader elected. The Conservatives in 1999 (Nick Bourne), Labour in 2000 (Rhodri Morgan) and the Welsh Liberal Democrats in 2007, all had leaders who were 'elected' unopposed. In addition, UKIP and the Welsh Conservatives have both never had a female candidate for their leadership. UKIP and the Welsh Liberal Democrats can also have a Welsh leader who is from outside the Welsh Assembly. In this respect, the Welsh party leadership passed to MP Mark Williams in May

2016, from Kirsty Williams AM. UKIPs Nathan Gill MEP AM also lost his party's Assembly leadership to Neil Hamilton AM in May 2016, but remained the Welsh party leader.

Box 2.4 Welsh party leaders' roles

It is the political party leader's central role to ensure that their party remains as popular with the Welsh electorate and as electable as possible. They also have a number of other roles:

1. to seek to gain political office in order to implement their party's manifesto pledges;
2. to work with their party nationally (UK-wide) or with sister parties in order to ensure that they follow the same ideological path, while also ensuring a Welsh distinctiveness;
3. to act as a rallying point and political figurehead for their party's Welsh members and supporters;
4. to keep the party united and seek to ensure that internal strife is minimised;
5. to appoint ministers, if in government, or spokespeople for various government functions, if in opposition;
6. to increase and develop their party membership into an electoral force;
7. to maintain, in conjunction with their party's chief executive/general secretary and national executive bodies, the running, administration, fundraising and campaigning actions as required;
8. to be a political figurehead, a recognisable public face, political dynamo and lead spokesperson for their party in Wales, the United Kingdom and wider world; and
9. with the exception of Plaid Cymru, maintain cordial relations with the party's UK leadership and party operations at Westminster.

If they fail in any of these roles they can be subject to a leadership challenge or endure the general dissatisfaction of their members, either elected or party members.

Party membership and structures

All the political parties in Wales have their own executive and ruling body. This is normally within the post of Welsh president/chair or both.

For the Conservative and Labour parties, the UK leader is their official party leader; their leader in the Assembly is only their official leader there. In reality, their Assembly leader is often seen by the public, media and their own Welsh party as also being the Welsh leader. For the Welsh Liberal Democrats, in a federal structure, and Plaid Cymru their Welsh leader is also the leader of their state party.

All the parties enjoy considerable autonomy in matters such as policy creation, internal party structures and sometimes candidate selection rules and regulations. The parties are structured locally on a geographical basis, which can be multi-layered – regional–constituency–ward or just one of those elements. Each structured sub-union also has a number of party executive posts with it, such as chair, secretary and treasurer. These are normally elected posts, for which local party members vote. It is these units that are registered for accounting purposes with the Electoral Commission under the regulations required by the Political Parties, Elections and Referendums Act 2000.

For decades party membership in Wales and elsewhere appeared to be in terminal decline. After the 2015 General Election and the 2016 Brexit referendum, however, there seems to have been something of a renaissance in party membership numbers. All political parties in Wales saw a rise in party membership. Some parties, such as the Welsh Labour Party and the Welsh Liberal Democrats, saw substantial rises.[23] As is the case in the rest of the United Kingdom, party members also play an important role in:

1. leadership and candidate selection/endorsement;
2. campaigning in elections and on specific issues;
3. fundraising for the party;
4. acting as a pool for election candidates;
5. policy formulation or policy soundings and endorsement;
6. keeping the party alive and active locally between elections; and
7. attending conferences, rallies and participating in other public shows of party support.

Manifestos and policy creation

Political manifestos are political parties' blueprints for office. They are made public during election periods. Manifestos allow both the electorate, business and other bodies, Civil Service and the political party themselves to know what their programme will be, should they gain office. For coalition governments, they also form the basis of negotiations for the joint agreements for power-sharing. For constructing these manifestos, policy-making methods vary considerably within the political parties. Policies and manifestos may also require endorsement at the party's Welsh party conference. Here they may also be amended or even not carried forward.

For UKIP and the Conservatives, manifestos can involve being written by just one or two individuals in consultation with elected AMs and senior party figures, whereas for the other main political parties in Wales this often involves a slower evolution of policy via policy committees and endorsement at party conferences. The political parties in Wales frequently seek to differentiate policies so they are more clearly 'made in Wales'. As noted earlier, this policy determination can also result in substantial policy differences from sister parties/regional parties outside Wales.

Box 2.5 Case study: UKIP and Welsh politics

Traditionally, it was the Conservatives in Wales who were the most significant Eurosceptics. They had campaigned vigorously against entry to the European Monetary Union and the Social Chapter. Conservative Welsh Secretaries John Redwood and William Hague were both prominent Eurosceptics during John Major's government. Both had, for instance, refused to fly the European flag over Welsh Office buildings as an indication of their Euroscepticism. From the late 2000s, however, their Euroscepticism was overtaken by a party that did not want to negotiate for a revised place in the EU, they wanted to withdraw from it all together: UKIP – the United Kingdom Independence Party.

UKIP's name sums up its central message of wanting the United Kingdom to withdraw from the EU. The party also campaign strongly on an anti-immigrant platform. Although the party was founded on an anti-Europe message, it has also sought office at all levels of political representation in Wales. Though it was founded in 1993, it was not until the 2005 General Election that UKIP started to contest a significant number of parliamentary constituencies in Wales, and in 2009 they won their first parliamentary seat in Wales at the European elections. In 2009, John Bufton, a long-time Welsh Eurosceptic, was elected in Wales and at the same time pushed the pro-European Liberal Democrats into fifth place.

Just like the Conservative and Labour parties in Wales, UKIP is a regional part of the UK party rather than a national (federal) party in its own right. The regional branch has one representative on the UK board of the party. Although the party has been active in Wales since 2005, it was only in 2014 that it held its first Welsh Autumn conference and its branch structure only started to become established across most of Wales in the run up to the 2015 General Election. Unlike the other parties, the leadership in Wales is not elected by the members of the party but appointed by the national UK leader. In this respect, Nigel Farage appointed its first Welsh leader, Nathan Gill, in December 2014, although its leader in the Welsh Assembly is Neil Hamilton AM, the former Conservative MP.

The ideology of UKIP

It is sometimes difficult to track UKIP's ideology from its own manifestos and campaigning members because they can be contradictory. In the 2010 General Election, for instance, UKIP pledged to introduce a dress code for taxi drivers, regularly deploy armed forces on the streets and repaint trains in traditional colours. Later, however, the entire manifesto was dismissed as 'obvious nonsense'.[24] As far as we can gather, therefore, UKIP can be defined by both its most recent manifestos and central mission statement as a Eurosceptic and anti-(EU) immigrant party.

Considering that it campaigns for withdrawal from the EU, it is perhaps ironic that much of the funding for UKIP actually comes from the salaries and office support costs from its MEPs. Although leadership is important in all political parties, within UKIP the role of the leadership is a vital part of its electoral appeal. From his appointment as leader in 2010 until his departure in 2016, Nigel Farage's own personality and projection has been central to UKIP's appeal in Wales and elsewhere. This was despite the fact that he did not get on, on a personal level with the Welsh Assembly UKIP leader Neil Hamilton. This also puts UKIP into the category of being a right-wing populist party, moving around the populist politicising and anti-immigrant policies of Nigel Farage, although this may well differ with the change in UKIP leadership or the projection of other UKIP figures in Wales.

Wales has a political tradition of being politically supporting left of centre parties. As recently as the general election of 1997, all forty Welsh parliamentary seats were won by centre or centre left political parties. Therefore, it is somewhat against this tradition and expectations that UKIP became the second political party in Wales at the 2013 European Elections, the third political party in Wales at the 2015 General Election and the fourth party of the Welsh Assembly in 2016. They were also central to the successful Leave vote in the 2016 Brexit referendum in Wales.

UKIP's largest increase in votes also often occurred in areas were the Labour Party is dominant, with the voters there traditionally reluctant to support the Conservatives Party, but now support a party in significant numbers that is to the right ideologically of that party. Despite the fact that there has frequently been internal feuding within the Welsh and UK party, UKIP seems to retain a constant share of the vote of between 10 and 15 per cent, which under Wales' proportional elections enables them to gain a number of elected members and the political resources that come with these. Ironically, many of UKIP's elected members have been former members of the Conservatives Party, sometimes as MPs. This means that they also often enjoy a close affinity with the Conservatives in Wales and nationally, particularly on support for Brexit.

Conclusions

On the whole, Welsh political parties and ideologies align themselves closely with those of England and the rest of the United Kingdom. There are, nevertheless, some distinctive Welsh elements, specifically those concerned with the Welsh language and the long-term dominance of one political party in Wales. The political parties in Wales, either before or after devolution, have developed their own structures, leadership and policy-creation mechanisms. This can sometimes put them at odds with their political counterparts elsewhere in the United Kingdom.

Nationalism is also weaker than elsewhere in the United Kingdom, and therefore the support for continuance of the union stronger. The type of nationalism in Wales is also much weaker than in other nation-states, with the real extremes of nationalism absent from most of the political scene. Nevertheless, Welsh politics is evolving and new parties are entering the political scene that have been absent until recently, notably UKIP.

Questions for discussion

1. How relevant is the 'Three Wales Model' in explaining political identity in Wales?

2. Explain where each political party sits on the political spectrum in Wales, and why it can be positioned there.
3. React to the following statements and explain your reasons:
   a. The appeal of left-wing politics in Wales is enduring and can be mainly explained by historical factors;
   b. although Welsh Labour has dominated Welsh Politics, its position looks more precarious now;
   c. right-wing politics has no appeal in Wales;
   d. Plaid Cymru has failed to achieve the level of success that the SNP has achieved in Scotland mainly because of the language issue.

Case study: UKIP and Welsh politics[25]

Read the case study in Box 2.5 and answer the following questions:

1. What are the two central differences between UKIP and the other main political parties in Wales?
2. Is UKIP a nationalist party or merely a more Eurosceptic branch of the Conservatives party?

Suggested answer points are provided in the Welsh Government and Politics online resource for both the questions and the case study. The web link for these answer points is given at the front of the book.

Wales in Westminster and Europe

Russell Deacon

Overview

For the Welsh Assembly it is a truism that many legislative and political powers still reside outside Wales, even though some political sovereignty has been delegated down from Westminster. Much of the political power that impacts on Welsh life, however, is still derived from outside Wales. Therefore, both Westminster and the EU remain central to the political life of the Welsh nation. Whereas the territorial department and Cabinet Secretary that covers Wales – the Wales Office and the Welsh Secretary – have had a considerable reduction in their powers and responsibilities since devolution, they still play an important role in Welsh and Westminster politics. Similarly, the EU plays an important role in both the political and economic development of the Welsh Assembly and wider Welsh nation. This chapter therefore examines these external legislative and political bodies, and explores both the contribution from Wales to these bodies and their own Welsh interests and interaction with Welsh domestic politics.

Key issues to be covered in this chapter

- How and why did devolution develop in Wales – the story of Wales and Westminster?
- What is the background to the development of the relationship between Wales and Westminster?
- Defining the role and nature of Wales at Westminster.
- What is the role of various Westminster committees and their strengths and weaknesses?
- How are Police and Crime Commissioners elected and what are their roles?
- Defining the nature of the Welsh Parliament Party and the specific role of the House of Lords and Wales.
- What is the extent of the Welsh government's presence in Westminster and the Westminster government's presence in Wales?
- How do we view the role and responsibilities of the Welsh Secretary and Wales Office?
- What is the nature of the interaction between Wales and various Cabinet committees?
- Indicating the role and nature of the Special advisers (SPADS) and the Wales Office.
- How do the role of concordats and committees/councils that govern Welsh government– Westminster government relations operate?
- Examining the role of Wales and Europe, including Welsh MEPs, the European Parliament, EU Commission and Wales.

- To what extent are there links and interactions between the Welsh government/Assembly and Europe?

The historical evolution of Welsh politics

In Chapter 1 we we covered a number of the events and processes that led to Wales becoming nation in its own right and evolving its own political institutions. In this chapter we start by examining Welsh history once again, but this time looking at how it relates to developments connected directly to Westminster and London. Ever since the Acts of Union in 1536 and 1542, Welsh governance has officially been drawn into that of England and specifically that based in London (Box 3.1). Over the 500 years that followed these Acts Welsh political distinctiveness at Westminster faded. Then, from the late nineteenth century, Welsh distinctiveness reasserted itself once more until by the mid-twentieth century there could be no doubt that both England and Wales were separate nations politically.

Box 3.1 Wales joins England in Wales Acts 1536 and 1543

These are the specific sections of the Acts that brought Wales formally into a union with England.

From *Y Deddfau Cyfreithiau yng Nhgymru*:

His Highness therefore of a singular Zeal, Love and Favour that he beareth towards his Subjects of his said Dominion of Wales, minding and intending to reduce them to the perfect Order, Notice and Knowledge of his Laws of this Realm, and utterly to extirp all and singular the sinister Usages and Customs differing from the same, and to bring the said Subjects of this his Realm, and of his said Dominion of Wales, to an amicable Concord and Unity . . .

That his said Country or Dominion of Wales shall be, stand and continue for ever from henceforth incorporate united and annexed to and with this his Realm of England.

The arrival of the Welsh Office and Secretary of State for Wales in 1964, followed at the end of the century by the new National Assembly for Wales, gradually transformed the relationship between Wales and London. This chapter therefore examines the background,

role and function of the various elements of the Westminster
government that interact with Wales and vice versa. The chapter
also examines those formal links between Wales and the European
Parliament/Commission. As Wales has failed to significantly reverse its
economic decline, this European link has become ever more important
as a financial resource, and therefore the Welsh government has striven
to ensure that it retains close links with the EU both in Wales and in
Brussels.

Background to the development of the relationship between Wales and Westminster

It was under the English King Henry VIII that the public administration
systems of Wales and England were united formally under the Acts of
Union or Laws of Wales Acts (1536 and 1542). During the following
centuries, Wales was dominated on the whole by powerful aristocratic
dynasties, often with close links to the monarchy based in London. Such
families as the Cecils, Butes, Windsors and Morgans would be at the
heart of British politics, as well as having a considerable influence on
Wales, over a period of almost half a millennium. More often than not
they backed Tory (Conservative) governments, who had little appetite to
stir up any feelings of Welsh nationalism there may be. Although these
same families were supportive of developing Welsh culture, this did not
extent to political institutions of a Welsh nature.

Even in the latter half of the nineteenth century, the Tories continued to see few differences between England and Wales, aside from the
Welsh language and some aspects of religion. In contrast, the growing
Welsh Liberal Radicals increasingly saw Wales as a distinct nation and
in this vision it also fired the flames of Welsh nationalism. It was during
this period that William Gladstone became the first Prime Minister to be
persuaded that there was indeed a different nation in existence called
'Wales'. The fact that he lived in Howarden Castle in North Wales
and was married to a Welsh woman (Catherine) helped Gladstone
come into regular contact with the growing Welsh Liberal nationalism
prevalent in North Wales. It was this period of Welsh Liberal nationalism that at various times sought all of the forms of devolution (Home
Rule) listed in Box 3.2. This was mainly through the *Cymru Fydd* (Young
Wales) movement led by the Welsh Liberal MPs David Lloyd George
and Tom Ellis.

Box 3.2 What are the different types of devolution?

1. *Administrative (executive) devolution*: this involves the transfer of administration. The devolved body then controls the allocation of public funds, is given its own budget by central government and may also be responsible for drawing up and monitoring certain rules and regulations. There is also ministerial representation of some type in order to run the devolved department. This was the most common types of devolution in the United Kingdom prior to 1999.
2. *Financial devolution*: this gives the devolved administration the ability to raise its own revenues, whether this is through direct or indirect taxation or the levying of fees.
3. *Legislative devolution*: this gives the administration the power to make its own primary laws.
4. *Political devolution*: in which members are elected to both run a devolved government and as a legislature to hold the executive in check and make new laws. Political devolution often also encompasses all of the three types above.

Although the nineteenth-century Liberal-inspired Cymru Fydd nationalist movement was a failure, it did get enough Liberal politicians into power in order to advance administrative devolution. With David Lloyd George in the Cabinet and a number of other prominent Welsh Liberal MPs and lords also aiding the Welsh nationalist cause, greater administrative devolution was provided to Wales. This included the establishment of the Welsh Boards of Education and Health, but the more general desire for a Welsh parliament, as part of 'Home Rule all round', and substantial administrative devolution did not occur until much later.

Although much weaker in Wales than either the Liberals or latterly Labour, the Conservatives were not immune to seeking political advantage from issues of Welsh nationalism, making Cardiff Wales' first city in 1905 and cementing this by making it the nation's capital in 1955. They also made Gwilym Lloyd George the first Westminster government Minister for Welsh Affairs in 1954, combined with his role as Home Secretary. Labour, in contrast, rejected notions of Welsh political devolution almost until the start of the 1960s. Until then it had moulded itself on being the most unyielding of the unionist parties. It dismissed attempts to establish a Minister for Wales under the first Welsh White

Paper in 1946 when in government.[1] In its thirteen years of opposition from 1951 to 1964, Labour only finally consented to establish a Welsh Office and Welsh Secretary due to the perseverance of the deputy Labour leader and MP for Llanelli, Jim Griffiths. It would be Griffiths who became the first Welsh Secretary in 1964.[2]

Political and then administrative devolution in Northern Ireland and administrative devolution in Scotland occurred fairly quickly, if not painlessly. In Northern Ireland, political devolution began for the first time in 1922 after the separation from southern Ireland, and in Scotland administrative devolution occurred in the late nineteenth century. In Scotland, there was also majority support for political devolution from the mid-1970s onwards. This was not, however, the case in Wales. Here there occurred a long period of political campaigning by groups of MPs, individuals and organised bodies, such as the Parliament for Wales Campaign, before the majority of Wales could be persuaded that political devolution was a viable and desirable political option. For three-quarters of a century various pressure groups (see Chapter 8), sought the same and /or sometimes different types of devolution (Box 3.2). This revolved around establishing:

1. A Welsh Office (a territorial Civil Service department for Wales) similar to that of the Scottish Office, which administered a number of areas of government policy in Scotland, having been established in 1885.
2. A Welsh Secretary (a member of government in the Cabinet to represent Wales), similar to that of the Scottish Secretary and later on the Northern Ireland Secretary.
3. An elected primary law-making and tax-raising parliament for Wales (similar to the one that existed in Northern Ireland at Stormont and in many of the British Imperial dominions of the British Empire)

As we have already noted in Chapter 1, after the establishment of the post of Welsh Secretary and the Welsh Office in 1964, there was a gradual evolution and acquisition of powers and responsibilities under each Welsh Secretary whether Labour or Conservative. This moved Wales from a system of government with limited administrative devolution over a few areas to one in which an elected legislature interacts with a Welsh government with primary law-making and tax-raising powers (see Box 3.3).

Box 3.3 Evolution of Welsh politics, 1998–2017

- July–October 1998: the Government of Wales Act was given royal assent, leading to the establishment of the Welsh Assembly a year later;
- May 1999: the first elections were held for the Welsh Assembly;
- May 1999: a minority Executive Committee of the Welsh Assembly (the official name for the Welsh government) was formed by Labour;
- July 1999: the majority of the Welsh Office Civil Service transferred over to the Welsh Assembly. The post of Welsh Secretary remained, albeit with a much reduced staff in a newly renamed Wales Office;
- October 2000: Labour–Liberal Democrat Coalition Government formed at the Welsh Assembly;
- 2002: the Fullerton Review determines that Welsh government civil servants should be spread more evenly across Wales and regional offices were set up;
- March 2004: Richard Commission recommended primary law-making powers for Wales, an increase in AMs and a change to the electoral system;
- 2006: Government of Wales Act separates the Welsh Assembly between the Welsh government (executive) and the remaining AMs (legislature). It also paved the way for primary law-making powers to be devolved to the Assembly;
- 2006: most major Welsh quangos were brought into the Welsh government's Civil Service;
- March 2011: Welsh devolution referendum on establishing primary laws for the Welsh Assembly won with a large majority of 63.5 per cent For and 36.5 per cent Against;
- March 2014: Silk Commission recommended major new responsibilities and tax-raising powers should be devolved to Wales;
- December 2014: Wales Act formalised the change of name from Welsh Assembly government to Welsh government and devolved tax-raising powers to Wales, stamp duty, business rates and landfill tax for the first time;
- February 2015: St David's Day agreement (command paper) – Coalition government allowed for greater Assembly powers over certain taxes, energy projects (up to 350 MW) and a lowering of the voting age to sixteen;
- March 2017: Wales Act came into force giving the Welsh Assembly and government substantial new powers, including the recognition of distinctive Welsh law.

Wales at Westminster

The British system of politics, like that everywhere else in the Western world, is divided up into the executive (government), legislature (law-makers) and the judiciary (those that interpret the law). Therefore, just as the executive role of government in Wales has changed, so too has that of the legislature. The central part of this legislature for the United Kingdom that concerns Wales is that of Westminster. This section therefore examines those aspects of the executive and legislature that can be found in the British Houses of Parliament in Westminster and the government in Whitehall. In particular, it explores how the British Parliament and government adapted itself, or not, for specific Welsh purposes.

The Welsh Grand Committee

Although the great Welsh politician David Lloyd George did very little in the form of creating tangible Welsh parliamentary events when he was Prime Minister, his daughter Megan was able help secure one that has lasted longer than any others. In October 1944, she was the first MP to speak in what became an annual Welsh Day debate. This debate had been introduced to the House of Commons to examine specifically Welsh issues. It is held on or around St David's Day each year. This debate has an open agenda, within which matters of a fiscal or admin-istrative nature can be debated. This is not always held in the House of Commons, however, despite continued pressure from Welsh MPs to see that it does. Even though devolved issues such as health and education are not supposed to be discussed at Westminster with respect to their delivery by the Welsh Assembly, they still are.[3] The Welsh Secretary also normally attends these debates. and there is much political point-scoring as various issues supporting or degrading government policy are discussed and debated.[4]

Box 3.4 The role of Police and Crime Commissioners

There are four Police Crime Commissioners in Wales covering the four police authorities. Police and Crime Commissioners (PCCs) were established in Wales after the 2010 General Election by the incoming Westminster coa-lition government. Both the Conservatives and Liberal Democrats believed that elected commissioners would in part address the perceived problem of a lack of democratic and public scrutiny of both police authorities and the police themselves. The PCCs are elected by the Supplementary Vote method, in which voters mark their first and second choice of candidate. Unlike the other national elections in Wales, the first were held in November rather than May or June, but in 2016 they reverted back to the traditional May slot. Once elected the PCCs have four-year term in office. Plaid Cymru and the Liberal Democrats failed to contest the elections, in part fearing losing the £5,000 deposit necessary to contest the seats.

PCCs' responsibilities include[5]:

1. appointing chief constables of forces and dismissing them when necessary;
2. holding the chief constable to account for the performance of a force's officers and staff;
3. providing a link between the police and communities, which includes consulting local people, the council and other organisations;
4. overseeing community safety and the reduction of crime, and ensuring value for money in policing;
5. setting out a force's strategy and policing priorities through the Police and Crime Plan;
6. setting out the force budget and community safety grants – taken together, the PCCs are responsible for £8 billion of spending on police in England and Wales;
7. reporting annually on progress.

Although they have maintained a fairly low profile, from time to time the Welsh PCCs have achieved headlines not just in Wales but also across the United Kingdom. In June 2013, Iain Johnson caused the resignation of the Gwent PCC Carmel Napier over her 'management style'. In April 2015, Christopher Salmon held a public poll asking people if they 'wanted officers armed while on everyday duties'. The result was that 61 per cent of residents who took part said they would like to see officers armed despite the fact that Dyfed Powys Police have one of the lowest crime rates in the United Kingdom.

Unlike Scotland, which has a national police force under the control of the Scottish Parliament, Wales still retains four distinct police forces. Although they remain under the direct control of the Westminster government, the four Welsh PCCs regularly meet together with their chief constables to plan their own cross-Wales crime agenda and also with Welsh government ministers and officials.

The Welsh government and various commissions have repeatedly called for policing to be brought under their control as is the case in Scotland, Northern Ireland, the London Assembly and a number of the mayoral regions of England, such as Manchester. This would mean that the future of the PCCs would then be in the hands of the Welsh government.

The Welsh Affairs Select Committee

The Welsh Affairs Select Committee is one of the numerous Westminster departmental select committees of the House of Commons. It came into being after the failure of the St David's Day referendum in 1979. The new committee was set up to help to strengthen scrutiny of governance and wider issues in Wales, partly to compensate for there being no Welsh Assembly to carry out this role. Today, the Select Committee has evolved and its main purpose is to examine any Westminster government policies that have an impact on Wales outside the remit of the Welsh Assembly. It does this through set inquiries. In the 2010–15 Parliament, these ranged from examining the work of the Welsh PCCs to cross-border issues, such as health arrangements and road and rail connectivity.

The Select Committee has six members, three from the government and five from the official opposition, plus one from Plaid Cymru. This means that there is an in-built majority for the opposition, if there is not a Westminster coalition. Once nominated, the members and the chair can serve for the whole Parliament. The Committee[6] has the power to:

- send for persons – who must attend, although in reality it normally just requests rather than compels them to attend – papers and records;
- hold its meeting outside Westminster and across Wales; and
- appoint special advisers to help support its specialist inquiries.

After the 2015 General Election there was some discussion about scrapping the Welsh Affairs Select Committee and having instead a committee that would deal with all of the devolved nations. The discussion was partly in response to events in Scotland, where the SNP's overwhelming victory meant that any Scottish Affairs Select Committee would have been wholly dominated by the SNP and become a 'nationalist base for themselves'. The issue, however, was dropped after the robust defence of the Welsh Committee by its chair, the Monmouthshire Conservative MP, David Davies, who projected it merits.[7]

The Welsh Parliamentary Party

The oldest specific Welsh body connected with Westminster is the Welsh Parliamentary Party (WPP). Founded in 1888, it is made up of all forty MPs from Wales but, unlike the Welsh Grand Committee, does not include any MPs co-opted from England. It was initially founded in a period of growing Welsh nationalism stoked up by Welsh Liberal nationalists such as David Lloyd George and Tom Ellis. Over its long existence it has had some very distinguished chairs, including Alfred Thomas, Liberal MP for East Glamorganshire, who used it to push unsuccessfully for a Welsh parliament.[8] Another former chair included the founder of the National Health Service, Aneurin Bevan. For almost a century, the WPP was on occasions the only parliamentary mechanism by which MPs could collectively try to determine distinctly Welsh policies at Westminster.

As the political parties in Wales developed their own Welsh structures, so the role or need for the WPP to represent them as a whole diminished. Therefore, it is now only on very rare occasions that there is enough cross-party consensus to enable the WPP to meet. Between 1996 and 2014, for instance, it only met twice. The latter time being in November 2010[9] when a request was made by Welsh MPs to hold a meeting of the Welsh Grand Committee to discuss plans to cut the number of Welsh MPs. The Welsh Secretary, Cheryl Gillan, refused the request, and the longest-serving Welsh MP, Ann Clwyd, called a meeting of the WPP instead. The WPP has little power, but can agree on a motion to pass to the government although this is only advisory. The request for meeting of the WPP, however, normally suffices to send a warning shot to the government in Westminster that there are sufficient problems in Wales over a specific issue that something needs to be done.

The Welsh Westminster leaders and Welsh Whips

All of the political parties that hold Westminster seats also have a Welsh parliamentary leader. For Labour and the Conservatives this person is the Welsh Secretary or Shadow Welsh Secretary, depending on who is in government. For the other parties, it is Plaid Cymru's 'Westminster leader' and for the Welsh Liberal Democrats it is their 'Deputy Leader'. It is they that play the central role in coordinating Westminster politics and policy with their party and AMs in Wales.

To ensure that the Welsh MPs play a central and loyal part in their own party's agenda at Westminster there is a Welsh 'Whip'. The larger number of Welsh Labour MPs means that they have Welsh government Whips. In consultation with their party's Chief Whip they seek to ensure that their Welsh MPs support their party's policy agenda when required. All MPs are given directions on how they should vote on specific issues. These range from one line under a voting instruction (one-line whip), which reminds an MP of the party's policy, to the three lines (three-line whip), which require that MP to attend the vote and support their party in that vote. Normally, MPs can rebel against their party only so many times before they face sanctions from the Whips and their party, which include deselection and/or withdrawal of the whip. This means that they are no longer regarded as a member of that political party either for a short period or permanently. It is unsurprising therefore that Whips have often been accused of bullying or using strong-arm tactics by MPs who for one reason or another do not wish to follow the party's required line in a vote.

Part of the role of a Welsh Whip, unlike their English counterparts, is ensuring that there is a working relationship established between the party's Westminster and Cardiff Bay politicians, even when they are in coalition government of opposing parties. In 2007, the then Welsh Labour Whip, Wayne David MP, defined the Welsh Whips' role:

> In our post-devolution Wales, Government is now based on part-nership between Cardiff and London. Before this year's election, this relationship was relatively straightforward as Labour formed the Governments in both the Assembly and Westminster. Now it is obviously more complicated with Labour sharing power in Cardiff Bay with Plaid Cymru. This new configuration will mean that Labour Ministers in Westminster will have to co-operate with Plaid Ministers in the Assembly to ensure the effective delivery of UK policies in Wales. Given the political differences between Labour and Plaid this will not be easy, but policy delivery must take precedence over worries about longer-term objectives.[10]

The Welsh Lords[11]

There are a numerous Welsh lords and baronesses in the House of Lords (Upper House). Unlike the House of Commons, however, they are not there as representatives of any specific Welsh region, but as representatives of either themselves and party or merely themselves. There are also no bishops in the House representing Wales as there are in England, because the Church was disestablished in Wales in 1922. From time to time there are also Welsh members of the House of Lords in the government or in the role of spokespersons on specific departmental areas for their own political parties. Some recent examples include Baroness Kinnock (Labour), who was a Minister at the Foreign Office; Baroness Randerson (Welsh Liberal Democrats), who was a Minister at both the Wales and Northern Ireland Offices; and Lord Bourne, who is a Minister at both the Wales Office and Department of Energy and Climate Change.

In the House of Lords there are no procedures that are specific to Wales. They also do not deal with matters reserved for Wales or cross-over areas between Westminster and Cardiff Bay. This is not peculiar to Wales, however, as the Upper House also has no specific procedures covering Northern Ireland, Scotland or England either. This means, therefore, that there are no questions to any specific Welsh minister in the Lords. Instead, specific thirty-minute slots at the start of the day are given over to questions on virtually any topic. Normally, four questions are heard, with time being given for answers and supplementaries from the questionnaire and relevant minister. As in the House of Commons, Welsh legislation must go through the Lords but the Upper House does not have a separate committee to consider the legislation. It considers it through the whole House sitting, but does not suffer the same time constraints as the Commons in this respect. The Lords do, however, often sit on any Bill Team (Government or Opposition) that undertakes the planning and scrutinising/amending of any specific Welsh legislation with their colleagues from the Commons. Unlike the Commons, the Lords are not affected by English votes for English laws (EVEL) and can therefore still block or amend legislation on matters that have been devolved to Wales, even though they are Welsh lords and their Commons counterparts cannot do the same.

The role, nature and development of the Wales Office and Welsh Secretary

As we saw in Chapter 1, it took over five decades from first starting the campaign for a Welsh member in the Cabinet until a Minister for Wales was appointed. It was then just over another decade until a Secretary of State for Wales was eventually appointed in 1964. Successive Welsh Secretaries, almost without exception, built up the various areas of responsibility for their department until it was eventually consumed into the Welsh Assembly government in 1999. A small residual department then remained to service the needs of the Welsh Secretary and his or her junior ministers – the Wales Office. The three ministers that serve in the Wales Office between them share out the portfolio (Box 3.6). It is then the responsibility of each minister to ensure that Welsh and Westminster government policy and legislation is covered appropriately.

Box 3.5 The Welsh Secretaries in facts and figures

By July 2016 there had been eighteen different Secretaries of States for Wales. There are a number of relevant overall facts about each:

- from 1964 to 2015 there were eighteen Welsh Secretaries: eight Labour and ten Conservative Welsh Secretaries;
- only three Conservative Welsh Secretaries were Welsh by birth: Peter Thomas (1970–4); Cheryl Gillian (2010–12); and Alun Cairns (2016–). Cairns is the only Conservative Welsh Secretary to have been born in Wales and to have a Welsh constituency;
- six of the ten Conservative Welsh Secretaries represented English constituencies whilst in post;
- for some Welsh Secretaries the post offered a training ground for bigger posts, notably William Hague (1995–7), who became Foreign Secretary; George Thomas (1968–70), who became Speaker of the House of Commons; and Stephen Crabb (2014–16), who then became Work and Pensions Secretary;
- the majority of Welsh Secretaries, however, ended their ministerial careers at the Welsh Office, and only two, Jim Griffith (1964–70) and Peter Walker (1987–90), came into post from more senior Cabinet posts;
- Jim Griffith (1964–6), the first Welsh Secretary, was also the oldest on appointment at the age of seventy-four; the youngest appointment

---

was Stephen Crabb (2014–16) at the age of forty-one and also the first Westminster Cabinet Secretary with a beard since 1905;

- there has only been one female Welsh Secretary for Wales, Cheryl Gillan (2010–12);
- two AMs have now become Welsh Secretary, David Jones (2012–14) and Alun Cairns (2016–); two former Welsh Secretaries became AMs, Ron Davies (1997–8) and Alun Michael (1998–99); Michael also became First Secretary of the Welsh Assembly (later called First Minister) between 1999 and 2000.

The role of the Welsh Secretary has changed considerably since it came into being in 1964. The central executive role of running a small government department ended in 1999 when these responsibilities were transferred to the Welsh government. Instead, the Welsh Secretary and their ministerial team now act mainly as the 'eyes and ears' of the Westminster government in Wales and also, to an extent, as a mutual lobbyist for Welsh government over agreed issues such as the electrification of the Swansea to London rail line. The post-holders have also come from different backgrounds politically and have had varied fortunes before and after holding the post (Box 3.5).

Box 3.6 The role and function of the Welsh Secretary[12]

The Welsh Secretary is based in London (always on Wednesday and Thursday during parliamentary sessions), and in Cardiff and their own constituency over the rest of the week. Traditionally, the Welsh Secretary maintained the role of 'the voice of Wales in the Cabinet and the voice of the Cabinet in Wales'. Today, their central role is based around constitutional affairs concerning Wales and the rest of the United Kingdom.[13] As members of the Cabinet they have the same collective and ministerial responsibility as any other minister in the government. Different Welsh Secretaries have also shaped this role according to their own agenda and personality. Officially, party politics aside, the Secretary of State is responsible for the overall strategic direction of the Wales Office. Within this role, responsibilities include[14]:

- overall strategic direction (Westminster government policy direction in Wales): the UK government's voice in discussion with the Welsh government;

- dealing with relations between Wales and non-devolved departments, such as the Departments of Work and Pensions and Transport (excluding roads);
- attending and speaking at sessions of the National Assembly for Wales;
- constitutional and electoral issues and promoting devolution arrangements in Wales. This includes Westminster government and PR work and explaining how devolution operates[15];
- developing economy and business (non-devolved issues);
- Welsh budget (concerning the overall funding for the Welsh government);
- infrastructure (major projects and transport infrastructure);
- foreign affairs (Wales' connections with the wider world and the EU, acting as an ambassador for Wales, often in conjunction with the Welsh government);
- health (monitoring of);
- defence;
- localism[16];
- justice (law and policing); and
- a Welsh voice on the UK government's budget and in dealing with any primary legislation that impacts on Wales.

We should note that, as with all government departments at Westminster, there is also a Shadow Welsh Secretary and Front Bench team who mirror the roles and duties of the Welsh Secretary and his or her ministers. They come from the official opposition at Westminster and also act as a central lead figure for their own political party and Welsh MPs at Westminster. We also note that the Welsh Westminster ministers also have special advisers – political civil servants like their counterparts in the Welsh government.

The Wales Office

Location

Ever since the establishment of the Welsh Office in 1964 there has been a need for those representing government in Wales to have an administrative base in London. This is for the purposes of:

- working with other Whitehall departments who have responsibilities that impact on Wales;

- ensuring that the Welsh voice is heard in government; and
- making sure Welsh interests are taken into account in any relevant legislation.

For these purposes the former Welsh Office used a mansion dating back to 1772 called Gwydyr House, Whitehall. This was located close to the three most important government centres: Downing Street, the Treasury and the Cabinet Office. Former Welsh Secretary David Jones has described it as 'an embassy for Wales in London . . . a shop window for Wales'.[17] This now houses the Wales Office, the section of the Ministry of Justice that services the Welsh Secretary and their ministerial team. The Wales Office's central role therefore is to 'ensure the smooth working of the devolution settlement in Wales, representing the UK government in Wales . . . (they) also represent Welsh interests in Westminster'.[18] The Wales Office is headed by a director who manages a number of civil servants. They are responsible for various aspects of monitoring constitutional relationships and policy related to Cardiff Bay and Westminster. Gwydyr House also used to contain the Welsh government's Civil Service representative in London, but they are now located elsewhere.

Meetings and policy monitoring and creation[19]

The Wales Office has a series of sections/staff that mirror those of the Welsh Assembly/government. Under their respective ministers they coordinate their activities through weekly Wednesday meetings. These are called *Prayers*, and cover any issues arising over the previous week, any issues planned for the coming week, and any problems that need resolving with respect to Westminster or Cardiff Bay. The modern Wales Office also has an important role as the 'eyes of Wales in Whitehall'. In this respect, they contribute to any government policy that might impact on Wales. When a Westminster government develops new policy ideas they are sent around all Whitehall departments. The Wales Office then examines these to note whether the policy is:

1. in an area that is already devolved to Wales and within the remit of the Welsh government, as they will need to be consulted as well;
2. there is a policy area that for some reason, such as geography or industrial, will not work the same way in Wales and will therefore need to be amended;

3. not in a devolved area, but will still have an impact on Wales and will therefore need some comment on it or amendment before implementation.

If when the policy reaches maturity it requires legislative amendments, then the Wales Office will also seek agreement with other relevant departments for this to go ahead. Although the process can sometimes be seen to move slowly there are mechanisms at Westminster that can move it rapidly if required by the intervention of the Wales Office, such as curtailing time spent on the legislative discussion at Westminster. Normally, there are two junior ministers at the Welsh Office who share the portfolio of the Welsh Secretary. In recent years it has become the custom to draw one of these posts from the House of Lords. Those ministers, however, also hold a ministerial post in another department. This is something that Welsh Secretaries have done before but never junior ministers at the Wales Office.

Whitehall Cabinet committees

In Whitehall, the Welsh Secretary attends the full Cabinet meeting in Downing Street chaired by the Prime Minister, normally on Thursday mornings. As they are traditionally one of the most junior members of the Cabinet, the Welsh Secretary is often not seated close to or even within direct eye contact of the Prime Minister in these meetings. This put them at a disadvantage in pushing forward Welsh issues. Outside the Cabinet meetings, the Welsh Secretary attends a series of subcommittees, the most important of which is the Parliamentary Business and Legislation Committee (PBL). This is the central committee for legislation as it is here that Bills are pitched by various departments and difficult questions are asked by other ministers (it has been likened to 'the Dragons Den of legislation' in comparison with the TV show of the same name). It is here that the Wales Office ministers and civil servants check the legislative programme and ask questions about 'how it could impact on Wales?'

There are numerous other Cabinet subcommittees that which the Welsh Secretary or their ministers may attend. During the 2010–15 Westminster coalition government the most important of these was called the QUAD because it was made up of the four key positions of the coalition government. This sorted out any coalition disputes and was attended by the Prime Minister, Deputy Prime Minister, George Osborne (Chancellor of the Exchequer, Conservative) and Danny Alexander (Chief Secretary to the Treasury, Liberal Democrat). It was they that dealt with difficult decisions and decided on whether it could go through. They made one of three judgements:

1. agreed jointly and proceed to action;
2. negotiated something all could agree on; or
3. the decision never came out of the QUAD and stayed undecided.

For the last point we should note that when things could not be agreed, for example, on the Press Complaints Commission (Calcott), where both parties took different lines on the regulation of the press, no agreement on government action ever emerged. The QUAD was felt to be useful because the rules avoided the 'back stabbing and counter briefing' of the previous Labour Blair and Brown government over divisive policy issues.

Box 3.7 Case study: do we still need a Welsh Secretary?

Expert opinion during the first decade of devolution frequently speculated that the time of the Welsh Secretary had passed. In future, they believed that there should be just one powerful Territorial Cabinet Secretary instead of separate secretaries of states for each devolved nation. In addition, in 2011, both Plaid Cymru's leader, Ieuan Wyn Jones, and the Assembly's Presiding Officer, Lord Elis-Thomas, also argued for the Wales Office and Welsh Secretary to be scrapped.[20] It was noted that most powers of the Welsh Secretary had now been transferred to the Welsh government and its fifteen Cabinet and junior ministers. So was such a post still needed? After all, across the six decades that the post of Welsh Secretary has been in existence there have already been a number of times when the job has been downgraded or shared with other government posts and junior ministers at the Wales Office continue to do this. The last time being when Peter Hain combined the post with that of Leader of the House of Commons between 2003 and 2005.

In the mid-2000s, therefore, with Labour in power at Westminster and also in Scotland and Wales, it looked as though Scottish and Welsh secretaries would indeed evolve into this combined post. Even as recently as May 2015, however, a major review of devolution by BIICL, a respected legal think tank, called for the scrapping of all territorial secretaries posts, including that of Welsh Secretary, and replacing them with a single 'Secretary of State for the Union'.[21] Therefore, is there still a need to maintain a Cabinet Secretary for Wales, two junior ministers and a Civil Service staffed office at an annual cost of £13.5 million (in 2014/15)? Perhaps the role 'Could be undertaken by just one junior minister and a much smaller team under a Cabinet Secretary that deals with all devolved governments?' It appears the answer is 'no', mainly because there is currently no political desire to abolish the role of Welsh Secretary from within any of the political parties in Wales. There are a number of reasons why:

1. Politicians from all parties think it is important to keep the three territorial secretaries separate. This is because the devolved nations are all distinctly different politically and have differing degrees of devolved powers and responsibilities. This lack of uniformity means that different Cabinet secretaries are needed to understand the complexities of the various devolved nations.
2. The Welsh voice is normally the quietest in UK politics and could get lost at Westminster. It is felt by Welsh politicians that Scotland 'shouts loudest and threatens independence and therefore gets better treatment', Northern Ireland in turn has its historic problems and therefore gets extra money to 'keep the peace', therefore if the Welsh Secretary was not there for them it would be much harder to hear the Welsh voice.
3. Outside devolved issues, it is also important to have a Welsh voice in the Cabinet to ensure that Welsh issues are noticed and dealt with.
4. For the governing party(s) in Westminster it important to have a link person to the devolved administration in order to ensure cooperation on issues, as opposed to conflict. This could be the Deputy Prime Minister (as was the case in part during the coalition government), but the role normally sits best with the Welsh Secretary.
5. In periods when the government in Westminster is not of the same political persuasion as that in Wales, it is important for the government to ensure that there is someone in Wales who can be there to project their own case and to act as a political counterweight to their political opposition there.

It therefore looks as though the position of Welsh Secretary will remain constant, as long as there is a Welsh Assembly/government for them to interact with.

The concordats and committees/councils that govern Welsh government – Westminster relations

When the Welsh Assembly was first established the relationship between the Assembly and Westminster/Whitehall was mainly informal. This was a system that was helped by the fact that the same party – Labour – ran the government at the UK and Welsh levels. Over time, however, a system of formal arrangements has developed. These are referred to as Memorandums of Understanding (MOUs). They are agreed by the UK government and the devolved administrations, and set out the principles which underlie relations between these administrations.[22] Although not legally binding and more a statement of political intent rather than law, they form the basis for intergovernmental relations and cooperation.

The coalition government provided a revised MOU September 2012, which superseded the initial agreement of 2001. This MOU allowed for the continuance of the Joint Ministerial Committees and concordats on the EU, Financial Assistance to Industry and International Relations. Importantly, it also provides an agreement on dispute avoidance and resolution should the Welsh government fall into a dispute over a devolved issue with the UK government.

The Joint Ministerial Committees

The most visible aspect of MOUs is the Joint Ministerial Committees (JMCs). These act as a forum for ministers of the United Kingdom, Wales, Scotland and Northern Ireland governments. The system is designed to coordinate relations between them. These often revolve around both devolved and non-devolved issues, as well as any disagreements between administrations. The JMCs normally result in some form of joint declaration on agreed activity, if only to update the MOU once more. On occasions, the First Minister may use this or another meeting with one of the devolved government leaders to make a joint statement on policy that is contrary to the UK government. In June 2015, for instance, Nicola Sturgeon (Scottish First Minister) and Carwyn Jones issued a joint statement saying that it would be 'unacceptable' for the UK to leave the EU against the wishes of people in Scotland and Wales. This was despite the UK government insisting it was a UK-wide vote.[23] Welsh ministers also attend JMCs with their UK and devolved government counterparts in Whitehall to determine a UK approach to some policies.[24]

Despite these mechanisms designed to ensure that Whitehall communicates with Cardiff Bay over relevant issues, there remain problems with communications and general consultation. When Cheryl Gillian was Welsh Secretary in 2013 she noted that 'we're operating constitutionally in too many tramlines and not allowing what I would consider to be better communications'.[25] The result is that sometimes it is unclear if Wales is following English policy, its own policy or a combination of both. This is a situation that continued to course concern even after Gillian left the Wales Office.

Wales and Europe: Welsh MEPs, the European Parliament, EU Commission and Wales

In order to promote itself as more than a British region but also as a nation-state, Wales frequently seeks to do this within the structure of the EU. Sometimes who represents Wales abroad is not always clear, however: is it the First Minister, Welsh Secretary, Prime Minister or even the Prince of Wales or all four? Thankfully, there is some clarification available on this. The MOU between the Welsh and UK governments in September 2012 states quite clearly that it is the UK government that retains sovereignty when dealing with the EU. It accepts, however, that the Welsh government and Welsh Assembly will wish to maintain their own relations with the EU and provides for them to do so.[26]

Lord Kenneth Morgan in his book *Reflections on Welsh Democracy* (2014)[27] noted that over the last thirty years Wales has gone from being a mainly Eurosceptic country to one that has become mildly Eurosceptic. In July 2013, opinion polls for Wales were showing that 39 per cent of the population were in favour of leaving the EU, while only 29 per cent wanted to stay in; although by March 2016 polls were showing a reversal of this, with 41 per cent wanting to stay and 36 per cent wanting to leave.[28] Yet, almost from its inception, Wales has benefited or at least received substantial structural funds from the EU. The reason behind this is that Wales has continued its steady economic decline for almost the last half century. It therefore attracts European monies in order to help boost both its economy and social and educational infrastructure. Nevertheless, on 23 June 2016 Wales voted to leave the EU. Much to the dismay of most of its politicians, 52.5 per cent of the Welsh population voted to leave the EU compared with 47.5 per cent who voted to remain within it.

Although Wales like the rest of the United Kingdom will leave the EU, for the moment it continues within it. Therefore, like all other parts of the EU, Wales also sends elected MEPs to the two European parliaments in Brussels and Strasbourg. In 1979, Wales elected its first MEPs for single-member constituencies across Wales. Under the FPTP electoral system, three Labour MEPs and one Conservative were elected. This rose to five members between 1999 and 2004, but back down to four members from 2004 onwards. It is interesting to note that although the five Welsh MEPs' constituencies disappeared at a European level in 2004, they were retained for the Welsh Assembly's list of members constituencies and therefore continue as an accidental reminder of this period. In 1999, elections for Welsh MEPs, like those in the rest of the United Kingdom, moved over to the Closed Party List System of elections (see Chapter 7). Despite their low media profile, MEPs still maintain active political roles (Box 3.8).

Box 3.8 The role of Welsh MEPs

The central roles of MEPs are to:

1. assist in the scrutiny of European legislation;
2. act as the official spokesperson for their party on Welsh issues in Europe;
3. take part in and secure a role in influential committees of the European Parliament;
4. act as a lobbyist on behalf of Welsh issues in Europe, such as ensuring that Wales is included in key EU priorities for spending and development;
5. spend about one week a month on constituency issues in Wales.

Despite their differing political parties all four MEPs sometimes work together on common Welsh issues, such as securing increased European funding for Wales. They also often work with the Welsh government in helping to get access to key committees or meetings with senior EU officials.

The Welsh Assembly/government and Europe

The EU and European Parliament maintain a number of connections with Wales. In this respect, the body at the heart of the EU, the European Commission, has kept a permanent office in Cardiff since 1976. This office acts as a voice of the Commission in the Welsh

Assembly/government and the wider world of Welsh governance, civic, educational and business sectors. But the interaction between Wales and the EU is a two-way process. In this context, the rest of this section will examine the processes by which Welsh government and the Assembly interact with Europe.

Welsh government

Both the First and other Welsh ministers can and do attend Council of Ministers meetings together with UK ministers in order ensure that there is Welsh input into the European issues, although they rarely, if ever, lead the UK representation at these meetings. They also meet directly with European Commissioners to ensure there is Welsh input on European issues and access to European monies for areas such as Welsh infrastructure projects.[29] At a UK level, they also attend quarterly meetings of the JMC on Europe, which involves ministers from the UK government and the other devolved administrations. It is this JMC that also agrees a common front for all governments across the UK on EU issues. As we noted earlier, it is through these JMC meetings that the UK line on EU issues is formulated.

The Welsh government also maintains a Civil Service office in Brussels, which undertakes a number of functions in support of the Welsh government and relevant Welsh Assembly committees. The most prominent of these are to[30]:

1. raise the profile of Wales in the EU and work with the Wales European Commission Office;
2. influence EU-related policy development and legislation;
3. maximise the benefits to Wales of EU membership;
4. ensure that EU legislation is complied with in Wales;
5. raise awareness of EU issues in Wales;
6. support Welsh Assembly Committee enquiries into EU issues.

Welsh Assembly and European issues

European Union issues are close to a lot of the policy, legislative and committee work undertaken in Cardiff Bay. European matters are also debated in plenary sessions of the Welsh Assembly, and a number of the committees deal directly with European issues either wholly or partially as part of their agendas. Sometimes these meetings are in Cardiff and on other occasions they are in Brussels. In November 2013, for instance, the Enterprise and Business Committee spent two days in Brussels as part of its report on EU funding opportunities. Many other committees must also take on a European perspective in their own respective agendas, particularly in areas such as Agriculture, Fisheries and the Marine Environment. With respect to the Welsh Assembly's legislative role and the EU, regulations automatically become law in Wales as they do in all EU member states without going through the law-making process of the Welsh Assembly. EU directives, however, must either go through the Welsh law-making process or be adopted from the UK Parliament via their legislation (known as a Sewel motion, see Chapter 6).

For European funding issues the Welsh government has a Wales Programme Monitoring Committee chaired by an AM. There are another twenty-seven members on the committee, which is responsible for examining how European funding is maximised to its best effect across a number of funding areas, including the European Regional Development Fund (ERDF), European Social Fund (ESF) and European Agricultural Fund for Rural Development (EAFRD).

Up until the end of the fourth Assembly in 2016, the political parties in the Welsh Assembly had been broadly pro-EU in terms of their own policy and actions. These elections saw a number of Conservatives, including the party leader Andrew R. T. Davies, declare themselves as pro-Welsh Brexit from the EU. They also saw the election of seven UKIP AMs, and the demise of the pro-EU Welsh Liberal Democrats. Both of these factors changed the pro-EU consensus that had previously existed in the Assembly.

Wales and international affairs

In the nineteenth and the first half of the twentieth century the large ports along the South Wales coast attracted many international sailors and crews. In turn, there were many foreign consulates there to support these maritime employees. This is not the case today as, unlike elsewhere in the United Kingdom, there are no full-time foreign or Commonwealth consuls (embassy staff) representing their nation in Wales today. The only full-time consulate in Wales in recent years, that of Ireland, closed after the economic crash of 2008. There is, however, an extensive network of honorary consuls in Wales, who represent a large number of nations. They have some duties connected with visas, ambassadorial visits, attending Welsh state occasions and acting as a friendly face to the citizen's of their respective nation should they need help. Therefore, the Welsh government either works directly with honorary consuls, the Foreign and Commonwealth Office, London embassies, the European Commission office in Wales or the Welsh Centre for International Affairs on bringing diplomatic staff to Wales for various reasons. The Welsh government has its own civil servants tasked with coordinating international relations. The same is true of the Welsh Assembly, which also has an international relations team that supports AMs in engaging with international parliamentary networks and overseas activities.

Internationally, the Welsh government also has its own offices overseas. In this respect, it has about fourteen representations located in seven countries in various offices. These are currently located in some of the world's largest trading nations/blocs: Belgium (EU), China, India, Ireland, Japan, United Arab Emirates and the United States. These are responsible for trade and investment, government relations, tourism, culture and education. Many are a legacy of the offices once run by the now defunct Welsh Development Agency.

Although the Welsh Assembly is only meant to discuss and comment on national rather than international political matters, it does on occasions break these rules. Carwyn Jones, in 2017, for instance, called for the proposed state visit of US President Donald Trump to be postponed until after a controversial visa block on certain Muslim countries had been lifted. This position was backed by some other Welsh political leaders, including Plaid Cymru's leader Leanne Wood. Normally, however, both the Welsh government and Assembly seek to promote relations with other nations in a positive sense rather than criticise them.

Conclusion

Despite the wishes of some people, Wales is not an independent country and, even though there is a Welsh Assembly, much of the political decision-making still occurs outside Wales. Therefore, the politics of Westminster and Whitehall, Brussels and Strasbourg continue to play a central role in developing both Welsh public and private life. In this respect, the processes and procedures with which the Welsh government and Assembly interact with the other British and European legislatures and executives can change quite radically in a small space of time.

Part of the central dynamic in the process of intergovernmental relations is this need for change. The first dramatic change was in 2010 when the government in Westminster was no longer of the same political party as that in Cardiff Bay. This meant new mechanisms had to be developed as Welsh and Westminster government issues could no longer be dealt with an inter-party way. The second big change occurred with respect to European governance in 2016 with the hardening of anti-EU attitudes within the Welsh Conservatives, the arrival of UKIP at the Welsh Assembly and the demise of the pro-EU Welsh Liberal Democrats. The Welsh Assembly's pro-EU consensus had ended. Both changes mean that the mechanisms for Welsh political interactions outside the country will continue to evolve.

Questions for discussion

1. To what extent has Westminster been adapted to reflect the interests and governance of Wales?
2. What is the Welsh Secretary's role in Westminster?
3. Wales only has four MEPs, with such a small number can they still play any significant role?

Case study: do we still need a Welsh Secretary?[31]

Read the text in the case study in Box 3.7, then answer the following questions:

1. Who believes that the post of Welsh Secretary should go and why?
2. Give three reasons why you think no Westminster government has scrapped the post of Welsh Secretary?
3. Examine the career of a recent Welsh Secretary and try to find a story in which they have 'fought Wales' corner' and another where they seem not to have done. For each story give a reason as to why the Welsh Secretary sought this cause of action.

Suggested answer points are provided in the Welsh Government and Politics online resource for both the questions and the case study. The web link for these answer points is given at the front of the book.

4

The Welsh Government: The Core Executive

Russell Deacon

Overview

At the heart of the Welsh political story is the Welsh government (also known as the core executive). The Welsh government is centred around the First Minister and his or her Cabinet. Although the Welsh Assembly was a new form of democracy in the United Kingdom, it follows closely many of the precedents of the government in London (Westminster/ Whitehall). Ministers are selected in similar ways to those in the UK government and also abide by the doctrines of ministerial and collective responsibility in the same manner. Each Welsh post also has its own roles and responsibilities, and these are examined within this chapter. The chapter also provides an overview of the relationship between ministers, their special advisers and civil servants. It concludes by examining how a long period of one party dominance by Labour has impacted on the evolution of Welsh government.

- What is the nature and structure of the Welsh government?
- How similar is the core executive in Wales to that of the UK government?
- How do you become the First Minister and what skills and attributes to you need?
- What are the limitations on the First Minister's powers?
- How is the Welsh Cabinet structured?
- To what extent do Welsh ministers have to observe the twin doctrines of Cabinet and collective responsibility?
- What is the role of special advisers in Welsh government?
- What is the role of the Welsh Civil Service?

The role and function of the Welsh government

The Welsh government in Wales is different from others anywhere else in the United Kingdom in that it has been dominated by one political party from inception – the Labour Party. From the outset, all three Welsh First Ministers have been from the Labour Party, as have the majority of the Welsh government Cabinet. This makes Welsh politics unique because since the arrival of devolution in 1999 no one political party elsewhere in the United Kingdom has been so dominant in any one legislature. At the heart of the Welsh government is what is known as the core executive (Box 4.1). The actions of the core executive are key to the running of the Welsh government not only on a day-to-day basis, but also with respect to short- and long-term policy planning.

Box 4.1 What is the core executive in Wales?

In the Wales the core executive consists of:

First Minister: assisted by his or her own political office, Cabinet, Cabinet Office, political advisers (SPADs), policy units, the Cabinet secretary and his or her staff.

Deputy First Minister: assisted by his or her own political office and political advisers (SPADs), their main area of responsibility is normally specific policy areas such as economic development.

Welsh government Cabinet: assisted by Cabinet committees, Cabinet Office, policy units, senior civil servants, deputy ministers. 'Experts' and external specialists may also be called to assist, as may senior civil servants and policy units.

Ministers (Cabinet and non-Cabinet): assisted by their own political office, senior civil servants, private advisers, policy units.

The role and function of the First Minister

When it comes to Welsh politics the most visible figure within Wales, nationally and internationally, is that of the First Minister. The Welsh government is led by a First Minister, who is also the leader of the majority party in the Assembly. The First Minister is the most politically powerful of all of the AMs. It is they who are also the public face of the Welsh government and the dynamo which keeps the Welsh government running.

At the Welsh Assembly's commencement, the First Minister (Secretary) and the Westminster Cabinet Welsh Secretary were the same man, Alun Michael. This was undertaken in order to maintain continuity in the government's running of Wales in its initial stages. Since then the position of Welsh Secretary has only been held by an MP. There is no equivalent of 10 Downing Street in Cardiff. In fact, early attempts to have a distinct building for the First Minister in the Pierhead were rejected at the outset of the Welsh Assembly and instead the First Minister's main office remains in Tŷ Hywel, the red-brick building at the back of the Welsh Assembly's Senedd Building.[1] The First Minister also retains an office at the old Crown Building in Cathays Park, Cardiff. Since 2007, the First Minister has been directly appointed by the monarch and represents the Crown in Wales.

As the evolution of the post has continued, each First Minister has been able to strengthen the role both in Wales and within the UK's own political structures (Box 4.2).

Box 4.2 The evolution of the role of First Minister

As the Welsh Assembly has evolved, so has the post of its First Minister so that now its status is considered comparable to that of a Prime Minister. Under the Government of Wales Act 1998, a post of First Secretary rather than First Minister was established. This was said to be for three reasons: first, that as the Assembly had been established as a corporate body rather than as a parliamentary executive the term Secretary was more appropriate; second, as the Welsh Assembly had been established as less powerful body than that created in Northern Ireland or Scotland the term was needed to distinguish between them; and, third, that that the Welsh term for First Minister, *Prif Weinidog*, means Prime Minister in English so a different title was needed to avoid confusion with the UK Prime Minister.

After the start of the first coalition Welsh government in 2000, however, it was decided to use the term First Minister. This was formalised by the Government of Wales Act 2006, which also gave the First Minister the title of 'Keeper of the Welsh Seal'. This same Act ensured that in future the First Minister would be directly appointed by the Crown and act on its behalf in Wales

The First Minister is also a member of the Privy Council, which means that he or she is formally addressed as the Right Honourable (Rt. Hon.) before his or her name. The Privy Council is attended by senior politicians and judiciary from across the United Kingdom. Its primary role is to advise the monarch and it has some judicial and ceremonial functions, but most of these are now delegated elsewhere and today it is mainly ceremonial in purpose. It does, however, have some practical purposes for the First Minister, and it was at a meeting of the Privy Council at Buckingham Palace, London, on 14 December 2011, that the Queen formally presented Carwyn Jones with the 'Welsh Seal', for the stamping of Welsh Acts.

The election of the First Minister

The First Minister is appointed by the Queen and represents the Crown in Wales. The constitutional significance of this is that the head of government in Wales is appointed by the Crown on the advice of the elected representatives of the Welsh people (the Welsh Assembly), without direct reference to the government in Westminster. This formal appointment therefore must be made after he or she has also received the endorsement of a majority vote of the Welsh AMs.

The First Minister, however, must normally undergo two elections. Both offer a restricted franchise of party members and/or elected AMs; neither are by the general public and are therefore not presidential in nature. The first election is for the Assembly leadership of their political party; the second election is by elected AMs to directly elect him or her as First Minister. This is either after the Welsh General Election or upon the resignation, death or dismissal of the previous First Minister.

After the first Welsh Assembly elections the leader of the largest political party – Labour – Alun Michael was elected as First Secretary (later First Minister). This process is then repeated after each new Welsh General Election or upon a resignation. Although at times the post is contested by other Welsh political parties, numerically only the candidate with the largest support from AMs can win. Therefore, it has remained within the domain of the Labour Party. If there is a sudden resignation, as was the case with Alun Michael in February 2000, the largest political party nominates a temporary First Minister to hold the post until there can be official re-elections. In that instance it was Rhodri Morgan. When Morgan's own resignation was announced, some years later, it was well in advance so a more orderly progression was enabled. Carwyn Jones was elected as leader by the Welsh Labour Party and Rhodri Morgan was therefore able to resign with his successor already in place.

The role of the First Minister

Both nationally and internationally, the First Minister is seen as the most senior Welsh politician. Often he or she lead the nation on occasions of importance, ranging from international military commemoration connected with the First and Second World Wars to home rugby internationals. Outside these occasions, however, the First Minister's role has been shaped over the duration of the post's existence. The role has therefore come to mean that he or she is there to[2]:

- lead the Assembly;
- lead their own political party in Wales;
- be the head of the Welsh government;
- act as a Welsh figurehead, representing Wales at national and international occasions;
- liaise with the Welsh Secretary and Prime Minister over issues of governance;
- lead and select the Welsh government's Cabinet, the Deputy Welsh Ministers and the Counsel General for Wales (law officer) with the approval of the Queen;

- liaise with the UK government, in particular the Prime Minister and the Secretary of State for Wales (and other Whitehall ministers as necessary), on fiscal matters, policy and legislation relevant to the Welsh Assembly;
- ensure that the party's Assembly manifesto or any coalition agreement is implemented;
- develop and coordinate new policy and legislative initiatives;
- take a lead in promoting AMs and selecting members of the Cabinet;
- represent the Assembly in European institutions and overseas;
- hold regular question times within the Assembly for AMs; and
- take part in some staffing and Civil Service matters in Wales.

What strengths does one need to have to become the First Minister and remain in post?

Up until the Welsh Assembly's fifth term in 2016 there have only been three First Ministers in Wales: Alun Michael, 1999–2000; Rhodri Morgan, 2000–9; and Carwyn Jones, 2009–. All have been members of the Labour Party. They also had some other factors in common:

1. they were all middle-aged, university-educated, married, white and male;
2. they had gained previous political experience in local government as councillors, and in the case of Rhodri Morgan and Alun Michael, their elected experience also included substantial periods as Westminster MPs. In fact, Alun Michael never stopped being an MP even while serving as an AM;
3. they were all fluent Welsh-speakers, a skill that may well be vital in a bilingual legislature such as the Welsh Assembly. It also enabled them to communicate their message across the entire Welsh population;
4. they had a background of loyalty and service to the Labour Party and Labour governments; and
5. their constituencies were all in South Wales, either in Cardiff or Bridgend, although Alun Michael was born in Anglesey.

Therefore, for the first four terms of the Welsh Assembly the key characteristics required of a First Minister could be said to be a male, south Wales elected Labour AM who was also a Welsh-speaker. While this may be true for getting the job in the first place, it does not adequately explain the skills a First Minister needs to have in order to keep the job.

So, what are the skills a First Minister needs to remain in office? Over the Assembly's first four terms a number of these skills became apparent. As no political party in Wales has ever achieved an electoral majority, the Welsh government must frequently get its own policy, fiscal and legislative agenda through with the support of other political parties. Therefore, in order to stay in office the First Minister must also develop and use the following skills[3]:

Command the respect and loyalty of their own members in order to avoid any party rebellion: the First Minister must always ensure that his or her own party is on-board with regard to any policy he or she wishes to implement. If they are not, then the First Minister may also seek to persuade them through some other inducement or reward for themselves or their constituencies. This could be the offer of promotion or a specific high-profile job implementing policy or something extra financially for their own constituency. This is also known by the US political term 'Pork Barrel' politics or providing an electoral sweetener.

To remain popular with the Welsh electorate: in order to enhance the status of the Welsh Assembly and help keep the Welsh public on-board with the devolution project in Wales, a First Minister needs to remain popular and respected by the Welsh population. Opinion polls concerning the popularity of both Rhodri Morgan and Carwyn Jones constantly show them with popularity ratings considerably above their own political parties. They also need to be aware that if this popularity is dented it could cause an electoral backlash. This was felt to be the case in 2004 when Rhodri Morgan decided not to attend the D-Day commemorations in France. This incident was later felt by himself and others to have dented his own popularity in what was seen by some as a 'snub to war veterans'.

To remain popular within your own political party: in order to stay in their role as First Minister, there is a strong need to retain the support of one's party members both inside and outside the Welsh Assembly. By February 2000, Alun Michael had lost the support of the majority of his party's AMs, which became evident in internal party meetings. He was therefore unable maintain the support of his own party before a crucial confidence vote in his Welsh government and had to resign. Both Rhodri Morgan and Carwyn Jones have therefore sought to ensure that they retain close links with their own party, particularly with their AMs. Unlike the government in Westminster, due to the fact that no one party has ever had a majority at the Welsh Assembly First Ministers cannot afford for even one of their members to rebel, otherwise they would not be able to put their policy through.

In 2005, the Labour AM and former Assembly Secretary for Local Government and Housing, Peter Law, fell out with his own party over the introduction of all-women shortlists for the election of Westminster candidates for his Bleanau Gwent constituency. Law felt that he was the natural choice to stand for election to the Westminster seat when the incumbent MP, Llew Smith, stood down. Yet when Smith did so, Law was barred from standing for the seat because it was open to female nominations only. In a complex process, Law then resigned from his party, stood as an independent and won the seat at the 2005 General Election. Law then sat as an Independent in the Welsh Assembly, reducing Labour's seats to twenty-nine, that is, less than half of the total. As Law, and later his wife (who took over his seat after his death), voted mainly with the opposition for the next two years, the Welsh Labour government was held hostage to negotiations with the other political parties in order to get any business through the Assembly. In the process, the Law affair illustrated clearly what can happen if just one member of the ruling party rebels against it.

To act as a statesman for their nation: in many ways the First Minister acts as the national figurehead, acting as a ceremonial figure on occasions of national importance, such as a major international event staged in Wales or the opening of a large-scale project or building. On these occasions, the First Minister performs the role of statesman above domestic Welsh politics and seeks to minimise any controversy.

What are the limitations on the First Minister's powers?

As in any democracy, the powers of the leader are limited and the First Minister is no exception to this. Although he or she is the most powerful politician based in Wales, there are a number of limitations on what the First Minister and his or her government can and cannot do:

1. Statutory and constitutional: what the Wales Acts (1998 and 2006) states that she or he can and cannot do. The policy areas the First

Minister and his or her government can pursue are defined in law and he or she cannot legally go outside these. To go outside these powers is known by the Latin phrase *ultra vires* (beyond the powers). If the First Minister does so, then his or her actions can be challenged as an illegal act (administrative review) in the UK Supreme Court or European courts.

2. The Welsh Assembly has the power to reject any Welsh government policy if it can get a majority vote against the government. At the same time, its various scrutiny committees can also advise against or severely criticise government policy. Between 2005 and 2007, for instance, the Welsh minority government was regularly defeated on issues of policy, which acted as restraint on the First Minister's own powers.

3. Fiscal barriers: the Welsh government's budget is restricted, it has limited tax-raising powers and is reliant on the money coming from Westminster. This therefore restricts the amount of money that can be spent on the First Minister's policy desires

4. Ruling party(s) barriers: the First Minister's own political party or coalition partner needs to be carried with them on policy issues. In the past the conservative nature of the Wales Labour Party, for instance, has led to a slower evolutionary process of devolutionary growth than that in Scotland. In addition, if the Welsh government is a coalition government the First Minister's powers can be restrained by the need to keep his or her coalition partners on-board.

5. The First Minister's own Welsh Westminster MPs or even his or her party leadership in London may seek to block policy. Welsh Labour MPs, for instance, can also act as a restraint on the First Minister's policies by blocking changes within the Welsh Labour Party

6. Not gaining an overall majority in the Welsh Assembly also acts as a constraint on the First Minister's powers as he or she will often have to bargain with another political party in order to get policies through. This is most common at the time of the Welsh government's annual budget negotiations.

7. Similarly, the government in Westminster, of whatever party, can considerably curtail the First Minister's scope for action either fiscally or through statutes or legal challenge testing or reducing his or her powers. In this respect, Westminster retains the legal sovereignty to reduce or curtail the First Minister's powers.

8. The Welsh Secretary scrutinises the actions of the Welsh government to ensure that they are legal. She or he may also add pressure

to change any actions seen as being contrary to the 'Welsh national interest'.

9. The loyalty of their own AMs: the First Minister needs to retain the loyalty of his or her own party. In 2000, First Minister Alun Michael lost the support of his own party and was replaced by Rhodri Morgan when he could not retain their loyalty. Therefore, the First Minister needs to ensure that all his or her AMs are kept on-board.

10. Events: both the Welsh media and Welsh public opinion can also impact on the powers and actions of the First Minister according to topical events or stories. In recent years, poor PISA educational score results, problems with the Welsh steel industry and the poor state of the Welsh NHS compared with England have pressurised the First Minister to concentrate on these areas rather than others.

11. Resources: Wales is a small country with limited resources, there-fore, the knowledge, experience or resources of the executive are not always available to pursue as a distinctly Welsh agenda as the First Minister may wish. The Civil Service may be ill-equipped to carry out the policy agenda or even advise against it being imple-mented at all. This may mean that the First Minister has to borrow or follow the English agenda on certain policy areas directly or not be able to implement them. In 2002, for instance, a policy pledge to give every school child an email account was dropped when civil servants advised that there could be child protection concerns.[4]

Choosing a Cabinet and the role of Cabinet and Deputy Ministers

The First Minister selects his or her Cabinet on a variety of different cri-teria. Due in part to young nature of Welsh democracy and the size of the ministerial pool of AMs, the experience of those joining the Welsh Cabinet is often nowhere near as significant as those that are appointed in the Westminster government. Few of those appointed have had any substantial experience outside Welsh local government before being appointed to run the Welsh government's departments. For the first Welsh Assembly Cabinet, the *Western Mail* journalist Martin Shipton noted:

Those chosen by (Alun) Michael to join the Cabinet were Rhodri Morgan (Economic Development), Andrew Davies (Assembly Business Manager), Peter Law (Local Government), Tom Middlehurst

(Post-16 Education), Rosemary Butler (Pre-16 Education), Jane Hutt (Health and Social Services), Edwina Hart (Finance) and Christine Gwyther (Agriculture). With the exception of Michael and Morgan, none of them had a national profile. Andrew Davies was a former party apparatchik who had worked in industry as a human resources and welfare officer and had latterly been working as a public affairs consultant (i.e. lobbyist) for a firm run by Leighton Andrews (later Welsh Education Minister), co-founder of the Yes for Wales referendum campaign in 1997. Law, Middlehurst and Butler were essentially full-time councillors, Hutt worked in the voluntary sector, Hart was a bank union official and Gwyther was a council officer. They had a steep learning curve to climb . . .[5]

Since the first Cabinet government ministers have continued to gain experience whilst in post, but few have come into the Cabinet with any prior experience of running a government department. Although they may not have previously run a department, in theory minister's are chosen because they have some knowledge or experience in respect of the department they are to run. At the start of the Assembly in 1999, however, there was considerable upset in the farming community when Alun Michael appointed Christine Gwyther as Agriculture Minister. Welsh farming is concerned mainly with livestock (meat) production, yet Gwyther was a vegetarian. In 1999, Tom Middlehurst, who was appointed to be the minister in charge of the Welsh language, was unable to speak or read Welsh, nor was his successor Jenny Randerson.[6]

Box 4.3 How are Welsh Cabinet members selected?

The first time a minister formally knows of their potential appointment is when they are phoned by a special adviser and asked to meet the First Minister at their Cathays Parc, Cardiff, offices. The appointment is made therefore directly by the First Minister after discussion with the candidate.

The minister is defined in law as a Welsh Minister of the Crown, which operates under Royal Prerogative powers.[7] This is the same status as that of a minister in the UK government. Cabinet members are chosen on the basis of:

1. the views of the First and, if applicable, Deputy First Minister;
2. their interest in doing the job;
3. their loyalty to the party and government;

4. tenure and experience as an AM or previous ministerial posts;
5. a balance between male and female;
6. their geographical location (which area of Wales they represent). The First Minister normally tries to ensure that minister's constituencies are spread across Wales and are not over-represented by one area such as South Wales Central.

As is the case with the UK government, Welsh Cabinet ministers are officially appointed by the Queen on the recommendation of the First Minister. We should also note that in a coalition government the Deputy First Minister decides on his or her party's Cabinet members.

Of all the Cabinet ministers, after the First and Deputy First Ministers, it is the post of the Business, Enterprise, Technology and Science (now Economy, Science and Transport) that is regarded as the most important ministerial post. The first holder of this post was Rhodri Morgan, the twice-failed Wales Labour leadership contender. His appointment was seen as a consolation prize for his failed leadership bids. Deputy First Ministers Michael German and Ieuan Wyn Jones have also held this post in conjunction with their wider Deputy role.

Another Cabinet portfolio, the Leader of the House and Chief Whip, formerly known as the Business Minister, is key to the running of the Welsh government. They have to ensure that the government's business agenda and legislative programme goes through smoothly and on time. At the same time, they also have to make sure that their own party backs the government in any votes in the Assembly chamber and remains publicly supportive of it.

All of the Assembly ministers hold regular question times within the Senedd Chamber, just as their counterparts do in Westminster. It is here that AMs can ask them oral or written questions. In addition to these questions, ministers are also scrutinised by the appropriate Assembly committee that covers their portfolio. Often, these produce extensive reports on areas that are relevant to developing policy or legislation.

At its outset in 2010, the Westminster Cabinet of the coalition government became infamous for its lack of female representation; in contrast, on the whole, the Welsh government has achieved a stronger balance. Although no female has been First Minister, there have been times when the Welsh government Cabinet had a female majority (five of nine ministers in 2003). In recent years, this has declined and the figure went back down to three of eleven in 2014, but rose again to six of twelve in 2016.

What is the Welsh government Cabinet?

The 2006 Wales Act allowed for the appointment of a maximum of twelve Welsh ministers. This includes the posts of Deputy Welsh Ministers, but, importantly, excludes the posts of First Minister and Counsel General. This means that the maximum size of the Welsh government is fourteen members. With respect to titles, those ministers that run a government department are known as the 'Cabinet Secretary for . . .', whereas those junior ministers that serve under them are referred to as the 'Minister for . . .' in order to distinguish their rank and status.

The term 'Cabinet' itself is derived from the Middle French word *Cabinet* meaning 'small room'. For the British government these came to be associated with the smaller gathering of ministers rather than the whole of the governing party. This term is now used generally for meetings of the senior ministers/councillors for any political governing body in the United Kingdom. As is the case elsewhere, the Cabinet in Wales is the main decision-making body of the Welsh government. In this respect, it provides the policy direction for the Welsh government. It also, however, acts as a sounding-board for new ideas, collective government planning, financial planning for departments and strategy (see Box 4.4).

The Cabinet is chaired by the First Minister, and it is he or she who therefore directs and determines the proceedings. They normally meet on Monday in Cathays Park, Cardiff. All ministers meet for the Cabinet. The Permanent Secretary, Cabinet Secretary, Cabinet Secretariat and about twenty advisers also attend, although they may not all be in the room for the entire duration of the ninety-minute meeting. Also in attendance are the special advisers, Cabinet Secretary, First Minister's Principal Private Secretary and Head of Strategic Communication (Press Officer). Added to these are the Cabinet Secretariat and often presentations by senior civil servants on departmental issues increase the number. All of this means that Cabinet Meetings can at any one time have thirty-five to forty people in attendance. Every month there is also a political Cabinet where the civil servants leave the room and purely party political issues are discussed.[8]

We should also note that the Assembly Cabinet has various subcommittees that deal with specific areas of policy and legislation. They then report back to the full Cabinet. The type and nature of these is determined as the need demands.

Box 4.4 The role of the Welsh Cabinet

1. Determining presentation of policy.
2. Making decisions that bind the government together collectively.
3. Settling departmental/ministerial disputes.
4. Legitimising decisions made elsewhere within the government.
5. Responding to events elsewhere, such as in Whitehall and Westminster and the relations with the Westminster government, through bodies such as the Joint Ministerial Committee (Domestic).
6. Setting up and/or responding to the work of major committees/commissions that are examining aspects of Welsh government policy.
7. Setting a political agenda for both electoral and strategic purposes.
8. Allowing any coalition or partnership government strategies or problems to be addressed and determined collectively.
9. Ensuring that they govern effectively enough to be re-elected.

The Welsh Cabinet and collective responsibility

The Welsh government has borrowed much of its procedures and structures from the precedents set by the government in Westminster/Whitehall One of the central rules the Welsh government follows is that of collective responsibility. This means that ministers are bound together by collective responsibility. In reality, this means that they are collectively responsible for all government decisions and policies. Interestingly, opposition parties also use the doctrine of collective responsibility when they wish to supress dissenting voices in their own ranks, even though they are not in government.[9]

At a UK level collective responsibility has been at the heart of Cabinet government since the 1850s, and is based on the concept of collegiality. Therefore, the Cabinet seeks to make decisions on the basis that they will all take responsibility for the decision, whatever their personal opinions or constituency obligations may be. Collective responsibility means therefore that ministers accept that they are part of a collective body. Lynch and Fairclough (2013) provide us with four conventions of collective responsibility for the Westminster government that can equally apply to the Welsh one, these are that[10]:

1. all Cabinet decisions must be defended by all ministers (in and out of Cabinet);
2. any minister who wishes to dissent in public must resign their ministerial post or face dismissal;
3. ministers are free to dissent from a policy or decision in private, but must then defend it in public; and
4. ministers who resign because they cannot support a collective Cabinet decision are normally considered honourable, and while their political careers may be adversely affected in the short run, they may return to office in the long run.

The Welsh Assembly is a much smaller body than Westminster with respect to the number of elected representatives. It is less than 10 per cent the size of the House of Commons so it is far easier for constituency issues to impact on Cabinet members. It is this area of conflict therefore that has caused some of the greatest problems for Welsh ministers (see Box 4.7). As the First Minister will often be constrained by the fact that he or she is leading a minority or coalition government, he or she cannot afford to alienate any member of the government, even after they resign. In this respect, the First Minister will often be obliged to leave the door open for a return to office in order to ensure the ex-minister remains loyal to the government.

We should also note that collective responsibility is taken in a far wider context than with Westminster governments, and is also applied to Assembly Committee chairs who are not directly in the Welsh government even if they still happen to be of the same party. In this respect, in October 2015, Labour AM Jenny Rathbone, publicly criticised the Welsh Labour government for spending millions on the M4 Relief Road rather than on other areas of policy. As a result, First Minister Carwyn Jones removed Rathbone from her chairmanship of the All Wales European Programme Monitoring Committee. In doing so, Mr Jones said: 'The chair of the programme monitoring committee is an appointment made by the First Minister, because that person, as is made clear in a letter of appointment, is a representative of the (Labour) Welsh Government.'[11] In this respect, the 'person is required to have particular regard to act in the spirit of collective responsibility, the main principle of the ministerial code'. This is not the same position as Westminster, where the legislature seeks to remain detached from the direct influence of the executive. To try to counter this, the Assembly Presiding Officer, Elin Jones, and the Business Committee, in June 2016, moved to a system of chairs being elected by secret ballot to remove some of the powers of appointment from the party leaders.[12]

Box 4.5 Case study: Education Minister Leighton Andrews resigns over collective responsibility[13]

On 25 June 2013, the Welsh Education Minister, Leighton Andrews, resigned after a conflict between his role as a constituency member and that of Education Minister. Whilst accepting his resignation, First Minister Carwyn Jones noted: 'I recognise very well that there is sometimes tension between the role of a government minister and the demands of a constituency assembly member . . . The ministerial code aims to define the boundaries between the two roles and, on this occasion, I believe those roles were confused.'

On this occasion, Andrews had breached the Cabinet's collective responsibility for the schools closure policy and therefore had to resign. He had campaigned openly against school closures in his own constituency, which was against his own government's policy.

The Welsh government and ministers

The Government of Wales Act 2006 limits the size of the Welsh government to twelve ministers, including deputies but excluding the First Minister and the Counsel General for Wales. There are currently (2017) ten ministers (including the First Minister) and three deputy ministers in the Welsh government. In addition, the Chief Whip and Counsel General for Wales also attend Cabinet meetings. Although the Counsel General is not an elected post, the other fourteen are serving AMs. This means that nearly half of all of the governing party in the Assembly serve in government.

Box 4.6 What is the role of the Counsel General?

In 2003, the Chief Legal Adviser to the Assembly, Winston Roddick QC, recommended that in future that post be referred to as the Counsel General.

In 2006, that was formalised in the Government of Wales Act and given statutory functions. This was at the same time that a parliamentary division was made between the legislature and the executive in the Welsh Assembly. Initially, it was a post that was held by elected members: Carwyn Jones, 2007–9, and John Griffiths, 2009–11, both of whom were former lawyers. The post, however, is the only one in the Welsh Assembly that may be held by an unelected official. From May 2011, the post was also open to a non-elected member of the Welsh government to sit in the Cabinet. The first holder of this new non-elected post was the Welsh barrister, Theodore Huckle QC. The position is commenced by a formal swearing-in ceremony undertaken by the Presiding Judge of the Wales Circuit on behalf of the Queen.

The Counsel General is appointed in the same as way as other ministers, albeit via a recruitment process, and must abide by the same ministerial code (Box 4.7). They also lead a team of other law officers, including the First Counsel to the Welsh Government who represents them in legal cases involving matters that raise issues of constitutional or major public importance.

It is the Counsel General who oversees the legislative process inside the Assembly (from Bills to Acts), monitors the extent to which the Assembly Acts are within its legislative competence and refers them to the UK Supreme Court for a decision if this is required. He or she may also represent the government directly there. The Counsel General is also responsible for the government's interaction with the legal processes and community within Wales. In addition, they help to follow through any legal action brought by or against the Assembly in the courts. These cases may be of constitutional significance. In 2017, for instance, the Welsh government Counsel General, Mick Antoniw AM, brought an unsuccessful case before the Supreme Court on the right of the Welsh government to be consulted on Brexit.

The role of the private office

Like the First Minister, the other secretaries and ministers have their own support team within the Civil Service, plus their own private office and staff. The private office has been seen as the political life-support machine that serves each minister from the moment they are appointed. Headed by a private secretary (chief of staff), the private office plays a central role in the core executive by ensuring that the minister is able to carry out his or her role effectively. The private office, however, is a facilitator for the wider government department rather than being a source of advice or expertise in its own right. This role falls either to the minister's own special adviser and/or the wider department or other experts. The private office therefore has two main roles:

1. to act as a doorway to the wider department, ensuring that the minister can make well-informed decisions and that these will be acted upon; and
2. to remain loyal and trusted by the minister, but at the same time remaining attached to the wider department it is serving.

Box 4.7 What is the Ministerial Code?

In order to ensure that ministers behave in the most effective and ethical manner there is a Ministerial Code issued by the First Minister. This applies to all secretaries, the Counsel General and ministers. It covers areas such as the details of ministers' own special advisers, ministers' own interests, any gifts ministers receive over £260 in value and any overseas travel costing more than £500.

The code states that: 'In the performance of their duties, Ministers are expected to behave according to the highest standards of constitutional and personal conduct. In particular, they are expected to observe the Seven Principles of Public Life and the principles of Ministerial Conduct.' It comes from Lord Nolan's Commission on Standards in Public Life, which, in the 1990s, stated that all public officials should adhere to the following seven basic principles: selflessness, integrity, objectivity, accountability, openness, honesty and leadership. Although this was before the establishment of the Welsh Assembly, the seven Nolan principles have become the benchmark for ethical codes in British public life.

In 2014, the then Natural Resources and Food Minister, Alun Davies, sent a letter to Natural Resources Wales (NRW) in which he said he was 'very disappointed' by the body's approach to the Circuit of Wales new racing track proposals for an application to build in Ebbw Vale. This was Mr Davies' own constituency and the opposition claimed he had broken the ministerial code by interfering on an issue for which he was also the minister. In response to this, First Minister Carwyn Jones asked the Permanent Secretary Sir Derek Jones to 'look into the facts' surrounding whether Jones had indeed broken the ministerial code. Mr Davies was deemed to have done so and therefore was removed from office by the First Minister.[14]

The Welsh government and ministerial responsibility

Cabinet secretaries and ministers are deemed to be responsible for what goes on in their own department and also how their own personal actions may reflect on the department or the government. As a rule, this means that they should not undertake any activity or sanction their department undertaking any activities that are either illegal, unethical or generally against their own ministerial or departmental codes of conduct or manifesto policy. The Cabinet Secretary or minister is therefore open to challenge if this is seen to occur. This is called ministerial responsibility and is as an important a constitutional doctrine as collective responsibility. Despite frequent calls for ministers to resign, actual cases of ministers doing so are limited because most seek to weather out any 'political storms' they have knowing that public and media attention may soon shift to another topic and forget their specific issue (Box 4.8).

Box 4.8 Case study: 'Smoke without fire': a case of Welsh ministerial responsibility[15]

In July 2008, the Plaid Cymru Welsh government Culture Minister, Rhodri Glyn Thomas, resigned after claims he walked in to a pub holding a lit cigar. Witnesses at the pub claimed that Thomas was reprimanded by staff for having a lit cigar in his hand as he walked in. There had been a smoking ban introduced in public houses in Wales from 2 April 2008. Thomas was the Welsh government Minister for Heritage at the time.

Previously, at the at the 2008 Wales Book of the Year Thomas incorrectly announced that Tom Bullough was the winner of a prize when it was in fact Dannie Abse. This generated a lot of negative publicity for Thomas and he resigned his minister post stating: 'In the light of the publicity that has been following me in the last weeks I feel that my position in the government is no longer sustainable.' Although no civil servant in his department had been responsible for any misconduct Thomas had taken personal ministerial responsibility for his action damaging his own department and the government and therefore resigned.

The role and nature of special advisers

Often the civil servant that works the closest with the minister works the same long hours and is normally even in the same party as the minister.

They are known as special advisers, also known by the acronym of SPAD. They are a politically appointed civil servant who existence is wholly dependent on both the electoral cycle and the term of office of the First Minister/minister they serve.

Whereas in the old Welsh Office there was normally only one SPAD, the Welsh government normally has around seven, a number that can increase if there is a coalition government. They may not necessarily cover all policy areas, however, and in 2013, for instance, there were no SPADS covering some of the biggest spending departments at the Welsh Assembly, such as Education, Local Government and Health. As we noted earlier, they also attend Welsh government Cabinet meetings.

Special advisers are often seen as the political civil servant who is most closely associated with the creative part of the policy process.[16] Sometimes they are also seen as a political dynamo creating much of the Welsh government's own manifesto or ongoing policy. The former special adviser to the Welsh Labour government, Sophie Howe, for instance, was seen as being central to developing the Welsh government's policy and legislative proposals for the Domestic Abuse Bill. This was something that was later to help her secure the post of Deputy Police and Crime Commissioner for South Wales Police.[17] An SPADs role can, however, be at times controversial (see Box 4.9).

Box 4.9 Does the Welsh Government really need special advisers (SPADS)?

There are arguments for and against the question set above.

Yes

There is no doubt that the Welsh government values special advisers and in this respect has continued to use them.

• The Welsh government views them as adding[18]:

[a] political dimension to the advice and assistance available to Ministers while reinforcing the political impartiality of the permanent Civil Service by distinguishing the source of political advice and support . . .

They are an additional resource for the Minister providing assistance from a standpoint that is more politically committed and politically aware than would be available to a Minister from the permanent Civil Service.

- In addition, they are useful to provide a balance to Civil Service advice.
- They can take forward ministers 'half-formed ideas' and deliver them as the party intends.
- They can liaise with the political party's central office and test the political waters concerning new policy initiatives.
- They can act as a 'roving commission' and warn on any political 'banana skins'.
- Unlike other civil servants, they only serve one party/government the minister knows therefore they will remain loyal to them.

No

- Civil servants are already expert in most areas and can offer neutral advice, why then is advice needed from elsewhere?
- If expert advice is required why can it not be brought in from academics or consultants on an ad hoc basis as often happens elsewhere in government?
- Not all special advisers are expert in anything, often they are less qualified in the department on which they are advising than the civil servants with whom they work.
- In the Westminster government special advisers have often been seen to 'spin' government policy and news to the government's own advantage, helping to avoid scrutiny. Perhaps the same is true in Wales?
- Their job description is often unclear, are they a politician or civil servant?
- Their input often remains unknown by those outside the ministerial circle. How much are they responsible for creating policy that is outside the political party's own formal policy-making processes.
- They are nearly always active party political members, so they also become party political activists funded by taxpayers.
- Are they politicians of the future or the past, to what extent is the post merely a well-paid resting place for politicians who have lost office and are waiting to stand for election again or those that are waiting for a vacancy to occur to contest their first election?

The role of the Welsh government

Civil Service

Just like the government in Westminster, the Welsh government is served by the same UK Civil Service. Their loyalty remains in principle primarily to the Crown and not the First Minister. The Welsh Assembly has a separate Civil Service from the Welsh government. In 2013, the Welsh government's Civil Service numbered around 6,100, about 6.8 per cent of the civil servants working in Wales. It does, however, still make them one of the largest employers in Wales and is the only devolved nation to have increased the size of its Civil Service since devolution.[19] The Welsh government's Civil Service is not seen as being top heavy, with between just 2 and 7 per cent of each department consisting of senior civil servants, which is about the same as the Whitehall average.[20]

The devolved Civil Service in Wales has been growing and evolving since the establishment of the old Welsh Office in 1964. Initially, it was an executive body covering a few functions with just over 200 civil servants, but, importantly, it was headed by a Permanent Secretary and a Secretary of State with a post in the Cabinet. By the time it was replaced by the Welsh Assembly in 1999, its functions had grown considerably, as had its staffing, and it had now also developed considerable experience in developing Welsh government policy.[21] Despite the growth of the Welsh government's Civil Service, there are still those that advocate increasing it still further to ensure that it has the capacity and expertise to cope with the growing range of new Welsh Assembly powers.[22]

We should also note that the Assembly itself employs around 300 staff responsible for supporting the AMs in vocational posts ranging from translators to clerks of the committees. Although their service conditions are closely connected to the Civil Service they are not civil servants themselves. Instead, they are independent of the Welsh government and therefore they act impartially mainly on behalf of the non-government AMs as employees of the Assembly. In addition. there are also a large number of public sector employees in what are called Welsh government sponsored bodies (WGSBs) or quangos (see Box 4.10).

Box 4.10 What are Welsh government sponsored bodies (WGSBs)?

WGSBs are bodies directly funded by the Welsh government, but not directly part of the Civil Service, although their internal structures are still based on the Civil Service. Before the Government of Wales Act 2006 they were also known as Assembly Sponsored Public Bodies (ASPBs). They are also known as quangos, and in England they are referred to as non-government department bodies. Examples include Qualifications Wales, Cadw, the National Library of Wales and National Museum of Wales.

They are headed by a chief executive and often have their own chair, vice chair and board. Their central advantage is that they can develop expertise and professionalism that is beyond the normal Civil Service. They are also able to operate in a more commercial field, if the situation dictates. Criticisms of them, however, are that some of them can be secretive, difficult for ministers to hold to account and scandal-prone. It is for this reason that a number have been scraped in the past and brought directly into the Welsh government.

The Welsh government's Permanent Secretary

The Civil Service in Wales is headed by a Permanent Secretary and is the most senior Civil Service post in Wales. The Permanent Secretary is ultimately accountable to the National Assembly for Wales, as opposed to the Westminster Parliament, to which their Whitehall counterparts still remain responsible. The Permanent Secretary is responsible for the 'management of the Government's resources'. They are accountable to the First Minister and his or her Cabinet. They also have the twin roles of chief policy adviser to ministers and Principal Accounting Officer for the Welsh government. They are the main link between Welsh ministers and the organisation. In this respect, the Permanent Secretary's department provides many of the services that directly support the First Minister and Cabinet.

As devolution has progressed, Welsh ministers have required broader support from civil servants, for example, their skills in drafting robust legislation. It is the Permanent Secretary's department that sets the specific direction to ensure the organisation is evolving and developing skills in line with this progress. The department also coordinates relationships with other parts of the United Kingdom, Europe and the world. This includes working with other governments on areas varying from constitutional issues to nurturing overseas trade and investment links. How they interact is specified in various MOUs between the UK government and the devolved administrations.

Traditionally, the Permanent Secretary in Wales has been regarded as one of the most junior permanent secretaries. This has changed during the period of devolution and they now sit on the powerful Civil Service Board (CSB). This is the management board for the Civil Service and is responsible for the strategic leadership of the Civil Service on all issues with a corporate impact, including topics such as talent management, departmental spending and budget allocation, and employee relations within the Civil Service.

The First Minister and civil servants

The chief Civil Service adviser to the First Minister is the head of the First Minister's private office: the Principal Private Secretary (PPS), a post currently held by Des Clifford. That makes the PPS one of Wales' most senior civil servants after the Permanent Secretary. As with Westminster Civil Servants, they are bound by the Civil Service code which states:

> Civil servants must not take part in any political or public activity which compromises, or might be seen to compromise, their impartial service to the Government of the day or any future Government.

As we have noted, just as the government in Westminster, the Welsh government is served by the same UK Civil Service. Their loyalty remains primarily to the Crown and not to the First Minister and his or her Cabinet, although as the First Minister is also the Queen's official representative in Wales it is difficult to distinguish between the two. Just as in the famous TV series *Yes Minister*, there is sometimes friction between ministers and civil servants, with ministers seeing civil servants as being risk-averse and not prepared to take tough decisions and civil servants, in turn, seeking to ensure that ministers do not undertake a 'reckless' course of action and advising them accordingly on restraint. Normally, however, the relationship remains cordial, and ministers and civil servants react closely on a daily basis. If there is any mistrust, however, and the minister wishes to hold a civil servant to account for any action they also have the power to summon them directly to explain their course of action and insist that their desired course of action is followed. This power, together with the virtual permanence of the Labour Party in office in Wales, has tended to mean that the Welsh government, unlike the ministers in *Yes Minister*, remain in charge. Although we should also note the inexperience of new ministers or experience of older ministers and sometimes the civil servants themselves can lead to an imbalance in this power relationship.

Conclusion

The Welsh government has evolved over a relatively short period of time. Much of its procedures and operating mechanisms have been copied directly from the government in Westminster. The principles of collective and ministerial responsibility, for instance, operate in broadly the same way as at Westminster, and the Civil Service structures that serve the ministers and Cabinet are mirrors of those for the UK government. There have been attempts to add a particular Welsh twist on occasions, such as with having more open government, but the realities of how these have actually improved democracy are open to question. The Welsh government does not have the variety and professional expertise of anywhere near as many civil servants as the government in London. This has meant that in order to develop their own policy agendas they have also drawn significantly on their own force of special advisers to the extent that they now form a significant part of the government and the Cabinet's policy operations.

The Labour Party has dominated the Welsh government since its inception in 1999. Although there have been two periods of coalition government, it is the Labour Party that has mainly shaped the positions and posts of Welsh government, and in that respect the Welsh government is a reflection of their devolution policy and agendas. In this respect, Welsh First Ministers have been able to maintain a popularity rating that has helped to ensure that they have enhanced their own position and that of the government in the public's eye.

Questions for discussion

1. In what way is it true to say that the First Minister is the Prime Minister of Wales?
2. The First Minister's post gives them unbridled power – discuss.

3. To what extent is the Welsh Cabinet merely an extension of the office of the First Minister?
4. To what extent is it true to say that the Civil Service in Wales can provide all the support any minister needs, therefore, there are no need for SPADs?

Case study: collective and ministerial responsibility[23]

Read the text in Boxes 4.5 and 4.8, and also the material in Chapter 4 that explores ministerial and collective responsibility. When you have done this address the questions below:

1. What is the difference between collective and ministerial responsibility?
2. Why do you think that Leighton Andrews may have campaigned against his own government's policy?
3. Why did Rhodri Glyn Thomas resign when no civil servant in his department had been at fault?
4. Examine the subsequent careers of Leighton Andrews, Rhodri Glyn Thomas and Alun Davies (Box 4.7) and determine whether ministerial resignation or sacking is ever really that detrimental to a politician's career?

Suggested answer points are provided in the Welsh Government and Politics online resource for both the questions and the case study. The web link for these answer points is given at the front of the book.

The National Assembly

Russell Deacon

Overview

The National Assembly for Wales is the legislative body around which much of the world of Welsh politics and government revolve. It is the place where the political parties undertake the role of both government and opposition. Although it is a new body, the Welsh Assembly borrows many of its practices and procedures from those in Westminster, but has altered them with a distinctive Welsh slant. Here, both the government, opposition and AMs therefore play similar but at times quite distinct roles to their Westminster counterparts. This chapter explores these roles from constituency to committee. It also examines the role of a typical AM from their interaction with constituents to the mechanisms that keep them ethical and honest and in line with their own party's political agenda.

Key issues to be covered in this chapter

- What is the role and purpose of the political opposition in Wales?
- How does an AM operate on both a daily and weekly basis?
- Why did devolution develop in Wales – the story of Wales and Westminster?
- To what extent are AMs similar to MPs?
- What ensures that Welsh AMs remain honest and ethical?
- When is there a need for a Whip in the Welsh Assembly?
- How does the Assembly operate with respect to its formal meetings, such as plenary or Assembly committees?
- Why is the Welsh budget important?
- What is the Barnett formula?

Government and opposition

If the role of government is to govern, what is the role and purpose of the political opposition? In this respect the Welsh Assembly mirrors the Westminster Parliament in that it has a government and an official opposition. There is no legal basis for having an official opposition and the term and status has just developed along with the Assembly itself.[1] The official opposition is the largest political party that does not also form part of the government. Since 2016, this role has been performed by Plaid Cymru. They are provided with their own budget to maintain their role as the official opposition. Resourcing is not unique to just the opposition; indeed, if any political party has more than three AMs it can be regarded as a political group and it is then allocated resources for additional support staff for the leader and the group.

The official opposition has a number of functions both inside and outside the Assembly, including:

1. to scrutinise and challenge the Welsh government on their policy implementation and government of Wales;
2. to provide alternative policy and administrative ideas for the government in Wales;

3. to act as an alternative government in waiting; and
4. to put forward their own debates for discussion in the Welsh Assembly.

As part of its role the official opposition also maintains a number of Shadow Cabinet posts, which again mirror those of the Welsh government. It is these shadow ministers that take the lead in scrutinising and challenging their counterparts.

The effectiveness of the opposition

The effectiveness of the opposition to the Welsh government varies. It is at its most vocal in the verbal sparring that occurs during First Minister or other Cabinet ministers question times. Here, the opposition seek to catch the government out on policy or other topical issues. When the Welsh government has a majority, however, there is little that the opposition can do to reverse or effectively alter government policy.

When the government does not have a majority the opposition is more effective in altering government policy, as we will see later, when it comes to the need to pass their annual spending budget. The combined opposition can also amend or even stop legislation completely as occurred in March 2016. In this instance, a public health bill, which included a ban on e-cigarette use in some public places, was rejected by AMs following a row between Labour and Plaid Cymru. Plaid Cymru voted against the bill in a last-minute move, meaning that the Assembly vote was tied 26:26 and the bill failed to pass as a result.[2] This also shows one of the main disadvantages of not having a majority government in that it makes implementation of government policy unpredictable and uncertain.

Being an AM

Before 1999, Wales already had three types of elected members who covered three quite distinct areas. They were local councillors, covering unitary authorities or community/town councils; members of the Westminster Parliament (MPs); and members of the European Parliament (MEPs). In May 1999, however, elections were held to the first National Assembly for Wales and a new generation of politicians arrived in Wales, with a whole new role to play. This section then explores the role of these new AMs.

What is an AM?[3]

The National Assembly for Wales is made up of sixty AMs. Elections are held in May every five years. Being an AM is a paid job and currently has a salary of £64,000 per annum (2016). Assembly Members are elected to represent a specific area of Wales as members of a political party (for example, Conservative, Labour, Plaid Cymru, Welsh Liberal Democrat, UKIP) or, occasionally, as independent members.[4] Of these sixty members, forty are elected in the same constituencies in which the Westminster MPs sit. There are an additional twenty members elected through the Additional Member System, and these are known as list members. There are four of these for each of the Welsh Assembly's five electoral regions (see Chapter 8). Assembly Members are not simply the same as Westminster MPs but based in Cardiff Bay instead of Westminster, rather there are a number of differences (Box 5.1).

Box 5.1 Case study: differences between being an AM and an MP

To many people being an AM in Wales and an MP at Westminster are the same thing. Assembly Members are elected for defined geographical areas (mainly the same as that of an MP), represent a political party, campaign on the same issues, hold constituency surgeries and follow the same party discipline. There are, however, a number of differences:

1. The Welsh Assembly is bilingual, which allows AMs to converse in English or Welsh; at Westminster you may only converse in English for official purposes.
2. Welsh MPs are currently allowed to vote on all non-devolved issues for Wales, which allows them to vote and take part in virtually any area of government policy from education to foreign affairs and defence, whereas AMs are limited to devolved issues and cannot get involved in areas such as law and order and social security.
3. Assembly Members are nearly all members of two or more committees plus holding either a government post or a spokesperson role, there are no backbenchers, whereas most Welsh MPs are backbenchers without a frontbench role.

4. Assembly Members and MPs are responsible for different areas of legislation and scrutiny, for example, AMs for education and health and MPs for defence and social security. Neither can legislate on the other's areas of responsibility.

5. There are forty MPs that cover Westminster from Wales, but sixty AMs for the same area.

6. At Westminster very few Welsh MPs are part of the government, normally less than 10 per cent and sometimes none at all in the Cabinet itself; for AMs it is around 30 per cent, including 15 per cent in the top Cabinet posts.

7. Not only does the proportional electoral system mean that the Welsh Assembly is more representative of the voting patterns of the Welsh population as a result, it is also more representative of the political support of the Welsh population as a whole.

8. The percentage of Welsh female MPs at Westminster is normally below a quarter of the total MPs, whereas for AMs it is between 40 and 50 per cent.

9. There have been no ethnic minority MPs from Wales in its parliamentary history, whereas the Welsh Assembly in its fourth term had three (5 per cent).

10. The working conditions are also different in Westminster to those in Cardiff Bay. In Cardiff Bay, the hours are designed to be more family friendly with the sessions being built around the school-holiday period and avoiding Monday and Friday sitting and evening work. In Westminster, the sessions are shorter but longer in terms of the hours worked within these.

What does an AM do?

Unlike virtually any other job there is no specific job description if you wish to be an AM. This is because in reality AMs have three different employers, all of whom wish to see different aspects of their role undertaken. These three employers are the electorate, their political party and the Welsh Assembly itself. These are the three groups that can help remove them from office, either directly or indirectly, should the need arise.

One of the central roles for legislative members in any democracy if they are not part of the executive (government) is to examine and scrutinise that government. The Welsh Assembly is no exception to this rule.

Therefore, an AM's role involves debating policies, asking detailed questions to ministers about policies and government actions, and holding inquiries into specific issues or the work of public bodies. Assembly Members therefore carry out the central role of the Assembly's democratic work. They are the only ones with a democratic mandate to do so. As a result, they represent the interests the Welsh people and nation. They have four main roles in this respect to:

1. represent their constituents;
2. make new laws or amend existing laws for Wales;
3. represent their political party and carry out its manifesto promises; and
4. hold the Welsh government to account (if they are not themselves a member of that government or governing party).

They undertake these four roles in a variety of ways, depending on whether or not they are also part of the Welsh government.

The AMs' working week

For those AMs not in the government, the working week is broken up into two constituency/regional days (Monday and Friday) and three Assembly days. Also, AMs will often cover events in their constituency at weekends and evenings throughout the week if they live close enough to Cardiff Bay in order to do this. It has been estimated than on average an AM would work around sixty hours a week. To this affect it has been being stated that their 'biggest challenge is finding time to eat during their busy schedules'.[5] Most AMs spend their constituency/regional days either attending events/meetings or holding surgeries. Assembly days are filled with meetings, plenary sessions and committees. They also need to attend relevant political party meetings either at the Assembly, nationally or within their constituency.

Throughout the week AMs must also cover their given portfolios, which nearly all have, and attend events relevant to these. The portfolios' coverage tends to be much larger in the smaller parties, such as the Welsh Liberal Democrats. It is worth remembering that small parties have to do the same work as the large ones (which can mean with just a quarter of the staff). This means that AMs often do not have enough time to cover all areas of legislation and scrutiny. This is also given as a central reason for the need more AMs and support staff in order to be able to scrutinise and hold the Welsh government to account. The current figure of sixty AMs has frequently been cited by many within and outside the Assembly as being insufficient for the tasks that a modern legislature has to undertake.

The difference in duties between constituency and regional AMs[6]

Technically, constituency and regional AMs have the same duties and responsibilities, and they have equal status as far as the Assembly and the relevant Wales Acts are concerned. In the past there has been some resentment between constituency AMs and regional ones, particularly in the Labour Party over the division of roles and functions. The Labour Party has the bulk of its AMs elected from constituencies, whereas the opposition parties have approximately half theirs from the regional lists. Therefore, those constituency Labour AMs have tended to see regional members frequently as 'failed constituency members', lacking the close links and bonds that they have with an individual constituency. They also note that it is the constituency AMs that get the vast bulk of case-work, whereas regional members see themselves as having the extra stresses of covering eight constituencies compared with the constituency AM's single constituency.

There is some justification for both sides on their respective views. In general, the public go to the constituency AM first for help as that is what they are familiar with from the Westminster system of MPs. This means that while regionals cover a far larger area they tend to have less casework. Those cases that they do tend to pick up can often be 'lost hope cases' from people who have already been to their constituency AM/MP. The regional AM then has the task of trying to help sort out a complex case. When it comes to representation, there is an important point to note, however. While members do represent the interests of the public, this does not mean that they have to do what the public wants or even demands. In the end, they are there to do what they think is best on behalf of the public and therefore to act on their consciences. At the same time, AMs are also aware of the need to be re-elected and therefore can be reluctant to associate themselves with unpopular vote-losing causes regardless of whether they are a regional or a constituency AMs. They are also bound by the manifesto and their loyalty to their political party.

Welsh AMs have an allowance to run an office and its staff both in their constituency and at the Welsh Assembly. This normally means that they will employ a constituency caseworker and an Assembly caseworker/researcher as a minimum. There are no rules to state that those employed cannot be related to you and a number of AMs have close relatives working directly for them, which from time to time can cause both media and public controversy (Box 5.2).

Box 5.2 Keeping it in the family: Welsh political employment practices

While Welsh members of the European Parliament are now barred from employing relatives, those at the Assembly are not. In 2009, an Independent Assembly Review Panel, chaired by businessman Sir Roger Jones, recommended that the practice of employing relatives by AMs should cease. At that time sixteen AMs employed their relatives. The Jones Report stated:

> We . . . object in principle to the employment of family members and believe this should be avoided. "The panel acknowledges that the current arrangements may work well on occasion, but as a general principle the panel considers this practice should cease over time, in the interest off public confidence and best use of public funds. We recognise, however, that family members who currently work for AMs will have existing employment rights which should be protected.

After 2009, Plaid Cymru AMs stopped employing new family members, as did the Welsh Liberal Democrats. This meant that by 2014 although the number of AMs who employed relatives had gone up to twenty, it was mainly in two political parties: there were ten Labour AMs, nine Conservative AMs and one Plaid Cymru AM who employed relatives. Therefore, one-third of the thirty-strong Labour group employed relatives, including a number of Cabinet ministers, whilst nine of fourteen-strong Tory group did, including the party leader Andrew R. T. Davies.[7] This did not alter greatly in the fifth Assembly with the arrival of the new Assembly grouping UKIP. In 2016, four of the seven UKIP AMs employed family members, including the party's leader Neil Hamilton.[8] Despite the obvious concerns about nepotism, the Welsh Assembly retains the view that imposing such a ban would be legally challengeable on the grounds that it would infringe the human rights of politicians' relatives. Whilst others point out the benefits of keeping a stable family life by being able to employ relatives closer to them in their often demanding jobs, with long hours.

Ensuring that AMs remain ethical and honest

For an elected legislature to work effectively in a democracy it needs to ensure that its elected members retain public trust as far as possible. To ensure that this is the case, the AMs are kept in check by a number of measures, both informal and formal. Informally, they are guided by their own ethical values and the norms of acceptable behaviour of Welsh society and the communities they serve. They are also kept in check by media scrutiny and the sanctions this can bring upon them, including persuading public opinion not to vote for them in future elections or by aiding their own party members in ensuring they are not reselected for their seat. To guide them in their ethical behaviour, the Welsh Assembly also defines what it means through a Code of Conduct (Box 5.3).

Box 5.3 What does being ethical mean for an AM?

According to the Welsh Assembly's Code of Conduct being ethical[9] means that with respect to their personal conduct Members of the Assembly:

(a) must comply with the Code of Conduct for AMs;
(b) should act always on their personal honour;
(c) must never accept any financial inducement as an incentive or reward for exercising parliamentary influence;
(d) must not vote on any Order or motion, or ask any question in plenary or a committee, or promote any matter, in return for payment or any other material benefit (the 'no paid advocacy' rule).

There are also a series of formal checks and sanctions that help to ensure the ethical and honest behaviour of AMs. As well as the civil and criminal sanctions of the law, there are two other important checks. The first is their political party, which has the ability to suspend or strip them of their party membership or get them deselected. The Welsh Assembly has also set up mechanisms to deal with allegations of misconduct by a member.

To hear any allegations of misconduct by members the Welsh Assembly has a Standards Commissioner, currently Gerard Elias QC, who is also a criminal barrister. It is his job to deal with any complaints made against AMs, but not against ministers, who have been accused of breaking the ministerial code. If the complaint is upheld, there are a variety of penalties, and these can vary from being censured to total exclusion from Assembly meetings and a withdrawal of all privileges, either temporarily or permanently. There are very few complaints, however, made against members. Between 2011 and 2014 there were fifty-four complaints, only three of which the Commissioner indicated were admissible and these were all in the year between 2012 and 2013.[10] None of these resulted in any sanction against a member beyond censure, and in 2013–14 the annual cost of this role was £21,244 in Commissioner and staff costs. To guide the Commissioner there are a set of general principles they should uphold (Box 5.4).

Box 5.4 How Welsh AMs must remain honest and ethical[11]

In the 1990s, in response to a series of scandals involving MPs at Westminster, Lord Nolan held a wide-ranging inquiry (Committee on Standards in Public Life) into the role of parliamentarians. As a result of this, his committee came up with seven general principles of conduct. These are relevant in the Welsh Assembly where Members should observe principles of:

(a) *Selflessness*: AMs should take decisions solely in terms of the public interest. They should not do so in order to gain financial or other material benefits for themselves, their family, or their friends avoiding conflict between personal and public interests.
(b) *Integrity*: holders of public office should not place themselves under any financial or other obligation to outside individuals or organisations that might influence them in the performance of their official duties. As part of this AMs should not ask civil servants to act in any way that would compromise their political impartiality.
(c) *Objectivity*: in carrying out public business AMs should make choices on merit.
(d) *Accountability*: holders of public office are always accountable for their decisions and actions to the public.
(e) *Openness*: AMs should be as open as possible about all the decisions and actions that they take. They should give reasons for their decisions, and restrict information only when the wider public interest clearly demands. This includes declaring any relationships to people or businesses in which they have a financial relationship.

(f) *Honesty*: AMs have a duty to declare any private interests relating to their public duties and to take steps to resolve any conflicts arising in a way that protects the public interest.

(g) *Leadership*: AMs should promote and support these principles by leadership and example.

Political party control in the Welsh Assembly

Like most other legislatures, the AMs elected are nearly always members of political parties. Each political group has their own leader, who normally also acts as their party's leader in Wales. The parties maintain their own communications and policy officers at the Welsh Assembly. It is their role to ensure that their party's political presence is felt not only by others in the Welsh Assembly, but also by the media and wider general public. The political groups also have spokespersons for each functional area covered by the Welsh Assembly. It is their role to present their party's own policy ideas at the same time as scrutinising and challenging those of the government and other political parties in the Assembly.

All political parties need to follow their own party's political agenda, whether this is from the manifesto, which they stand on at the Welsh Assembly elections, or the position that has been determined within their group meetings. If they do not do so, it can cause internal party splits, which nearly always result in a negative impact at the ballot box as voters tend to reward unified parties over disunified ones., There are a number of mechanisms in place in order to ensure this cohesion, the most important of which is the party whipping system.

Who are the party Whips and why are they important?[12]

Each political party has one or more AMs who act as a political Whip responsible for ensuring that members vote in the direction determined by the party's leadership. It is they who circulate the whip. This is a piece of paper that tells the AM which way they should vote in committee or on a piece of legislation. It is given each week to members and follows the party's own policy agenda/manifesto or group meeting discussion. For party discipline it important that members follow the party whip. If they do not, the party may not be able to follow its own policy agenda or get its policies and laws passed. Also because the Welsh government has frequently been a minority government it has not be able to allow even one of its members to vote against its own policies or legislative agenda. The penalties for ignoring the party whip can be severe for a member and may include de-selection as a candidate for that party at the next election or having their membership suspended.

Sometimes an AM is not in agreement with the party whip because it goes against a constituency issue or pledge, which may damage them electorally or personally. They may also be personally opposed to the voting direction because of an ideological, moral, religious or ethical reason. They may find a way of avoiding the conflict. Sometimes it is possible for a member to pair off with another member from another party. They agree not to vote and therefore they can cancel out each others votes and therefore the issue of not following the whip does not occur. If this is not possible when they are in government, then they can discuss options with the Chief Whip. If they are not happy with an issue they also may be able to get it changed after discussion with the relevant minister. If they still disagree, then they will have a conversation with the First Minister or their party leader, who will seek to find some compromise or they may force them to vote in the required direction. If they are in opposition the same discussions are normally held with their party leader and Assembly party manager.

The formal meetings in the Welsh Assembly

When it is in session the Welsh Assembly has a number of formal meetings. These act as both the public and legislative face of the Welsh Assembly's operations. The two most important meetings are Plenary and Assembly committees and are covered in this section.

Plenary

The most public face of being an AM is in the televised meeting in the Senedd Chamber. Here they meet twice weekly when the Assembly is in session to discuss issues relating to the governance of Wales or constituency issues. The full meeting of the Assembly, when all members are present is called the Plenary. Here Members can ask questions of Welsh government ministers, debate issues such as government policies and committee reports, and examine any proposed new Welsh laws. Opposition parties can also have debates on issues of their choice. These debates are on Tuesday and Wednesday afternoons, and are allocated depending on the size of that political party in the Assembly. Although both the plenary and Assembly committees are televised, it is normally only the Plenary session and particularly First Minister's Questions that find themselves reported in the Welsh print and broadcast media.

Without running a Plenary the Assembly cannot function or even start operations. This is due to the fact that in law after an Assembly election Members must meet in Plenary to agree key items of business, and also to hold elections for the Presiding Officer and Deputy and nominations for a First Minister. The organisation of Plenary itself is determined by the Business Committee, which is chaired by the Presiding Officer. The Business Committee is not concerned with commercial businesses (that is, confusingly, called the Enterprise and Business Committee). It is instead concerned with the weekly running of Assembly business and any future planning, such as the revision of Standing Orders or the timetable for any proposed new Welsh Acts. This committee therefore includes representations from each political party and the government Minister for Business. One of its key roles is to ensure that every area of responsibility of the government, new laws and any associated public bodies are subject to scrutiny by a committee or committees.

Assembly committees

Perhaps the AM's most important role in both scrutinising Welsh government policy and helping to develop new policy in Wales is through the role of the various Assembly committees. These have been set up for specific tasks, including examining laws, scrutinising policy, running the Assembly's business, holding ministers to account and carrying out other tasks necessary to run a legislature. Committees can also introduce new legislation (see Chapter 6). As part of this role of open scrutiny, committees nearly always meet in public and are televised. In 2016, there were twelve committees in operation in the Welsh Assembly, chaired by members of different parties and ranging in size from four to ten members. The membership of committees approximately matches the overall representation of the parties within the Assembly. Since June 2016, the chair of each committee has been elected by secret ballot in order to stop party leaders from removing the chairs of committees when they contradicted their own party's policies, which had been done on a number of occasions in previous

Assembly sessions. It also brought it in line with how chairs are selected at Westminster.[13]

The committees are normally named after the areas of government policy they cover; thus, the Public Accounts Committee scrutinises Welsh government expenditure and is chaired by an official opposition member. The central benefit of the committee system is that more time can be taken for scrutiny outside the Assembly debating chamber. At the same time, Members are able to carry out work more quickly and specialise in particular fields which enhances scrutiny. The main drawback is that there are too few members to develop expertise in any one area, and as a result Members are often on a number of committees and do not have the time or resources to develop the expertise to scrutinise quite complex issues. To get around this problem, the committees can also establish smaller subcommittees 'task and finish groups', which work in a smaller group on a specific issue.

Box 5.5 Cross-party groups: what do they do?

The Welsh Assembly has around fifty cross-party groups that cover areas that may or may not be within the Assembly's remit, but are of interest to members. Importantly, these are not formal groups and are not therefore bound by the Assembly's Standing Orders. This means that they can also include membership from outside the Assembly, and a lobbying group or another body interested in that issue often provides the secretariat.

Therefore, the secretary of the Cross-Party Group on Small Shops is from the Association of Convenience Stores, while the Nursing and Midwifery group has its secretary from the Royal College of Nursing. This support is in part required because although these groups can use Assembly rooms for meetings, the Assembly does not provide them with a budget for their operation. All the groups produce minutes, elect officers and publicise their meetings. It does, however, also allow many lobbying groups much closer access to AMs and a subsequent influence on policy than may be apparent to the public.

The Welsh budget

Each year the Welsh government must pass its budget through the Assembly in order to allocate funding for the coming year. The fiscal resources for this comes down from Westminster in the form of the Welsh block grant or through the Barnett formula. It is the intention of both the Welsh Assembly/government and the Westminster government that in future the Welsh government should also use direct and indirect tax-raising powers to raise more of its own money. In this respect, a Welsh Treasury has been created in Wales to enable the Welsh government to raise its own taxes.

When it comes to the setting of the Welsh budget to ensure its own programme, the Welsh government needs to gain a majority of the AMs' votes for it to pass. For more than half of the Assembly's existence the Welsh government did not have a majority. Therefore, they had to get the support of one of the other political parties in order to ensure their budget passed.

When the Labour government did not have a majority in the fourth Assembly (2011–16), in their first budget they struck a deal with the Welsh Liberal Democrats to get the budget passed. The result of this deal was that the Welsh Liberal Democrats required a pupil depriva-tion grant to be introduced to schools in order for them to vote with the government. In their second budget, the Labour government then did a deal with Plaid Cymru. Their condition for voting for the budget was a two-year investment in apprenticeships. Both political parties, however, realised that the Labour government was playing one party against the other to get a better deal for itself. In order to gain more for themselves, however, both Plaid Cymru and the Welsh Liberal Democrats negotiated together in order to gain more from the Labour government in a dual opposition partnership and continued to do so for the last three years of the fourth Assembly.[14] Although this joint negotia-tion is beneficial for the smaller parties in the Welsh Assembly, there is also some criticism that it leads to back-door deals with the party elite rather than open and transparent politics in view of both the public and party members.

Barnett formula

The Barnett formula has been in place Westminster since 1978, and was introduced originally as a mechanism for the proposed devolution in 1979 that never arrived. The formula is not just used for Wales, but also helps to determine the budget for Wales, Scotland and Northern Ireland. The formula is based on the expenditure of Whitehall departments based on the population of England. This, in turn, determines the allocation of money based on population size rather than actual spending needs.

The main advantage of the formula is that it allows devolved government's considerable autonomy in determining funding priorities, as they do not have to spend it on the same area as Whitehall departments do. It is generally accepted, however, that the Barnett formula underpays Wales in comparison with Scotland and Northern Ireland. There is therefore considerable pressure to reform the funding arrangements for Wales from the Welsh political parties.

Conclusion

Across the chapter we have seen how the Welsh Assembly operates in its non-legislative functions. This has included the work of both AMs and their political parties when in government and in opposition. This process has evolved over the period of the Assembly's existence, as have matters such as the ethical conduct of Members. One issue that is often apparent is that AMs are stretched across their variety of functions both as the powers of the Assembly grow and as public expectations of their role increase. In this respect, various commissions and reports that have looked at the role of AMs have constantly recommended that their numbers be increased to between eighty and a hundred. Yet successive governments in Westminster and Cardiff Bay have declined to do so, fearing a public backlash over an increase in politicians. Without the increase in AMs, however, it may become impossible to ensure that the Assembly functions in the way it was designed to, with the stresses and strains on AMs becoming too great.

Questions for discussion

1. In what ways are the both roles and nature of the regional (list) AMs different from those of the constituency?
2. What safeguards are there in place to ensure that AMs remain ethical and honest?
3. How do the political parties ensure that their AMs follow the party line both inside and outside the Assembly chamber?

Case study: differences between being an AM and an MP[15]

Read the text in Box 5.1 and answer the following questions:

1. List four ways in which AMs are like MPs.
2. List four differences between AMs and MPs, and give the reasons for these differences.
3. Which legislature do you think is most suited to a modern democracy and give reasons for you answer?

Suggested answer points are provided in the Welsh Government and Politics online resource for both the questions and the case study. The web link for these answer points is given at the front of the book.

6

The National Assembly and the Law-making Process

Russell Deacon

Overview

One of the central distinguishing areas of a democratic system is the ability of a legislature to actually legislate (make laws). In Wales, for almost the first decade of its existence the Welsh government and Assembly were limited to making secondary legislation or relying on Westminster to pass Acts of Parliament on its behalf. Over time, however, through statute and referenda Wales has evolved its own primary law-making powers. By July 2015, the Welsh Assembly had passed some twenty primary legislative Acts. Which means that this three-year period produced as much purely Welsh legislation as the previous 150 years combined. In March 2017, the convention that Westminster could no longer make laws on devolved matters in Wales without the permission of the Welsh Assembly was enshrined in law.[1] This has not fixed the law-making process in Wales, however. From the perspective of studying the law-making process in Wales, it is still important to note that it is an evolving process and that its methods and processes are still subject to fluctuation.

Key issues to be covered in this chapter

- How has the law-making process in Wales evolved to its current status?
- What is the constitutional nature of Wales?
- How does the monarchy interact with Wales?
- To what extent have the various constitutional commissions in Wales impacted on the law- making process?
- Why has the devolution of law-making powers taken longer than elsewhere in the United Kingdom?
- What are the arguments for and against establishing a Welsh legal jurisdiction?
- What are some of the differences between Welsh and English law?
- What were Legislative Competence Orders (LCOs) and how did they operate?
- How does the current law-making process in Wales operate?
- How many ways can a Bill become an Act in Wales?
- What are the stronger and weaker parts of the processes of making a Welsh law?
- How can legislation be speeded up or emergency legislation passed?
- Can we see an exploration of an Act as its goes through its various stages?
- How does a backbencher get their own legislation through the Welsh Assembly?

Both the old departmental Welsh Office and the new Welsh Assembly had law-making powers from the outset. These, however, were not the primary law-making powers held by the UK Parliament or those given to the Scottish Parliament and Northern Ireland Assembly. It was instead an inferior type of legislative power known as secondary legislative power or statutory instruments (SI). This meant that the Welsh Office and later the Welsh government were left determine exactly how an Act was to be implemented through SIs, although this had the advantage of some flexibility for the Welsh government in its implementation. Sometimes, an Act may even leave it up to the Welsh Assembly as to whether or not the legislation is implemented at all. This did not, however, allow for new policy initiatives by the Welsh government or backbench AMs as these still had to go through the Parliament at Westminster. However, by the time that the fourth Assembly had started in 2011, the legislative system in Wales had evolved into one that could create its own primary (original) civil laws (Box 6.1).

Box 6.1 The evolution of the law-making process in Wales[2]

From its inception it took just over thirteen years for the Welsh Assembly to be able to develop its own primary law-making powers. This box charts the main events on that journey.

  6 May 1999: first elections held, National Assembly starts work. At this stage it can only implement secondary legislation.

  1 July 1999: Welsh Office staff transfer to the Assembly serving both the Welsh executive and Assembly.

12 July 2000: an all-party review group set up to look at the Assembly's organisation and ways of working with respect to legislative practice.

24 July 2000: first attempt made to amend secondary legislation with respect to pre-paid prescription charges by the Welsh Liberal Democrat Group.

27 November 2001: the first attempt to point out the difference between the government (the executive) and the parliamentary (legislature) parts of the Assembly. From now on, the term Welsh Assembly government will be used to describe the Cabinet and its work

14 February 2002: the Assembly votes for 'the clearest possible separation between the Government and the Assembly'.

18 April 2002: a Commission is set up under Lord Richard to make recommendations about the powers of the Assembly.

31 March 2004: the Richard Commission report is published, recommending that the National Assembly should have more powers to make laws (Acts), that is, primary powers.

  6 October 2004: the Assembly votes in favour of separating the government and the Assembly and for more law-making powers. This would mean there would be a formal divide between the executive (government) and legislature (AMs not in government).

25 July 2006: Government of Wales Act is published. It provides for a further referendum on full law-making powers and for the UK Parliament to give the Assembly the right to make laws Bill by Bill through Legislative Competence Orders.

6 June 2007: Commissioners elected to oversee staff and business matters for the Assembly.

12 June 2007: the first Legislative Competence Order (LCO) is published – on special needs education.

6 May 2008: the Assembly passed its first law, the NHS Redress measure – believed to be the first internally passed Welsh law passed since the tenth century.

9 July 2008: the first Assembly Measure, the NHS Redress (Wales) Measure 2008 becomes law in Wales following its approval in Privy Council by the Queen.

19 November 2008: the first Assembly Commission proposed Measure – the National Assembly for Wales (Remuneration) Measure 2010 – is introduced.

21 July 2010: the National Assembly for Wales (Remuneration) Measure 2010 becomes the first Assembly Commission proposed Measure to receive Royal approval. It provides for the establishment of an independent panel, which will have future responsibility for setting AM salaries, allowances and pensions.

9 February 2011: the Welsh Language (Wales) Measure 2011 receives Royal approval in Privy Council and becomes part of Welsh law.

4 March 2011: the official result of the 2011 referendum on Assembly law-making powers is announced: 63.5 per cent voted 'Yes' and 36.5 per cent voted 'No'. The turnout for the referendum was 35.6 per cent.

15 December 2011: Her Majesty the Queen approves and presents the Welsh Seal to the First Minister in Privy Council. The Seal will be placed upon each Act of the Assembly, signifying that the Queen has given Royal Assent to an Assembly Bill (also see Chapter 4).

12 November 2012: the first Welsh Bill passed under the Assembly's new powers, the National Assembly for Wales (Official Languages) Act 2012, receives Royal Assent.

2017: Wales Act recognises the distinctiveness of Welsh law and establishes the position of President of Welsh Tribunals, although England and Wales still share the same jurisdiction.

The constitutional nature of Wales

As the United Kingdom does not have a codified constitution (all in one document), tackling the exact constitutional nature of Wales can be an uncertain and unclear process. As there is no specific power that Wales can exert to push forward its own issues, it is often subject to the need to acquiesce to the agenda set by its more powerful English neighbour.[3] In addition, although Wales is described as a principality (see Box 6.2.) this is only a courtesy title and has no constitutional status. Thus, constitutionally the people of Wales are equal to those living in the rest of the United Kingdom. In fact, it is this legal identity as citizens of the United Kingdom rather than Welsh citizens that they have officially overseas. At the same time, however, Wales is recognised as a nation internationally and has a status equal to sovereign states in that respect, particularly in the area of sports such as football, rugby and athletics.

Wales is one of the four constituent countries of the United Kingdom and Northern Ireland. It has been politically joined with England since the Acts of Union in 1536 and 1542. As we saw in Chapter 1, it was not until the late nineteenth century that Wales was again recognised as being separate from England. The recognition in parliamentary legislation that England did not automatically also mean Wales did not occur until the late 1960s. Because Wales' assimilation with England had been much smoother than that of both Scotland and Ireland, the nature of Welsh distinctiveness, language aside, remained more ambiguous.

Today, much of Wales' constitutional distinctiveness has been built upon what are referred to as constitutional conventions. These are political practices that become more binding over time and form part of our uncodifed constitution. It has become a convention that the UK government should not actively interfere in the Welsh government's domestic policy and vice versa, although both may still criticise each other in this respect. It is through conventions such as these that the constitutional position of Wales develops. The UK Parliament has therefore ceded legal sovereignty to the Welsh Assembly to make laws over specified areas, but still retains parliamentary/political sovereignty, that is, the right of Westminster to govern Wales as permitted within international law. Nevertheless, despite Westminster retaining ultimate sovereignty, this ceding (loaning) of legal sovereignty is an important constitutional precedent in the evolution of the Welsh political process.

There have also been attempts to clarify the constitutional position of the Welsh government through the Government of Wales Acts 1998 and 2006 and the Wales Acts 2014 and 2017. These have covered the legal status of the Welsh Assembly and government and its powers. The St David's Day Agreement 2015 and the subsequent Wales Act 2017 enshrined the permanence of the Assembly and the Welsh government in law. This means that despite the Westminster Parliament in theory being able to abolish the Welsh Assembly and government by an Act of Parliament, constitutional convention would require that a further Welsh referendum would be required. This is because referenda are now deemed to entrench a measure far more deeply than an Act of Parliament.

Box 6.2 The monarchy and Wales

In the Middle Ages there were numerous princes in Wales, but none whose territory covered the whole of Wales. This, however, still gave rise to the title of principality of Wales. We should note, however, that this is an honorary title and Wales is not a principality in practice because this would require the Prince of Wales to be the head of state in Wales (also see Chapter 1). After the Acts of Union in 1536 and 1542, the title of the principality remained and the heir to the throne, either male or female, bears the title Prince/Princess of Wales, but has no constitutional power with respect to Wales. The Prince of Wales, however, has still become the linchpin for the monarchy in Wales and is its most visible sign; the Royal Investitures of the princes of Wales at Caernarfon Castle in 1911 and 1969, for instance, attracted worldwide attention. Today, the titleholder, currently Prince Charles, also continues to command worldwide attention and recognition, although this often has little to do with Wales directly.

Although the Prince of Wales discusses political issues with the Welsh government he does not have a formal role in this respect. As we saw from Chapter 4, it is the Queen (the monarch) who therefore retains the formal constitutional royal role in Welsh government, including appointing Welsh ministers and signing Welsh legislation into law.

The evolution of Welsh devolution and law-making through the impact of the Commissions: from Richard to Silk

When it was first established the National Assembly was more like a local authority with respect to its structure and operations than a legislature. Its legal status was as a single body corporate with a 'first secretary' and 'assembly secretaries' responsible for general executive administration. Rather than having a government Cabinet, the Assembly Government was designed to work mainly through committees. For these the various departmental assembly secretaries were also to be members. Even before it came into existence, however, this local authority model of government had already become outdated. Local authorities themselves had moved over to a cabinet system of government based on the Westminster model, so the Welsh Assembly did likewise. In 2002, as part of the coalition agreement in the first Assembly government between Labour and the Welsh Liberal Democrats a wide-ranging commission was set up under Labour peer Lord Ivor Richard (the Richard Commission). When the Richard Commission reported back in March 2004 it recommended that the Assembly should have its own primary law-making powers and also that there should be a clear split (separation of powers) between the Welsh government (executive) and the Assembly (legislature). After some deliberation the Labour governments in both Wales and Westminster accepted the need to give Wales both primary legislative powers and to divide the government from the Assembly. Therefore, the Government of Wales Act 2006 recognised what was already occurring in reality. The National Assembly was now formally divided into two, creating 'a deliberative and legislative Assembly and a separate executive, accountable to the Assembly'.[4] This was to be called the Welsh Assembly government, later Welsh government.

The second key change made by the 2006 Act was to provide for the Assembly to exercise law-making powers through Legislative Competence Orders (LCOs). As we will see later, these proved to be unpopular in practice, but the Act also allowed for a referendum on whether the Welsh Assembly could also make its own primary laws directly. The All Wales Convention, chaired by Sir Emyr Parry-Jones, reported back in 2009 that the time was right for the move towards direct primary powers and that a referendum on this could now be undertaken. This was held in March 2011, won by a significant majority, and enables the Assembly to exercise primary law-making powers over twenty 'subjects', as listed in Schedule 7 to the 2006 Act. These twenty areas mainly cover those over which the Welsh government has direct competence, such as education, health and local government. Yet, as these events were occurring, elsewhere in the United

Kingdom, particularly in Scotland, devolution was continuing to evolve at a more rapid pace. Both the government in Wales and Westminster now sought to ensure that Wales was not left too far behind in the evolution of devolution.

In October 2011, the Welsh Secretary, Cheryl Gillan, set up the Commission on Devolution in Wales under the chair of Sir Paul Silk. He was a former senior House of Commons Clerk and also Clerk to the National Assembly between 2001 and 2007. The Commission then became widely known as the Silk Commission and reviewed two distinct areas: (1) fiscal, including tax-raising powers; and (2) legal powers, including civil and criminal law. The Silk Commission's first report brought forward various proposals about tax-raising powers, which then became part of the Government of Wales Act 2014. The Silk Commission's second report (November 2014) resulted once again in a debate as to how many devolved powers the Welsh government should have. Just like the All Wales Convention some five years previously, the Silk Commission also recommended that the Assembly be given power over policing, but this request was again ignored by Westminster.

The more fundamental of the Silk Commission's sixty-one recommendations were[5]:

- The introduction of the reserved powers model for legislation in Wales. Wales should now adopt a reserved powers model, making clear the powers reserved to the UK Parliament. Anything not reserved would be devolved, and the National Assembly for Wales would be able to pass laws in those areas.[6] This is already the case in Scotland and Northern Ireland.
- The devolution to the National Assembly of the power to determine its own size, electoral arrangements and other operational matters, including its name, along with putting the Sewel motion (a way of adapting Westminster laws for Welsh use) into statute and recognising the Assembly's permanence (as in Scotland). There would also be the removal of the rights of the Secretary of State for Wales to take part in Assembly proceedings.
- Silk also indicated that there should be around twenty more AMs in order to cope with the increase in legislative responsibilities, just as the Richard Commission had done a decade beforehand.
- The establishment of a 'Welsh Inter-governmental Committee' to improve coordination between the two governments.

- The devolution of powers over drink driving and speeding, policing and youth justice (criminal law) and a review in ten years to see if criminal law should come over to the Assembly.
- Devolution of a number of additional functions, including planning approval for certain energy schemes, speed limits, bus and taxi regulation, rail franchising and functions in relation to water and sewerage.

The national day of Wales, celebrating its patron saint, St David, is 1 March. Although neither the UK government nor the Welsh government has been able to make this a national holiday, despite numerous manifesto commitments, both still use this day, or days near to it, to announce major policy decisions or to hold referenda connected with the Welsh Assembly. Therefore, in line with this, on 27 February 2015 the UK coalition government announced at the Welsh National Rugby Stadium, Cardiff, that they would accept most of the Silk recommendations. This was called the St David's Day Agreement, also known by the UK government command paper *Powers for a Purpose: Towards a Lasting Devolution Settlement for Wales*. It also set out that the Welsh Assembly should have power over its own and Welsh council elections, the type of electoral systems used and the number of members elected. There then occurred various attempts to put Silk into a new Government of Wales Act, but consensus between Westminster and Cardiff Bay proved to be elusive for a while.

Box 6.3 Why has the devolution of law-making powers taken longer for Wales than elsewhere in the United Kingdom?

By the time the Silk Commission had produced its second report in 2015, the Welsh Assembly was in the process of transforming itself for the fourth time. As the Silk II Report noted, Wales has been subject to more changes in its devolution settlement since 1998 than have Scotland or Northern Ireland. There have been three phases in Welsh devolution: the first two National Assemblies operated under the Government of Wales Act 1998; the 2007 National Assembly operated under the first devolution model contained in the Government of Wales Act 2006; and the National Assembly elected in May 2011 operates under the second devolution model in the 2006 Act.[7] The Welsh Assembly now had within its grasp a fourth change – the ability to become a tax-raising and primary law-making body – which could also change its name to the 'Welsh Parliament'. Yet Scotland had already gained much of this in 1999, so why was Wales so slow in developing? There are three main reasons for this:

- First, devolution has not always been that popular in Wales. In the 1979 devolution referendum, those who were anti-Assembly outnumbered those in favour by almost five to one. In the 1997 devolution referendum, 'Yes' won by only a few thousand votes. Therefore, devolution has had to evolve with public opinion supporting it.
- Second, the two main political parties in Wales, Labour and the Conservative, are substantially more pro-unionist and less devolutionist with respect to their membership, both elected and party membership, than those in Scotland. Therefore, devolution has had to go at a pace acceptable to their members, which has been a slower incremental process than elsewhere in the United Kingdom.
- Third, Wales represents the least 'troublesome' of the three devolved nations. The political troubles in Northern Ireland have meant that special attention has had to be directed there in order to prevent the outbreak of another civil war. In Scotland, the rise of both the SNP and Scottish nationalism has meant that a lot of Westminster attention has been focused on avoiding Scottish independence. Wales, in contrast, remains much more firmly in the political mainstream. Here some 90 per cent of its MPs are in one of the two main Westminster parties, as opposed to none in Northern Ireland and approximately 40 per cent in Scotland. Therefore, there often appears to be no need to hurry on Welsh devolution with its electorate so committed to the union.

The arguments for and against establishing a Welsh jurisdiction

The Acts of Union of 1536 and 1542 abolished Welsh law and replaced it with that of England. Since then England and Wales have shared a single legal jurisdiction. Therefore, strangely, this means that the laws made by the Assembly or by the UK Parliament still form part of the law of England and Wales, even if they are intended to apply only in Wales.[8] The advent of Welsh primary law-making powers in 2011, however, brought about the need to examine whether Wales should have its own legal jurisdiction once more. The three central reasons why it might need do so are that:

- nowhere else in the world do two primary law-making bodies inhabit the same jurisdiction;

- the amount of separate Welsh legislation has been growing considerably since 2007, and therefore it will become increasingly difficult to follow a single 'England and Wales' jurisdiction; and
- as devolution in Wales evolves, it is possible that not only policing but elements of the criminal law may also be devolved to Wales, making a separate jurisdiction even more important to achieve.

We should also note that through its legislative processes, whether primary or secondary, Wales has managed to develop distinctive policy and laws to those in England. As these increase this may also advance the need for Welsh jurisdiction (Box 6.4).

Box 6.4 Examples of differences in Welsh and English laws

Wales has free NHS prescriptions;
unmanned coin-operated sunbeds are banned in Wales;
there is a 5p levy on each carrier bag in Wales, there are many exemption to this law in England;
organ donation is an opt-out process in Wales, in England it is opt-in;
shock collars for dogs are banned in Wales;
Welsh students pay much lower tuition fees than those in England;
Wales only has primary and secondary schools under local authority control; it has no academies or grammar schools; it also has a different educational awarding structure on qualifications such as AS and A2 examinations (Qualifications Wales).

Those arguing against the need for a Welsh jurisdiction point out, however, that a common jurisprudence system and procedure already allows the courts to operate differently in England and Wales. Therefore, to alter the status quo would only make the law more complex to interpret. They point out that you would also need to develop a separate legal profession and deal with central unanswered questions, such as would decisions made in English courts still be binding in Wales and vice versa.

In December 2013, the Welsh government reported back on a consultation exercise to ascertain the necessity to establish a separate Welsh jurisdiction. In their response, they came down on the side of waiting to see how Wales develops constitutionally. They wish to see it develop more fully into criminal law before they pushed for a separate jurisdiction.[9] The volume of Welsh legislation coming forward, however, will mean that the civil law in Wales will become increasingly distinct from that of England, and therefore this may in itself increase the pressure for a separate jurisdiction to be enacted

What were Legislative Competence Orders (LCOs) and how did they operate?

There have been very few purely Welsh Acts made within the Westminster Parliament over its long history. For both the Welsh Secretaries and later on the Welsh government it was very difficult to get Welsh legislation passed at Westminster. This was because of the lack of parliamentary time and also the lack of UK government will to devote parliamentary time to any law that would be contrary to its own political agenda. Therefore, legislation that did occur was principally concerned with the powers and responsibilities of the Welsh Assembly itself, restructuring of local government, the NHS in Wales and issues related to the Welsh language. As the Assembly evolved, however, there was an increasing desire by the Welsh government to implement its own primary legislation without the need to have to rely on the goodwill of the UK government. This pressure resulted, after the Richard Commission in 2004, in changes to the way that the Welsh Assembly could create its own primary legislation. From 2007, therefore, under the Government of Wales Act 2006 the Welsh Assembly created its own laws through Westminster in a process known as Legislative Competence Orders (LCOs).

From the outset, despite pleas from the UK government to let the process 'bed in', LCOs seemed to be impractical. They often took years to complete through a complex eleven-stage process involving the Assembly, UK government and Westminster. They also tended to be enacted only on non-controversial issues. The request to have legislation to introduce a bank holiday for St David's Day, for instance, was never allowed to go forward in an LCO by the Westminster government. One of the boldest moves by the Welsh government, the introduction of a 5p charge on plastic bags in Wales, was not even done through an LCO, but instead through the use of the power the Assembly gained under the Westminster Climate Change Act 2008. Therefore, both the Welsh government and Assembly opposition were soon pushing for direct primary law-making powers without the need to go through Westminster, although the then Labour government in Westminster still sought to let the LCO process continue for as long as possible, with a 'give it time to bed in' rationale being advocated.

How does the current law-making process in Wales operate?

It was not until its fourth term that the Welsh Assembly, via a referendum in 2011, was given its own primary legislative powers. When the Welsh electorate voted 'Yes' in the referendum in March 2011, it effected wide-reaching changes on the Welsh Assembly's powers. This law-making power was in relation to all devolved areas, such as health and education. Importantly, it also meant that it was no longer necessary for the Welsh Assembly to gain the consent of the UK Parliament before the Assembly could legislate. From now on, the Assembly had the power to pass primary laws (Acts) in the same way that the UK Parliament could (see Box 6.5).

We should also note that Westminster continues to be able to legislate for Wales, including on devolved matters, even though it has ceded some legal sovereignty. This is because the Assembly has the option to legislate itself or just take an Act or some parts of it directly from Westminster through the use of the so-called Sewel motions. This means that if they are deemed to be relevant and suitable, then the Welsh Assembly can also consent to them applying to Wales without the need for further legislation. This can occur because the Westminster Parliament retains political sovereignty within the UK's uncodified constitution.

Box 6.5 How the Welsh primary legislation process works: stage by stage[10,11]

Just like the other devolved bodies in the United Kingdom and unlike Westminster, there is only one body of representation in Wales (AMs) as opposed to two in Westminster (MPs and Peers). This makes the Welsh Assembly a unicameral body with no revising (second chamber). Its legislative process therefore reflects its unicameral nature.

From 2011 onwards, laws made in Wales have been known as Acts, previously they were known as Measures. The power to undertake primary legislation was provided by the Government of Wales Act 2006 and endorsed by the Welsh population in a referendum in March 2011. As with the

---

other legislatures in the United Kingdom and Northern Ireland, a 'Bill' is the name given to the proposed law before it becomes an Act. Welsh Bills can be created on any area devolved to the Welsh Assembly, specified in Schedule 5 of the Government of Wales Act 2006.

Welsh Bills follow a five-stage process in order to become an Act. These consist of:

Stage 1: consideration of the general principles of the Bill by an Assembly committee, after which these must be agreed by a majority of the whole Assembly. This can take between 95 and over 350 days, depending on the nature of the Bill. The Holiday Caravan Sites (Wales) Bill, for instance, took over 350 days to complete stage 1, whilst the Regulation and Inspection of Social Care (Wales) Bill took less than 100.
Stage 2: the Bill committee considers the Bill and any amendments tabled in detail.
Stage 3: the Welsh Assembly then considers the Bill and any amendments tabled on that Bill.
Stage 4: a vote by the whole Assembly to pass or reject the final version of the Bill.
Stage 5: the Bill is given Royal Assent and comes into law as an Act of the Welsh Assembly. The Act then has the word 'Wales' inserted at the end to distinguish it from Westminster legislation, for example, the Higher Education (Wales) Act 2015.

There is also an optional additional stage for amending the legislation between stages 3 and 4. This occurs if the AM proposing it requests this and the request is agreed by the majority in the Welsh Assembly. Bills can be introduced to the Assembly by the Assembly government, an Assembly committee, an individual AM through a members' ballot or the Assembly Commission.

A Bill is given Royal Assent after a four-week waiting period, although it may take longer. During this period the Counsel General for Wales or the Westminster government's Attorney-General could refer the measure to the UK's Supreme Court for a decision as to whether it was in the Assembly's legislative competence to pass into law.

We should also note that, unlike Westminster, a Bill does not have to be passed in the one parliamentary session. For public Bills, the only time limit is that the Bill has to be passed before the end of the Assembly in which the Bill was introduced. So it could in theory have almost five years in which to do so. Even then, a Bill can still formally receive Royal Assent after the end of an Assembly if it was passed by the Assembly before that Assembly ended it five-year term. For example, the Tax Collection and Management (Wales) Act 2016 received Royal Assent on 25 April 2016, whereas the Assembly had broken up some two weeks before that.

How many ways can a Bill become an Act in Wales?

There are presently five different ways a Bill can progress in Wales to become an Act. These mirror those of the other legislating bodies across the United Kingdom. The number of Acts passed can be seen in Table 6.1. The five different types of Bills are:

- *Welsh Government Bill*: the vast majority of Welsh Bills are government Bills. This is the normal practice in most legislative bodies because the government has both the need, resources, legislative time and elected majority to push through its own bills in priority to others.
- *Committee Bill*: these originate from the Assembly's various standing Committees. Although there were none of these in the fourth Assembly, in 2015, the Finance Committee did recommend that 'a bill is introduced into the Assembly to extend the role of the Ombudsman'.[12]
- *Assembly Commission Bill*: these are Bills produced by the Assembly itself through the Assembly Commission. The Commission consists of the Presiding Officer and four other Members nominated by the main political parties. It has produced just one Act – the National Assembly

Table 6.1 Welsh Acts by legislative type, 2012–15[a]

Method of legislation	Year			
	2012	2013	2014	2015
Welsh Government Bill	1	6	7	4
Committee Bill	–	–	–	–
Assembly Commission Bill	1	–	–	–
Members Bill (private)	–	1	–	–
Private/hybrid Bill	–	–	–	–
Total	2	7	7	4

[a] National Assembly for Wales, List of those Acts that have received Royal Assent during the fourth Assembly (from May 2011), 2015.

for Wales (Official Languages) Act 2012, which placed the Welsh
Assembly's obligations for bilingual duties on a statutory footing.
- *Members Bill (private)*: this is the process for non-government
  members to introduce legislation. After government Bills it forms the
  second largest number of Bills. Although few make it to the statute
  books.
- *Private/hybrid Bills*: these are undertaken by a public body or local
  authority. There were no Bills in this format between 2011 and 2016.

As the Welsh Assembly develops and evolves it is likely that all five of
these methods will be able to provide an increased variety and type of
specifically Welsh laws.

What are the stronger and weaker parts of the processes of making a Welsh law?

The primary legislative process in Wales is still relatively new. The power
to pass primary legislation is still in its infancy in Wales and therefore
the processes and methods by which legislation goes through are constantly being revised and tested. Over the first period of new law-making
powers a number of strengths and weaknesses in the legislative process
in Wales have become apparent.

Strengths of the Welsh legislative process

The main strengths/benefits of the Welsh legislative process are:

1. *The legislative process has flexibility*: it is not necessarily set in stone
   and therefore it is being reshaped and redesigned in Wales to make
   it better for Welsh needs. This may well help overcome some of its
   initial flaws.
2. The whole legislative process is now *much closer to daily Welsh political life* and therefore the perceived needs of Wales. Legislation can
   now be determined by the Welsh government, Assembly and Welsh
   policy community. It is shaped for Welsh circumstances within the
   nation-state, itself.
3. The legislative process is on the whole *much quicker and more open
   than the Westminster processes*. There is limited UK parliamentary
   time and other barriers meant that, mainly, only non-controversial

legislation could pass through Westminster. Even this would often be limited to a single Bill each year.

4. Although still sometimes difficult to follow, the current Welsh legislative process is *much easier to understand than the LCO* procedure that preceded it.
5. The *process has been given the endorsement of the Welsh electorate* through the referendum of 2011. This gives it a popular legitimacy not enjoyed by the UK Parliament.
6. The legislative process has a number of scrutiny mechanisms to ensure that any legislation is extensively examined from inside the Welsh Assembly
7. There are *additional checks and balances from* outside of the Welsh Assembly from the UK government from both the Welsh Secretary and the Attorney-General. They can both also help to ensure that any legislation is within the competence of the Welsh Parliament and is not subject to future legal challenge.
8. Welsh Bills can be *passed over a much longer time span* than those at Westminster (see Box 6.5). This helps to ensure that legislation is not 'rushed' in order meet a short deadline, helping to enable it to be scrutinised more thoroughly.

Weaknesses of the Welsh legislative process

The main weaknesses/drawbacks of the Welsh legislative process are:

1. *Welsh legislation is dominated by Government Bills*: over 90 per cent of Acts passed come from the Welsh government despite the fact that this is only one of the five different methods by which legislation can be made. Backbench (Private Members) legislation has little chance of progressing and the other types of legislation are limited or non-existent.
2. The whole process of Welsh legislation is *lengthy and difficult to follow* (even emergency legislation (see Box 6.6). For those examining the process from outside it is not always clear who, for instance, has made the numerous amendments and the reasons why some pass and others fail. In turn, awaiting Royal Assent or for a Bill to have a decision on its legality by the Supreme Court can lengthen the time it takes for an Act to come into law by a year or more. The Social Services and Well-being Act, for instance, was introduced on

28 January 2013, was passed by the Assembly on 18 March 2014 (458 calendar days), and received Royal Assent on 1 May 2014,[13] making the process nearly 500 calendar days from start to finish.

3. *Most legislative amendments are over issues of wording rather than the general principles of the Bill*: they are therefore rarely challenged or debated. Of those amendments that are about principle, unless they are from the governing party(s), very few are ever passed, meaning that the legislation often goes through unhindered.

4. *The AMs* who are either in plenary or the committee that scrutinises the legislation often *lack both the knowledge, expertise* and time to effectively scrutinise. This means they must rely heavily on the information provided by civil servants whose central objective is to pass the government's legislative programme.

5. The *UK government can still interfere with Welsh government legislation*: this is not only because it retains political sovereignty, but is also due to the fact that Wales currently has a conferred powers model of government. The UK government can thus delay or stop legislation by referring it to the Supreme Court for a judgment as to whether the legislation is within the Welsh Assembly's conferred powers remit.

6. As the Welsh Assembly is only a single chambered legislature it *lacks the expert scrutiny and reflection of a second chamber*, which occurs in most national legislatures.

Box 6.6 How can legislation be speeded up or emergency legislation passed?

Bills in the Welsh Assembly can sometimes take up to a year or more to progress. Thus, there is sometimes a need to speed the process up because the legislation is needed as soon as possible. Therefore a Bill can proceed without stage 1 consultation if the Business Committee agrees. This helps to speed its passage. This tends to happen with uncontroversial Bills or those that have already been widely consulted on (for example, a draft of the Bill may have been thoroughly consulted on beforehand).

Emergency Bills, however, are another category altogether and practice here is still subject to debate. The Welsh Assembly's Standing Order 26 deals with emergency legislation, but this is still up to the interpretation of various parties. The Welsh government believes that it should be used when there is a need for quick action on an issue. The Presiding and Deputy Presiding

Officer, however, believe it should be reserved for 'genuine emergencies'. The whole process is currently still under review, as even current emergency legislation is not that quick. At Westminster emergency legislation can be passed within a few days; in Cardiff Bay, the quickest so far, has been over three months.

Examples of two emergency Bills which can be cited as such are:

- The Control of Horses (Wales) Act which was introduced on 14 October 2013, and was passed by the Assembly on 10 December 2013 (fifty-seven calendar days). Royal Assent was given six weeks later on 27 January 2014.
- The Agriculture Sector (Wales) Act was passed by the Assembly in a shorter time, but due to a Supreme Court referral took longer to receive Royal Assent. The Bill was introduced on 2 July 2013, and was passed by the Assembly on 17 July 2013 (fifteen calendar days). The Bill was then referred to the Supreme Court, which found the Bill to be within the competence of the National Assembly for Wales. Royal Assent was given on 30 July 2014 (that is, a year after being passed by the Assembly).

The move to a reserved power model of legislation, however, may remove some of the barriers to the problems noted above.

Box 6.7 Case study: exploring the journey of a Welsh Bill to a Welsh Act

The process of Welsh legislation can seem lengthy and complex in its stages. To understand it more fully it is best to follow a worked example. The Welsh Assembly itself provides this information online referring to each specific Bill, but we will work through an example here to get a better grasp of the processes. In July 2015, the Qualifications Wales Act received Royal Assent after going through forty-two different stages. The Act provides for the establishment of Qualifications Wales as the independent regulatory body responsible for the recognition of educational qualification awarding bodies for non-degree qualifications in Wales. It was part of the Welsh government's process of separating qualifications in Wales from those of England.

Although the development times vary considerably on Welsh legislation, this Act can still provide us with an indication of the typical stages and the timescale a Bill needs to go through to become an Act:

28 September 2014:   The Welsh Assembly's Business Committee agrees an initial timetable for the Qualifications Wales Bill.

11 November 2014:   The Business Committee agrees to refer the Bill to the Children, Young People and Education Committee to consider and report on the general principles.

1 December 2014:   Qualifications Wales Bill by Huw Lewis, Minister for Education and Skills, Presiding Officer confirms that it is within the legislative competence of the National Assembly for Wales. The Welsh government sets out the reasons and purpose of the Bill in a Policy Intent Statement that provides a shorter and more readable explanation of what the government is planning to do.

11 December 2014–
5 February 2015:   Children, Young People and Education Committee examine and discuss the Bill in five meetings across this period. In March they produce a report on the Bill's progress (stage 1 report), as does the Constitutional and Legislative Affairs Committee on the Bill's legality.

24 March 2015:   There is a full debate on the Bill in plenary. There is also a Financial Resolution passed. This is the end of stage 1 of the Bill.

25 March–30 April 2015: The Committee Stage in which amendments are considered from the government and opposition. The Bill is examined line-by-line to ensure that it is fulfilling its intention. In this instance, for this Bill, of the government's amendments all fifty-five were passed; of the opposition's twenty-one amendments only one succeeded. This stage 2 allows for the government to ensure that its own legislation is fit for purpose and results in an amended version of the Bill going forward.

29 May–16 June 2015:   For stage 3 further amendments were published by Huw Lewis, for which a rationale in pro-

	vided for each. The vast majority are to make the textual explanations less ambiguous. The opposition also publishes a series of amendments. These are then debated in plenary on 16 June. The vast majority of amendments are uncontroversial and go through without a vote (Standing Order 12.36). Ten are voted on and for four the vote is tied, so the Presiding Officer casts his vote to ensure a decided vote (Standing Order 6.20) in order to ensure the government wins the vote.
16 June 2015:	Huw Lewis, in agreement with the Presiding Officer, proposes that the Bill be passed in accordance with Standing Order 26.48. A final version of the Bill is now passed (stage 4).
16 June–15 July 2015:	The UK government's Attorney-General and Secretary of State for Wales then consider whether the Bill is constitutional (within the powers of the Welsh Assembly) over a four-week period. If it is, it is referred to the Supreme Court for a judgment (section 114 of the Government of Wales Act 2006), if not, they write to the Clerk of the Assembly to say that they have no objections – as is the case with the Qualifications Wales Bill (post-stage 4). Royal Assent Qualifications Wales Act 2015 becomes law.

From the example above we can see the Presiding Officer has voted a number of times to ensure that the vote is not a tie (votes balanced equally). It is therefore worth noting their role in determining of the acceptance or rejection of amendments to a Bill. The Presiding Officer and the Deputy Presiding Officer do not vote unless it is to break a tie, when one of them is in the chair. The casting vote is exercised in accordance to the parliamentary practice first established in the late eighteenth century in Westminster. This means that the Presiding/Deputy Presiding Office votes against any proposition (vote) on the ground that it has not gained a majority (so a tied amendment is voted down). The sole exception is when the Assembly would be able to consider/discuss the proposition further and therefore potentially come to a majority. Therefore, in that case they would vote in favour of a Bill that is tied after the debate on the general principles of that Bill have been discussed.[14] With most Welsh government's not enjoying a majority this can occur quite frequently.

How does a backbencher get their own legislation through?

The non-government (Assembly backbencher) legislation process

In the third National Assembly (2007–11), AMs were able to put forward their own legislation in the form of a proposed Assembly Measure. Ten measures were put forward and half of these became law, with the others being rejected or falling out of time. In the fourth National Assembly (2011–16), a new method of legislation came into being – the Private Members' Bill. This means that any AM who is not part of the Welsh government is able to submit their own Private Member's Bill for consideration by the Welsh Assembly. To get their Bill into the legislative process, they must submit it to a ballot undertaken by the Presiding Officer. If they succeed in being selected in this ballot, they must submit their Bill for discussion within nine months. The member then opens and closes a debate in the plenary session and it goes to a vote. If the vote is successful, the Bill will then go forward to all the same stages as a normal Bill before becoming an Act.[15]

Although quite a few Private Members' Bills are put forward, very few get passed. In 2013, a Bill by the Welsh Liberal Democrat Peter Black, the Mobile Home (Wales) Act 2013, became law. This Act, which improves the regulation of mobile home sites, became the first Private Members' Bill to become law in 2015. Another Private Members' Bill, the Recovery of Medical Costs for Asbestos Diseases (Wales) Bill by Labour AM Mick Antoniw, was agreed by the Assembly, but was subsequently referred to the Supreme Court, which found that the Assembly did not have the legislative competence to enact the Bill in its present form. Aside from Peter Black's 2013 Act, only one other Private Members' Bill was passed in the fourth National Assembly (2011–16), the Nursing Staffing Levels (Wales) Act 2016, which set minimum staffing levels for hospital wards, put forward by another Welsh Liberal Democrat, the party's leader Kirsty Williams. This was the second and last Private Members' Act of the fourth Assembly.

Why do so few Private Members' Bills become law?

Of the nine ballots for Private Members' Bills held during the fourth Assembly, as we have seen, only two actually made it into law. So why have so few become law? There are a number of reasons for this:

- The AM *needs to secure the support of the majority of AMs*. This normally means they need the support of both their own party and others (called 'cross-party consensus'). If a majority of AMs oppose the principle of the Bill, it will fail to go beyond even the 'leave to proceed' motion.
- If the Presiding Officer decides that the *Bill needs a financial resolution* (as it will result in significant expenditure, which will be charged to the Welsh Consolidated Fund; WCF) a motion needs to be put forward by a government minister. This is despite the fact that it may be an opposition Bill. If the motion is defeated or the government declines to put forward the motion within six months of the stage 1 debate the Bill will fall.
- Private Members' Bills are sometimes *dropped by the Member* because another method of achieving that Bill's objectives comes forward, such as a commitment by the Welsh government to tackle the issue concerned. The process of putting forward a Bill may also have already given publicity to the relevant cause(s), and thereby achieved the member's main objectives(s).
- The Bill may also fail for a number of *technical reasons*,[16] meaning that it will run out of time. Unlike in the UK Parliament, however, it is almost impossible to stop a Bill by Members using obstructive techniques in order to use up the allocated legislative time because Bills can take such a long time to progress (see Box 6.6).

Conclusion

The legislative process in Wales has already undergone four distinct evolutionary changes since the establishment of the Welsh Assembly in 1999. It has gone from a legislature that could merely endorse or reject secondary legislation, to one that can determine its own primary legislation. Now it is equal within its own conferred powers on the legislative process in civil matters to the other devolved bodies and the UK Parliament. At the same time, however, the process is still bedding-in and evolving, and there are still some flaws that need ironing out. The Welsh Assembly remains weaker than the other legislative bodies in the United Kingdom in that it does not have its own jurisdiction and also does not have power over the criminal law.

Questions for discussion

1. What are the central reasons behind the legislative process in Wales evolving so much more slowly than that in Scotland?
2. Is there a need for a separate Welsh jurisdiction?
3. To what extent could the process of creating a legislative Act in Wales be described as a perfect process?

Case study: exploring the journey of a Welsh Bill to a Welsh Act[17]

Read the case study in Box 6.7 on the Qualifications Wales Act 2015 and answer the following questions:

1. Draw a flow diagram of the main stages of a Welsh Bill and next to each stage provide an indication of the time each can take.
2. What are Amendments and how do they become law?
3. Who decides if a Welsh Bill becomes an Act?
4. What happens if there is a tied vote on either an Amendment or the passing of the Bill itself?

Suggested answer points are provided in the Welsh Government and Politics online resource for both the questions and the case study. The web link for these answer points is given at the front of the book.

Wales and Elections

Alison Denton and Russell Deacon

Overview

When it comes to the electorate there are just over 2 million eligible voters in Wales. The average electoral size of a single seat constituency in Wales is just over 54,000 voters.[1] It sometimes may seem as though Wales is in a constant state of elections to various political bodies or voting for referenda on specific issues or new Assembly powers. It is true that there are currently elections for a legislature in three of every five years (Welsh, UK and European elections) and other elections for local government or by-elections occur in the other two years. The electoral cycle has now been set, with the exception of those for Police and Crime Commissioners, so that each institutional election has its own space. The electorate in Wales therefore has had the opportunity to vote regularly for representatives for four different tiers of government:

- European Parliament (which will end with Brexit);
- UK Parliament at Westminster;
- National Assembly for Wales; and
- local councils in Wales (community/town councils and unitary authorities).

Electoral systems used in Wales are similar to those used in England, but different from Scotland or Northern Ireland (which uses the Single Transferrable Vote in some elections). It is not exactly the same as England, however. Since 2000, for instance, it has been possible for mayors to be directly elected, and while a significant number of local authorities in England have adopted this model, so far none in Wales has done this, despite campaigns to do so.[2] As we will see later, the systems for electing representatives at different levels of government in Wales vary significantly, with some being far more electorally proportional than others. The Wales Act 2017 gave control over elections in Wales to the National Assembly, and these may well be shaped in a variety of different directions over the next decade.

Key issues to be covered in this chapter

- What type of elections are held in Wales?
- What are the type of electoral systems used in Wales, including their frequency and how each operates?
- How can we define the pros and cons of each system?
- When can a by-election occur?
- Where and what are the electoral constituencies in Wales?
- What does the Electoral Commission do in Wales?
- How can we define the nature and significance of UK General Elections in Wales?
- What is the nature and significance of Welsh General Elections?
- Has the political make-up of Welsh governments altered much since 1999?
- Do the electoral systems have an impact on party systems in Wales?
- What is the nature and importance of referenda in Wales?
- Do coalitions have specific advantages and disadvantages?

- How have coalition governments in Wales differed since the Assembly's inception?

Types of election and electoral systems in Wales

Up until the mid-1990s Wales only ever used the 'First Past The Post' (FPTP) electoral system.[3] As part of New Labour's constitutional reform agenda, in the late 1990s Tony Blair's government introduced new electoral systems for European Parliament elections and for elections to the devolved assemblies and Parliament in Scotland. This was in order to make the systems more proportional so that the percentage of seats won more closely reflected the percentage of votes cast. In this respect, the proportional Party List system, for instance, arrived for European elections and the partly proportional Additional Member System (AMS) was used for the new Welsh Assembly elections in 1999.

With the arrival of these new electoral systems it became apparent that no electoral system is perfect, and each has its own supporters. This helps to explain the variety and number of systems used in Wales today. The three different types of voting system used in Wales are (also see Table 7.1[4]):

- *Majoritarian/plurality voting system* is one in which the candidate who gains more votes (plurality) than the others contesting the election is elected. It does not seek to be proportional, but normally to reward the party with the highest number of votes with the highest number of seats. This is the FPTP system used for Welsh elections to the Westminster Parliament.
- *Mixed electoral (hybrid) system* is one that combines elements of majoritarian-style systems and elements of proportional representation. This is done in order to reduce some of the distortions that can occur with plurality voting, in which a party can gain the majority of seats with well under half of the popular vote. In Wales, the two different hybrid systems used are those held for the Welsh Assembly elections (AMS) and the Police and Crime Commissioner elections (the Supplementary Vote system).
- *Proportional Representation system (PR)* is one where seats are distributed according to vote share, as proportionally as the electoral system chosen allows. In Wales, the Party List system used for the European Parliament elections is a system of PR. It is a closed list system,

however, which means that candidates are elected in the order determined by the political parties rather than the voters. The system favoured by most advocates of PR – the Single Transferrable Vote (STV) – is not used for elections in Wales even though a number of Welsh Assembly Commissions, such as the Sunderland Commission on local government and the Richard Commission on the Welsh Assembly, recommended its use for elections in Wales. These recommendations, however, have not been implemented.

We will look at each system in more detail below.

How does each electoral system work?

All voting in Wales is by secret ballot (anonymous voting) either in person at the polling station, through a proxy vote (where somebody votes on your behalf) or through a postal vote. The origins of the use of the secret ballot itself come from Wales. Prior to the 1870s, voting was open and various Welsh landlords were notorious for evicting tenants who did not support their preferred candidate on election day. This issue was examined by a Parliamentary Commission, whose findings concerning events in Wales resulted in the Ballot Act 1872.[5] This made it a future requirement for all elections held to be by secret ballot. These days nearly all residents of Wales over the age of eighteen, with some exceptions such as foreign nationals, can vote in elections in Wales. As with the rest of the United Kingdom, Welsh elections are normally always held on a Thursday. Each of the voting systems used in Wales works in slightly different ways to the others. In this section we will take a short look at the distinctiveness of each system.

First past the post

The FPTP system is also known as Single Member Plurality, Simple Majority Voting or Plurality Voting. This is the oldest voting system still in use for public elections in the United Kingdom. Each elector has one vote only and votes in a named constituency, for example, Cardiff Central. The votes for each candidate are totalled, and the candidate with the most valid votes wins. There is no need to gain 50 per cent of the votes cast, just a majority of one (hence, 'first past the post').

Table 7.1 Types of electoral system in Wales

Type of election	Frequency	Years held if outside the norms	Number of representatives elected to serve Wales	Electoral system used
European Parliament	Every 5 years (since 1979): in June.		4 (Wales is one constituency returning 4 MEPs, since 1999).	D'hondt system for all-Wales Party Lists
UK Parliament at Westminster	Every 5 years (since 2010): in May	Periodically on the dissolution of Parliament prior to 2010; fixed 5-year terms since 2010.	40 (it is proposed that this falls to 29 by the 2020 election).	FPTP
National Assembly for Wales	Every 4 years (1999–2011); every 5 years from 2016: in May.	1999, 2003, 2007, 2011, 2016, 2021* (*to avoid clashes with UK general elections)	60	AMS; D'hondt system used for the list element.
Local councils in Wales	Every 4 years: in May.	Can be extended by a year if it clashes with the Welsh Assembly elections.	Just over 1,200	FPTP; councils are now allowed to move towards the STV system if they so desire.
Police and Crime Commissioners	Every 4 years (since 2012): in May.	Initially held in November, but moved to May in combination with other elections in order to boost turnout.	4	Supplementary Vote
By-elections	In a defined time after the seat has become vacant.	Only normally held if the system used is FPTP or the constituency element of AMS.	Normally one at a time.	FPTP, or vacancies are filled from the next party member on the relevant list.

Party lists

For the European elections the whole of Wales represents just one constituency. For this election each political party puts forward a list of candidates and electors vote for a party. Seats are allocated according to the percentage of the vote received by that party. The candidates on each party's list are elected in order and this is used in the European Elections for Wales' four MEPs. It uses the same method of apportioning the seats that is used for the AMS system of regional lists, detailed below. With the advent of Brexit this electoral system will now end in Wales, as there will be no more elections for MEPs.

Additional member system

The AMS is a hybrid mixed electoral system that uses the Party List proportional representation system for its proportional component. For Welsh General Elections to the Assembly, forty of the sixty AMs are elected by FPTP for single member constituencies. The other twenty AMs are elected by Party Lists for one of five regional constituencies. Each elector votes twice: once for a constituency AM from a list of named candidates from a variety of parties (one will be elected); and once for a party in their region (four will be elected). Each party has a list of candidates for the regional seats that they have prepared in advance, and which is publicly stated but is a 'closed' list, that is, the electors have no choice about which candidates on that list are elected, seats are allocated to candidates in the order in which they appear on the party list, in proportion to the percentage of votes received by that party, with a few adjustments to take into account the constituency result.

   The vote for the parties in each region is calculated after the constituency results have been dealt with. Each party's total from the regional ballot is divided by 1 plus the number of AMs already elected for that region for that party in the constituencies to begin with and then in the constituencies plus the region. The party with the highest total after this calculation in each region gets the first regional seat (the person at the top of their list is elected). This process is then repeated until all the regional seats have been filled. This is known as a 'top-up' because it evens out the inequalities of representation inherent in the FPTP system (lack of correlation between votes cast and seats gained), and gives the AMS its element of 'proportionality and fairness'.

Supplementary vote

The Supplementary Vote system is a shortened version of the AV system. In Wales, it is the system used for electing the four Welsh Police and Crime Commissioners. In this election the ballot paper has two columns: in the first column the voter puts an 'X' under their preferred candidate; in the second column they put an 'X' against their second preference. Voters must put an 'X' in the first column, but do not have to put one in the second. When the votes are counted, if no candidate receives a majority, then the top two candidates go on to a second round with the candidates being eliminated. Even though they have been eliminated, the second-choice votes of the eliminated candidates are then allocated to the two remaining candidates. Whichever candidate has the most votes becomes the winner. If only two candidates stand, as was the case in Dyfed Powys in 2012, there is no second round and the candidate is elected only from the first round.

We should also note that from 2021 Welsh unitary authorities can move from FPTP to the Single Transferable Vote (STV) if they wish. This system has also been advocated by a number of commissions for Welsh Assembly elections. It is the most proportional type of electoral system and is used in elections in Northern Ireland and for local government elections in Scotland. As there are no elections by STV at the moment in Wales, this chapter does not examine it in an operational context.

By-elections

When an elected member resigns, dies or is disqualified from office a by-election is held to elect a new member for their seat. In Wales, if a regional (list) Assembly seat becomes vacant the position is simply filled by next person on that party's list. There is no need for a by-election in this case, but in the Welsh Assembly single member constituencies, Westminster elections and for council seats a by-election must be held. The incumbent party is normally able to play a central role in the timing of the election, either choosing the date itself, as at Westminster elections, or by timing the resignation to ensure the maximum chances of their party's own electoral success. By-elections are nearly always held on a Thursday. The historic reason behind this is that this was traditionally a market day when most of the voting population would come into town. This would therefore maximise turnout. In the period leading up to whole council elections or General Elections a by-election is not called and the election simply occurs during the period of elections that are held across the whole of Wales.

Welsh constituencies

Except for Welsh MEPs, who stand for just one all-Wales constituency, elections occur for smaller geographical areas of Wales called regions, constituencies or wards. For the Welsh Assembly there are forty constituencies that each return one AM, and five regions that each return four AMs. The regions are North Wales, Mid and West Wales, South Wales West, South Wales Central and South Wales East. The exact size and nature of these constituencies was determined by using the boundaries from the former five MEP seats for Wales before those elections became for a single all-Wales constituency. For council elections the size of the wards can vary from one- to five-member wards. From 2020, for Westminster elections there will be twenty-nine constituencies as opposed to the forty in 2015.

The electoral boundaries are determined by the independent Boundary Commission for Wales. This seeks to ensure that parliamentary and Assembly constituencies are, as far as possible, equally matched in terms of population size. From 2020, for example, every Westminster constituency in Wales must have an electorate that is no smaller than 71,031 and no larger than 78,507. Although the Boundary Commission pay some attention to geographical distinctiveness of constituencies, this is not always paramount and the only limit to a constituency's geographical size is 13,000 km², or 61 per cent of the whole of Wales. The new parliamentary constituency for Powys, Brecon, Radnor and Montgomery, for instance, is about 40 miles wide and 80 miles in length, or 3,624 km².[6] Needless to say, such large geographical constituencies can put considerable stresses on the elected members in terms of travel distance and time to visit constituents.

Box 7.1 The work of the Electoral Commission Wales

The Electoral Commission is the independent elections watchdog and regulator of party and election finance in the United Kingdom. It is an independent body set up by the UK Parliament to regulate party and election finances and to set standards for well-run elections. It offers support and guidance

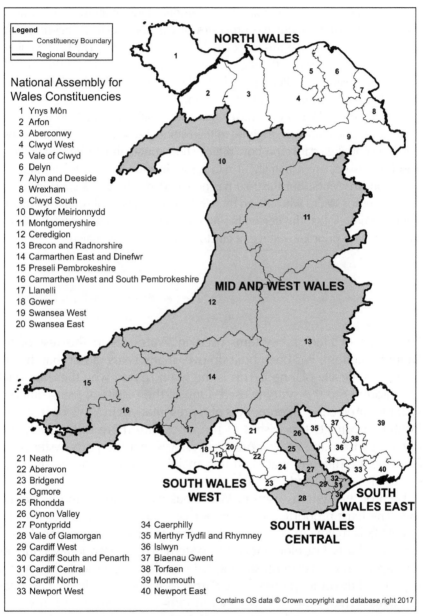

Legend
— Constituency Boundary
— Regional Boundary

National Assembly for
Wales Constituencies

 1 Ynys Môn
 2 Arfon
 3 Aberconwy
 4 Clwyd West
 5 Vale of Clwyd
 6 Delyn
 7 Alyn and Deeside
 8 Wrexham
 9 Clwyd South
10 Dwyfor Meirionnydd
11 Montgomeryshire
12 Ceredigion
13 Brecon and Radnorshire
14 Carmarthen East and Dinefwr
15 Preseli Pembrokeshire
16 Carmarthen West and South Pembrokeshire
17 Llanelli
18 Gower
19 Swansea West
20 Swansea East

21 Neath
22 Aberavon
23 Bridgend
24 Ogmore
25 Rhondda
26 Cynon Valley
27 Pontypridd
28 Vale of Glamorgan
29 Cardiff West
30 Cardiff South and Penarth
31 Cardiff Central
32 Cardiff North
33 Newport West

34 Caerphilly
35 Merthyr Tydfil and Rhymney
36 Islwyn
37 Blaenau Gwent
38 Torfaen
39 Monmouth
40 Newport East

Contains OS data © Crown copyright and database right 2017

Figure 7.1 Welsh Assembly electoral map

Gorwel is a Company limited by guarantee. Registered in England and Wales
Number: 8180087. Mae Gorwel yn Cwmni cyfyngedig trwy warant. Cofrestredig yn
Lloegr a Chymru Rhif: 8180087.

for candidates, voters and parties, and produces information so that voters are well informed about the processes of elections such as registering to vote, how electoral systems work and how to cast a ballot. The Commission maintains and publishes the registers of political parties in Great Britain and Northern Ireland. A political party has to be registered with the Commission in order to field candidates at an election.

The Office in Wales undertakes this role for all elections held in Wales with a specific emphasis on those to the National Assembly. It also provides all the central guidance on how the election counts should be undertaken and results declared. Initially, it had a role in promoting voter turnout at elections in Wales, but this role has now ended. There is a specific commissioner for Wales who sits on the UK board. The central requirement for appointment is that the person has no connection with UK political activity and often no prior knowledge of electoral systems or campaigns.

The advantages and disadvantages of the electoral systems used in Wales

The range of electoral systems used in Wales (as in the rest of the United Kingdom) has been built up over many years rather than having been strategically planned. This is the main reason why there is a lack of uniformity to the systems used. One of the results of using different systems for electing different tiers of representatives in Wales is that each institution reflects the wishes of the electorate more distinctively and differently from the others. Another result is that the party systems can also operate differently at each tier, mainly as a result of the disparate electoral systems used.

Each of the systems used in Wales has its defenders and its detractors. The least proportional system for elections used in Wales is FPTP. The AMS is mainly majoritarian, but delivers a more proportional result using the Party List element of the system. This is frequently criticised for significantly over-representing Labour Party representation at the expense of the other parties.[7] The Party List system used in the European elections remains the only wholly proportional system in use in Wales, but even here the small number of MEPs elected (four) means that a candidate still needs to get around 20 per cent of the vote in order to win a seat. With each election new advantages and disadvantages become apparent. These pros and cons can also differ depending on what one wants to see from the electoral system, for example do you want it to provide strong government or strong opposition? In this respect, the major advantages and disadvantages of the electoral systems used in Wales are shown in Table 7.2.

Voter turnout

Voter turnout at elections is important for politicians and for democracy overall. This is because the number of votes cast acts as a popular mandate for the endorsement of the political party and, if they form the government, for the implementation of the party manifesto and policy pledges. Second, voter turnout is a gauge of the popular interest and engagement in and understanding of the institution's elected representatives that are being voted in.

As voting is not compulsory in the United Kingdom, it is a voluntary process, it can mean that turnout levels are frequently less than 50 per cent (or one in two of the *electorate participating*). In Wales, as elsewhere in the United Kingdom, turnout remains highest for Westminster elections and lowest for council and EU elections. Political parties seek through various methods to ensure that the maximum number of their supporters turn out in those seats that they deem to be 'winnable'. At the same time, the media in Wales seek to ensure that voters are aware of the elections and specifically the day they are on. Turnout in General Elections in Wales has tended to be very slightly higher than the UK figure in each General Election since 1945. However, the 2010 and 2015 elections saw turnout in Wales fall below the UK figure.

Elections to the National Assembly for Wales: The 'Welsh General Election'

Elections to the Welsh Assembly are also known as the 'Welsh General Election'. The term 'general' is used because it refers to all sixty Assembly seats being elected at the same time (general). The first elections to the National Assembly for Wales took place in 1999 (see Table 7.1). Presently sixty AMs are elected at this election; forty are constituency AMs and the other twenty are regional AMs (list), though in law there is no difference in their role. The Welsh government emerges from these elections to the National Assembly, and is accountable to the National Assembly

Table 7.2 Advantages and disadvantages of the electoral systems used in Wales

System	Main advantages	Examples	Main disadvantages	Examples of problems
FPTP	*Voters can easily understand what they need to do to cast their ballot.* *The result is known relatively soon after the polls close.* *It generally leads to strong single-party governments that are accountable and legitimate and that can implement their manifesto promises.* *It allows a strong MP–constituency link, and for voters to clearly express their preference.*	In the 2015 UK General Election the Electoral Reform Society calculated that 20 of Wales' constituencies were 'safe'.[a] The full result was known in Wales by the morning of 8 May 2015, just 24 hours after polls had opened for the UK General Election. The FPTP section of AMS has delivered more seats in the National Assembly for Wales for Welsh Labour than for any other party since 1999. Welsh Labour has formed the government or been the main partner in a governing coalition since the first Assembly elections in 1999.	*All votes for candidates who do not win are wasted, as are all votes for winning candidates over and above those they needed to win.* *Parties with concentrated support, and larger parties, are rewarded disproportionately, whereas parties with support that is spread out, and smaller parties, are disadvantaged.* *Many representatives are elected on a minority of the votes cast in their constituency. Governments are often formed based on a minority of the total votes cast.* *It encourages tactical voting. It discourages the selection of a range of diverse candidates. It can lead to whole regions of the UK feeling under-represented at Westminster.*	Male bias: in the UK General Election 2015, only 26.6% of the candidates in Wales were female. In the 2003 National Assembly for Wales elections, Welsh Labour gained 50% of the available seats with 36.6% of the total votes cast. The reason for this was that Welsh Labour did well in the constituency (FPTP) part of the AMS. In the UK General Election 2015, Labour won 65% of the seats in Wales with 36.9% of the vote.[b] Websites such as Voteswap and Swapmyvote informed voters on how best to vote tactically in the 2015 UK General Election. UKIP won 13.6% of the vote in Wales in the 2015 General Election, but secured no seats. In the 2015 General Election the Welsh Conservative candidate won in Gower by securing 37.1% of the votes cast, 0.1% ahead of the second placed Labour candidate.

Party Lists (closed)	*The choice before the voter is simple as the vote is cast for a party.* *Female and ethnic minority candidates have more opportunities to be elected from a Party List.* *There is a high degree of proportionality between the percentage of votes cast for a party and the percentage of seats it receives.* *Multi-member constituencies offer more flexible representation for voters.* *Each vote counts equally – there are few if any wasted votes.*	In 2003, 50% of AMs elected to the National Assembly for Wales were female. The regional AMs elected for North Wales in 2011 were from the Welsh Conservative Party (2), Welsh Liberal Democrats (1) and Plaid Cymru (1). In South East Wales the 4 regional AMs elected in 2011 were from the Welsh Conservative Party (2) and Plaid Cymru (2). In the European Parliament elections of 2014 Wales returned 4 MEPs: Labour (1), UKIP (1), Conservative (1) and Plaid Cymru (1).	*All the power over who is on the list, and (crucially) in which position on the list, rests with the party.* *Independent voices within the party may be stifled, and minority candidates may not get a position near the top of a list.* *Multi-member constituencies weaken the link between the voters and the representatives.* *List candidates are selected by the party rather than the voters. The list is closed so voters have to accept who is positioned on the list even if they prefer other candidates.* *Multi-party governments are more likely as a result of more proportional systems like party lists. These can have disadvantages (see below).*	In the 2011 National Assembly for Wales elections, 38 of the 102 candidates were female, 4 identified as BME and one as LGBT.[c] The National Assembly for Wales has 20 regional AMs elected for 5 multi-member regions. The European Parliament has 1 constituency that covers Wales (called 'Wales' since 1999) and it elects 4 MEPs. Since 1999 there have been three periods of coalition/partnership government in Wales and three periods of Welsh Labour minority government.

Table 7.2 (Continued)

System	Main advantages	Examples	Main disadvantages	Examples of problems
AMS (this system is a combination of the two systems above and therefore has most of the advantages and disadvantages of those systems, as listed above).	*The unfairness of the FPTP part of AMS in terms of votes cast and seats won is rectified by the 'top-up' Party List part of AMS. This hybrid system rarely leads to strong one-party government. There is a need for compromise and negotiation with other parties which makes government in Wales pluralistic and more representative of the electorate's wishes.*	As the FPTP system can make Welsh political results highly disproportional all the political parties in Wales have gained most of their AMs by this method at one time or another. UKIP gained 100% of theirs via AMS in 2016.	*The same disadvantages as above plus the FPTP constituency ballot favours Labour in Wales. Welsh Labour has thus been over-represented in Welsh Assembly elections and has formed or been the major party in every Welsh government since 1999. Minority and coalition governments can be weak and/or can pursue policies that are driven by the junior party in the coalition partnership. This is perceived as not being 'open' or democratic by some. It leads to defeated candidates in the constituency who although receiving a low number of votes are still elected to the Welsh Assembly because they top their party's list, thus appearing to circumvent voters wishes (the so-called Clwyd West question).*	The hybrid system is still quite non-proportional. In the 2016 Welsh Assembly election, for instance, Labour won 34.7% of the constituency vote and 31.5% of the regional list vote across Wales, yet gained just under 50% of the total AMs elected.

SV				
	It is an easy system to understand *It encourages candidates to reach out beyond their partisan support base because obtaining the second preference is important.*	Used in Wales to determine the results of the Police and Crime Commissioner elections – also the likely system should there be any elected mayors in Wales.	*Is not proportional and the winning candidate does not have to have the support of 50% of the voters.* *Promotes voting for mainstream parties.* *If there are more than two strong candidates voters find it difficult to provide their second vote.* *Many votes cast in the first round cannot be cast in the second.* *Encourages tactical voting.*	Only on rare occasions does the second preference make a difference, and on no occasion in Wales has the candidate with highest number of first preferences not been the winning candidate – making the second preference unnecessary. The dominant regional party in 2016 was also the winner in each election. 2012 had record low turnouts for this SV election which meant the next one was connected to the Welsh Assembly election, overshadowing these elections almost entirely.

(a) Electoral Reform Society at: https://www.electoral-reform.org.uk.

(b) Deacon, *The Welsh Liberals*.

(c) Wyn Jones, 'How Welsh Labour became the UK's most Invincible Electoral Machine'.

in the same way that the parliamentary system works at Westminster. As is the case in the Westminster Parliament, it is constitutionally the largest political party that gets the first go at forming a government after the Welsh General Election. The Labour Party has always been the largest political party in the Welsh Assembly and consequently has led various governments since the Assembly's establishment in 1999.

Box 7.2 Case study: the effects of the AMS system on party systems in Wales

If we look at the effects of the electoral system across Wales we can see that in almost all elections it benefits the Labour Party over the other parties. This can be seen in virtually all Welsh elections. It is a consistent factor, so if we go back to the Welsh General Election of 2010, Table 7.3 shows the extent to which the FPTP element of the elections (the constituency seat allocation) favours the Labour Party in Wales. Indeed, for UK General elections where the voting is all done under the FPTP system all parties across Wales other than the Labour and Conservative parties have struggled to gain seats, despite quite often having a reasonable number of votes cast for them. It is this proportional injustice that the AMS seeks to rectify in elections to the National Assembly for Wales.

What positive and negative effects therefore does the AMS system have on both the political parties and governance in Wales? There are numerous examples of how the AMS system has shaped Welsh politics. The main ones, which are worthy of note, are that:

- It has led to a dominant party state with the Labour Party as the dominant party in Assembly elections and has been the lead partner in coalitions. This is because forty of the sixty AMs are elected using FPTP, which constantly rewards the Labour Party.
- The 'nationalist' parties in Wales, Plaid Cymru and UKIP, have been better represented in the Assembly than at national level in Westminster. However, Plaid Cymru has not managed to emulate the success of the Scottish Nationalist Party in either the Assembly or Westminster elections. The greater or 'fairer' representation achieved by Plaid Cymru in the Assembly has been largely due to the 'top-up' Party List part of AMS. Plaid have also won more constituencies in the Assembly than they have in UK General Elections. Outside the European elections, the proportional element for UKIP, with their seven AMs, has allowed them to break into

UK politics. This is to an a far greater extent than the FPTP system allows them to do anywhere else in the United Kingdom.

- The nature of opposition in Wales at the Welsh Assembly is different to that at Westminster. This is because, although there is an 'Official Opposition' made up of the party that has the second largest number of Assembly seats, as at Westminster, there has been no chance that they could act as an alternative government. This is because, aside from 1999–2003, the Official Opposition's total AMs has only been between a third and a half that of the ruling Labour Party's total AMs.

- Unbroken Labour electoral dominance since 1999 has led to a distinctive left of centre political 'Welshness' emerging in many areas where policy is different to that in England. For instance, Wales has retained comprehensive schools, resisting the introduction of academies/grammar schools, and in addition established a separate Welsh examinations system in 2015. Other distinct policy areas mean that the private sector has been kept out of the NHS and prescriptions were made free in Wales in 2007. Wales was also the first part of the United Kingdom to enforce a smoking ban and to have a dedicated Children's Commissioner. This same distinct political agenda, however, has also been blamed for Wales' continued economic decline and problems in the Welsh NHS that are not mirrored in England.

- It has acted as a lifeline to political parties who find it difficult to win constituency seats. The Conservatives in 1999, Welsh Liberal Democrats in 2011 and UKIP in 2016 won all or nearly all of their seats through the regional lists. This enabled them to become an all-Wales political party despite the fact that their electoral voice was limited to one or no individual constituencies.

Referenda in Wales

A referendum is not an election. It is a form of direct democracy, and in this respect it is normally a vote on a specific question, usually to decide a single important question of public policy. The use of referenda is increasing in the United Kingdom, but their occurrence is not as frequent as in some other European countries. In Wales, it has been used on local matters, such as to decide whether to have an elected mayor (Ceredigion is the only area in Wales to have held one), the abolition of community councils, transferring ownership of a park from one

Table 7.3 The effect of the 'top-up' regional list in correlating percentage of seats won overall to the percentage of votes cast for each party in the 2011 Assembly election[a]

Party	Votes won in the regional list ballot (%) percentage won in the regional list and constituency ballots combined)[b]	Seats won overall in the Assembly (%) (percentage of the total 60 seats)	Seats won in the constituency ballot: the 40 FPTP seats (%) (percentage of vote in the constituency ballot)
Welsh Labour	36.9 (39.6)	50	70 (42.3)
Welsh Conservatives	22.5 (23.8)	23.3	15 (25.0)
Welsh Liberal Democrats	8.0 (9.3)	8.3	2.5 (10.6)
Plaid Cymru	17.9 (18.6)	18.3	12.5(19.3)

[a] Martin Jennings, '2011 Assembly Election Results May 2011', National Assembly for Wales, Paper 11/023, Welsh Assembly Research Services, 2011.
[b] The total is not 100% as 14.7% of votes were cast for 'other' political parties in the regional ballot (8.7% in the regional list and constituency ballots combined), but no seats resulted from this.

authority to another or opening hours for licensed premises. The latter was allowed from 1881 until 2003 in order to make a county 'dry' or 'wet' for the sale of alcohol in public houses. It ended with the introduction of the Sunday Licensing Act 2003.

Referenda can also be used on a local and national (Wales or UK) basis. For a long while, however, nationwide referenda were not used because it was believed that:

1. they were primarily a method used by dictators to harness populist opinion to carry forward mainly unlawful acts, as had been used by Fascist/Nazi and Communist dictatorships;
2. the mandate of a political party's manifesto and their winning of the majority of seats in Parliament was deemed to be sufficient to ensure that any policy was undertaken without the need for a referendum.

Prior to 1997, there were only three national referenda of note: in Northern Ireland, on whether to remain part of the United Kingdom or not; in the United Kingdom, on whether to join the European Economic Community; and in Wales and Scotland, on devolution. Only the referendum on Europe, however, was held across the whole of the United

Kingdom and Northern Ireland. There was a sea-change in attitudes to referenda under Tony Blair's Labour Party in 1996, however. Here they reversed previous Labour policy and decided to hold referenda on establishing devolution across the United Kingdom and Northern Ireland. This was done mainly to establish a constitutional rule whereby if a new legislature is established by a referendum then it can in future only be abolished by one, although, this is not technically true because the UK Parliament remains sovereign and cannot be bound by any referenda. It was thought, however, that it would entrench the devolved institutions strongly enough to prevent them being abolished by simply passing another Act of Parliament through Westminster.[8]

Since 1997, there have been national UK referenda on changing the voting system for elections to the UK Parliament to an AV system (2011) and on the UK's membership of the EU (2016). A Scottish referendum was also held on independence in 2014, which decided that Scotland would remain part of the United Kingdom. In Wales, the key referenda are shown in Box 7.3.

Box 7.3 Key referenda specific to the whole of Wales

1 March 1979: 'St David's Day referendum', the first devolution referendum. The people of Wales were asked to decide whether to support devolution for Wales. Turnout was 59.01 per cent and the majority vote was against devolution by 79.7 per cent to 20.3 per cent.

September 1997: second devolution referendum. The result this time was a narrow majority in favour of devolution, by 50.3 per cent to 49.7 per cent, with turnout at 50.1 per cent.

March 2011: a referendum on extending the law-making powers of the National Assembly for Wales. Turnout was at 35.6 per cent, with 63.49 per cent voting for and 35.51 per cent voting against = YES.

We should note that referenda in Wales, as well as elsewhere, are a form of direct democracy. The results of referenda are not legally binding (this is something of a constitutional grey area) and there have therefore been criticisms of referenda where the turnout has been less than half of the electorate. This is because less than half of the population have decided on a key issue, and this in turn it may mean that under a quarter of the population have decided on the eventual result. Government's also seek to hold national referenda only when they think they can win them and if they do not think they can win them they will either be delayed as long as possible or not held at all. One Welsh example concerned the plans for a referendum on introducing tax-raising powers to the Welsh Assembly, which failed to get cross-party support and was therefore dropped in November 2015.[9]

Coalition government in Wales

Politicians in Westminster considering their new coalition government and wondering how to cope with the demands of a very new and different style of governing at Westminster in May 2010 needed to look no further than Wales. Viewpoints in the past have suggested that there has been greater support generally in Wales since devolution for the principle of strong government than for the idea of a representative result. However, this has not been the main experience of elections to the National Assembly since 1999. The AMS used to elect representatives to the National Assembly for Wales delivers a more proportional result, meaning that the Welsh Labour Party has never been in a position in which it could form a single-party, majority government and govern alone without the cooperation of other parties. This has often forced it into coalition or partnership government.

There have been periods of minority and 'majority' Welsh Labour government, and periods of coalition government. All this has had a noticeable effect on the parties in Wales and has led to the creation of a particularly Welsh way of doing politics in Cardiff Bay. This has been encouraged by the small and fairly familiar environment of the Senedd, where tradition and ceremony give way to practicality and modernism in conduct, and by the electoral system which makes coalition and minority government frequent occurrences. This has been dubbed 'The Welshminster consensus' and embodies 'soft-nationalist cultural politics and political rhetoric; devo-maximising constitutional reform; and a social democratic policy agenda', a consensus within which all the Welsh political parties operate to varying extents.[10]

A short history of Welsh coalition governments

The Welsh Labour and Welsh Liberal Democrat coalition, 2000–3

The first elected Welsh Assembly in 1999 did not deliver half the seats to Labour (they won twenty-eight) and their period of minority government until 2000 was marked by instability and uncertainty. First Secretary Alun Michael resigned and was replaced by Rhodri Morgan, and a coalition with the Liberal Democrats was established in October 2000. The influence of the Welsh Liberal Democrats was overall less than they might have hoped. They had an existing model of policy-making that involved party members, but these mechanisms were found wanting when policy-making in government required flexibility and speed.[11] The experience was a rather disappointing one for the Welsh Liberal Democrats, who although they were able to secure some of their manifesto promises, for example, on tuition fees and free museum entry, were unable to secure policies that would have benefited them electorally, such as STV for Welsh local government elections. It was also unclear to the electorate which party in the coalition was responsible for which policies, meaning either party could claim credit for them.[12]

The 'One Wales' (Red–Green) coalition of Welsh Labour and Plaid Cymru, 2007–11

The result of the 2007 Welsh Assembly election meant that a coalition government of some sort looked inevitable: Labour lost two seats overall, leaving them with twenty-six, not enough to go it alone. However, a Labour–Plaid Cymru coalition looked unlikely. An opinion poll for the BBC after the 2007 National Assembly for Wales elections revealed that 48 per cent of those questioned favoured a 'rainbow coalition', whereas only 28 per cent favoured a Labour–Plaid Cymru coalition government (which was the eventual outcome). Indeed, it took two months to achieve, and only after other coalition possibilities had been explored and had failed, including a so-called 'rainbow coalition' of all the other parties, excluding Labour.

It became known as the 'Red–Green' coalition because of the respective parties political colours, although Plaid Cymru have subsequently changed their green to yellow. This coalition delivered the support of forty-one of the sixty AMs and was a partnership of the two largest parties in the Assembly, a 'Grand Coalition' (rather than the largest party and a small one), although outside the Assembly both parties remained politically hostile to each other. For Plaid Cymru, it had an impact on implementing their policies in the fields of agriculture, transport and the Welsh language as well as many other areas during this administration, which lasted until the elections in 2011.

So, while coalition government is more 'normal' in Wales than in Westminster, it has yet to cement itself as the natural inclination of parties there. In many ways the adversarial nature of party politics at Westminster still prevail in Wales, despite their inappropriateness for the national political environment in Wales. The most obvious demonstration that old habits are hard to kick is the reluctance to form a coalition government, unless every other avenue has been explored. Indeed, more generally, there appears to be reluctance on the part of parties to accept that single-party majority governments are the least likely outcome of Assembly elections, and to anticipate the need to co-operate.'[13] However, neither coalition government was so warmly enjoyed by any of the political parties that they were in a hurry to reform them at the first opportunity. This was particularly true of the Welsh Liberal Democrats in 2007 and Plaid Cymru in 2016.

However, one of the criticisms of coalitions – that they are inherently unstable with a small party effectively holding a larger one to ransom – has not materialised in Wales. Each period of coalition government has been entered into by way of a formal agreement and the 'smaller' party has not withdrawn its support from the government and forced its downfall. We should also note that plans to increase the number of AMs in Wales to seventy, eighty or even a hundred will mean that coalition government becomes even more likely in future.

Conclusion

The electoral systems in use in Wales are diverse rather than rationally planned. One of the results of this is that each type of election has its own context and will not always be that predictable using the results of the last election for a different tier of government. It is entirely possible that the voters of Wales are feeling election 'overload'; turnout rates are nearly always below 50 per cent and are worryingly low for some types of election and referenda. Control over elections in Wales is an issue, like many others, that is gradually being transferred to the National Assembly for Wales as part of the devolution process. Nevertheless, the electoral systems in Wales have ensured that all parties, with the exception of UKIP, have enjoyed periods in government either in Westminster or in Cardiff Bay. Prior to 2000, only the Labour and Conservatives parties had any experience of governing in Wales.

The politics of Wales is heavily influenced by the electoral arrangements there. Each system brings different pros and cons to each party's electoral fortunes. New ways of working have also been found and cooperation, made necessary by the system used to elect AMs, has characterised the workings of the National Assembly. The relationship between the parties in Wales no longer mirrors that in England or the rest of the United Kingdom, and Wales is developing a distinctive political culture and Welsh policies. Differences of emphasis and style exist within parties, with the Welsh party and the UK party often having different perspectives on the same general issues.

Questions for discussion

1. How has the electoral system for the National Assembly affected the inter-relationships of the parties in Wales?
2. What impacts on policy in Wales have been caused by the Additional Member electoral system for the National Assembly and the outcomes it produces?
3. Are referenda a good way of deciding issues?

Case study: the effects of the AMS system on party systems in Wales[14]

The case study in Box 7.2 pays particular attention to those elements concerned with the Additional Member System (AMS) and its impact on party systems. Read the case study and then answer the following questions:

1. What sort of electoral system is AMS?
2. In what ways could it be said to be good for democracy in Wales?
3. What arguments can be used against AMS?
4. How has it altered the fortunes of specific parties in Wales?

Suggested answer points are provided in the Welsh Government and Politics online resource for both the questions and the case study. The web link for these answer points is given at the front of the book.

Civil Society, Pressure Groups, Lobbying and Local Government in Wales

Rob Southall

Overview

Civil society involves the activities of individuals and groups operating outside formal governmental structures. Wales, like other democratic nations both inside and outside the United Kingdom, operates a pluralistic democracy whereby a multitude of representative organisations seek to influence political party and government policy formulation, the framing of legislation by the legislature and the implementation of legislation, and allocation of funding by government. The groups involved are often the same as those in England, but increasingly there are groups unique to Wales coming to the fore.

This chapter seeks to provide an overview of the activities of pressure groups in Wales, their nature, resources, the coalitions they build with other groups in order to determine whether Wales is beginning to see the emergence of its own civil culture that is separate and distinctive to Wales, and whether this has come as a response to the increased powers of the Welsh government. We will also consider the part played by think tanks, lobbying firms and social movements to civil society in Wales, and try to assess the positive and negative effects of devolution on groups and group activity in Wales. The chapter concludes with a look at local government in Wales and the particular conflicts that have arisen since the creation of the National Assembly for Wales in 1999.

Key issues to be covered in this chapter

- What is the nature of pressure group activity in Wales?
- How can we define civil society and the question of whether Wales has its own civil society?
- What is the third sector and what are third sector organisations?
- What are the main strengths and weaknesses of civil society in Wales?
- Who are the main targets for lobbying and what are the key access points when seeking to influence government policy in Wales?
- To what extent is there a 'devolution dividend' and how has this affected the work of groups in Wales?
- What have been the effects of devolution on the work of the groups?
- Why do we have Welsh local authorities and what is their role?
- What are the main points of conflict between central and local government in Wales?
- What is the role of the Public Service Ombudsman for Wales?

Prior to the coming of devolution in 1999, Wales formed an integral, although distinct, part of British political society. Most pressure group activity in Wales was within the wider context of group–governmental relations in the United Kingdom, and the system of local government largely mirrored that of England. The forty years prior to the establishment of devolution brought many changes, and it is important to appreciate that these have helped to shape civil society in contemporary Wales.

In 1964, the UK Cabinet position of Secretary of State for Wales was established and the Welsh Office was created as a separate UK government department with offices in Cardiff. The Welsh Office took on a number of important governmental functions in Wales, including local government, town and country planning, economic development, housing, national parks and historic buildings, and culture including the promotion of the Welsh language. As a direct result of this a small number of distinctly Welsh organisations emerged to directly lobby the UK government in Wales.

One of the results of this lobbying was that Wales began to develop its own distinctive approaches in a range of policy areas, with notable examples in local government through the establishment of a unitary system of local authorities, economic development through the work of the Welsh Development Agency (WDA), historic environment via Cadw and promotion of the arts and culture through the Arts Council of Wales. The last seventeen years have continued, and in many respects, accelerated this process.

In turn, both the Welsh government and the Welsh Assembly openly seek to include many pressure groups in their formal and informal processes. This ranges from the creation of new policies, adjusting or reviewing existing ones, creating new legislation, consultation exercises, membership of task-and-finish groups, the work of Assembly committees or cross-party groupings, and the launch of campaigns by various pressure groups.

Pressure groups and civil society in Wales

Many organisations and bodies now have specific staff within them with a dedicated role in public affairs, which includes working directly with the Welsh government/Assembly in order to promote their own body's central aims. Some are businesses, but many are organisations that have a 'pressure group' role as a central part of their work. There are no accurate figures for the total number of pressure groups operating in Wales as these vary greatly in both structure, focus and aims. However, the Welsh Council for Voluntary Action, which represents the voluntary sector in Wales, the sphere where most pressure groups and charities operate, states on its website that it has 'an ever growing membership of more than 2,500 organisations comprising thousands of staff, volunteers and trustees, and is in contact with many more through national and regional networks'. In contrast, Public Affairs Cymru (see Box 8.7), which represents lobbying firms operating in the 'Cardiff Bay Village' (see Box 8.11), currently has over 100 members, although this includes a variety of public bodies and private companies, who employ public affairs or 'liaison officers' to manage their relations with government and other stakeholders, in addition to traditional pressure groups. In addition, there are a number of formal coalitions of voluntary groups, such as Age Alliance Wales, and public affairs firms under the umbrella of Public Affairs Cymru.

Box 8.1 What are pressure groups?

Pressure groups, sometimes called interest groups, are organised groups who seek to influence the policies and actions of government in modern representative democracies.

They generally differ from political parties in that they tend to have very limited, or specific, interests and they rarely stand for directly election, preferring to exert an influence from outside the corridors of power usually occupied by politicians and political parties. They tend to be linked to just one or two policy areas.

They differ from social movements because they have a high degree of organisation.

Many of these groups and organisations are termed Non-governmental organisations (NGOs), and may also have charitable status. Examples include Shelter Cymru, NSPCC Wales and Groundwork Wales. Charitable status can restrict the type of lobbying and campaigning that occurs. Often the 'pressure group' part of their work is just one of the operations they undertake, with their core mission lying elsewhere.

Theories of group activity

Government policy is not all derived from party manifestos and the Civil Service. It is important to appreciate that there are other sources that contribute to policy output. Therefore, for those seeking to understand distinct Welsh policy it is important to be aware of the role that pressure groups, academics and other specialists play. According to political theory of pluralism, political power in Britain is widely dispersed, and the interests of a large number of groups are taken into consideration by government when making policy decisions. Implicit in this concept is that for every group seeking to influence government in one way there will be another seeking the alternative course of action, and that every government decision is a result of compromise and consensus-building on the part of government and the groups concerned.

Political pluralism is an inclusive approach that tends to consider that there are no elite groups who dominate either the policy-making or decision-making processes. In contrast to pluralism, is the exclusive approach of societal corporatism. This asserts that in liberal democracies there is a tendency for organised interests to be granted privileged access to policy-making. Some political commentators have suggested that the Welsh government has become increasingly corporatist in its approach to group relations. However, this may be seen largely as a consequence of the small size, and limited capacity, of the Welsh government's Civil Service, which has resulted in a situation where government has been reliant on specialist groups and academics to provide expert advice

Types of pressure group in Wales

Given the plethora of different types of organisation now seeking to exert an influence on government in Wales, it might be appropriate to distinguish between the main types of group. The variety of groups reflects the almost infinite diversity of interests in modern Welsh society, and that not all groups fit neatly into one particular category so it is also appropriate to consider the following: sectional and cause groups, and insider and outsider groups. In addition, we will consider peak associations and formal coalitions, temporary groups, direct action groups, public affairs or lobbying firms, think tanks and social movements.

Sectional/cause classification

This is the best known and widely used of all pressure group typologies. It divides groups, according to their membership and aims, into 'sectional groups and cause groups.

Sectional groups

Sectional groups lobby government (see Box 8.2) in order to protect and promote the economic interests, terms and conditions of employment, social status and influence of their members. Examples of such organisations are Unison Cymru/Wales, which is Wales' largest trade union; CBI Wales, which represents employers; and the BMA, which represents doctors working in every branch of the medical profession in Wales as well as medical students. These groups are also referred to as protective groups. They tend to be long-established, well-connected and well-resourced organisations who are key players in their policy networks. They are also very influential as a result of their specialist knowledge.

Cause groups

Cause groups are those that seek to promote certain issues and interests above all others, for example, the environment or animal rights. Such groups have an open membership in that anyone can join or donate to them, and they tend to have support from a wider cross-section of the population. Examples of these groups include the Royal Society for the Protection of Birds, which is Wales largest cause group with about 50,000 members; Cymdeithas yr Iaith Gymraeg (the Welsh Language Society), which seeks to protect and promote the usage of the Welsh language; and Shelter Cymru, which works on behalf of people with housing needs in Wales. There are also some religious groups, such as Cytûn, which represents the Christian churches in Wales. These groups can be influential as a result of their specialist knowledge, staff and resources. Government often relies on their assistance in writing specific policy and, sometimes, implementing government decisions.

Box 8.2 What is lobbying?

The academic Duncan Watts defines the act of lobbying as 'the practice of meeting with elected representatives to persuade them of the merits of the case you wish to advance'.[1] Lobbyists are the employees of organisations who try to influence policy decisions especially in the Executive and legislative branches of government. Although lobbyists, and the act of lobbying, has had a negative press in the past in general both are viewed as beneficial as they serve as a checks-and-balances safeguard on the policy-making and legislative processes, however there is a realisation that individual lobbyists are not necessarily equal in the influence they wield. Some people think lobbyists in general have too much power and that special, that is, sectional, interests dominate government policy-making and legislation.[2]

Insider/outsider classification

The academic Wyn Grant (1989)[3] divides groups into two types according to their relationship with the key decision-makers in government, that is, insider and outsider groups.

Insider groups

Insider groups are those that, as regular members of the policy community (see Box 8.3), experience regular access to government and enjoy a close working relationship with decision-makers, often at all levels of government. They are often involved in government consultations on new legislation and on pre-legislative policy formulation. Some of these groups are considered as a first point of contact by politicians and civil servants who rely on their specialist knowledge. Examples of insider groups in Wales include the Wales Trades Union Congress (Wales TUC); business bodies such as the Federation of Small Businesses (FSB Wales), the Confederation of British Industry (CBI Wales) and the Institute of Directors (IoD Wales); and the Wales Council for Voluntary Action (WCVA), the organisation that represents the voluntary sector (see Box 8.12) in Wales and has a statutory commitment under the Third Sector Scheme to facilitate the bi-annual meetings between the sector and Welsh government ministers. Expert groups such as Shelter Cymru, which represents the homeless in Wales, have regular meetings with Welsh Assembly government ministers, and have built strong relationships with AMs and other parts of the Assembly such as Welsh Assembly Members Research Services and committee clerks. Insider groups are usually sectional groups who are most often better resourced and well connected. Ultimately, it is their specialist knowledge, or technical expertise, and willingness to engage in relationships with government that contributes most to this success. These insider groups are also often consulted directly by the political parties when shaping their own election manifestos

Outsider groups

Outsider groups are typically those groups that are held at arm's length by government/political parties or are denied government access to the policy community or issue network (see Box 8.3). This may be because of their beliefs or values, the methods they utilise or because they are unable to gain recognition within the wider community. There are also a number of groups who do not wish to have close or regular contact with decision-makers as they fear their values or cause may be tainted by the compromises usually expected by government and mainstream politicians. Cymdeithas Yr Iaith Gymraeg has been the most prominent of all outsider groups in Wales due to its use of direct action in support of the wider use of the Welsh language. However, as this cause is now shared by many people in Wales, both inside and outside the National Assembly and Welsh government, so Cymdeithas is now regarded as a legitimate lobby group for the promotion of language.

Box 8.3 Case study: what are policy networks, policy communities and issue networks?

Policy networks are the relationships between political actors who share a common interest. These typically include ministers, civil servants and key members of the legislature, along with specialist pressure groups, lobbyists, sympathetic academics and sections of the media.

These networks 'cut across formal institutional arrangements and the divide between government and non-governmental bodies'. The concept recognises the importance of 'informal processes and relationships' on policy-making and initiation, but highlights the sometimes closed and exclusive nature of the policy process.[4] This closed nature is best illustrated by the 'iron triangles' found in US politics.

Policy communities are small, stable and consensual groups of senior civil servants and key members of specialist pressure groups who are involved in decision-making in a particular area of policy,[5] for example, housing.

Issue networks are more open and inclusive than policy communities. They involve more people and organisations involved in a particular area of policy, for example, how to tackle poverty. In Wales this also forms what is known as the 'Cardiff Bay Village' (see Box 8.11).

Other types of group in Wales

There are various other ways of classifying groups and we will now examine some of these and their relevance to Welsh politics. Some of these also fall into the other categorisations that we have just explored.

Peak associations

Peak associations, also called umbrella groups, represent a number of groups working in a particular economic sector or policy environment. The best known of these in Wales would be 'Wales TUC Cymru', established as a distinct organisation in 1973, which represents over fifty affiliated trade unions and nearly half a million workers. The Confederation of British Industry, which has a director and regional organisation in Wales, speaks for 190,000 businesses in the United Kingdom. In Wales, one of the largest peak associations is the Wales Council for Voluntary Action (WCVA), which represents thousands of national, regional and local voluntary organisations throughout Wales.

Formal coalitions or partnerships

Formal coalitions or partnerships, which are umbrella organisations covering discrete areas of policy, have largely emerged in Wales since 1999 to campaign and coordinate member organisations' relations with the Welsh government and National Assembly. Examples of this type of organisation can be found in Box 8.4.

Box 8.4 Case study: examples of formal coalitions, partnerships or networks

Homes for All Cymru (previously known as Housing Forum Cymru), which brings together key organisations involved in housing-related matters in Wales and 'aims to maximise the contribution housing makes to the health and wellbeing of communities'.[6]

End Child Poverty Network Cymru (ECPN Cymru), which is a coalition of organisations focused on the eradication of child poverty in Wales. Membership includes Barnardo's Cymru, Children in Wales, Save the Children Wales, NSPCC Cymru, Welsh Local Government Association

---

(WLGA), Citizens Advice, Oxfam Cymru, Public Health Wales, Shelter Cymru, Prince's Trust Cymru, TUC Wales and Welsh Women's Aid, among others.

Children in Wales is the national umbrella body for organisations and individuals who work with children, young people and their families in Wales.

Disability Wales is an independent, not-for-profit organisation, established in 1972. It is a membership organisation of over 100 disability groups and allies from across Wales and champions the rights, equality and independence of all disabled people regardless of physical or sensory impairment, learning difficulty or mental health condition.[7]

Wales Environment Link (WEL), established in 1990 as the Wales Wildlife and Countryside Link, is the umbrella body for environmental and countryside NGOs in Wales and tends to be considered the main environmental stakeholder by Welsh government.[8]

All the groups in Box 8.4 work collectively for their members by campaigning, leading and running projects, securing funding, hosting training events and conferences, and engaging in advocacy in meetings with government ministers, civil servants and with AMs on a personal level in Assembly committees and in cross-party groups. They have become very much a part of the machinery of government in post-devolution Wales and an essential component of what is now termed the 'Cardiff Bay Village' (see Box 8.11).

Temporary groups

Temporary groups tend to be non-political and short term in nature, often forming in response to a particular problem and usually disbanding when their aim has been achieved or cause defeated. Typically, these are community-based groups fighting a local planning decision, such as the location of a traveller's site or waste disposal facility. Some recent examples are 'The Keep Caerphilly Mountain Green group' and 'Gwern Y Domen Conservation group', both of whom are fighting a controversial plan setting out the future of housing development in Caerphilly County borough and have called for the Local Development Plan (LPD) to be withdrawn.

Direct action groups

Direct action groups are organisations that tend to utilise either non-violent direct action, such as civil disobedience, sit-ins or strikes, or violent direct action, such as political assassination, the destruction of property, rioting, hunger strikes, terrorism and armed insurrection, as their main campaigning technique. In Wales there are a number examples of each, including those discussed below.

Non-violent direct action

Wales' best known protest group is Cymdeithas yr Iaith, the Welsh Language Society, which has often utilised non-violent direct action in the course of its campaigns. Since its founding in 1963, over a thousand people have appeared before the courts for their part in various protests with many receiving custodial sentences, making it the United Kingdom's most prolific direct action group since the suffragettes both in terms the number of activists sent to prison and those receiving fines. Typical actions have included sit-ins, daubing slogans on buildings and road signs, and other minor criminal damage. Notable successes have included the establishment of Radio Cymru in 1977. Many would agree that Cymdeithas' campaigns over the years have been successful as they have raised awareness of the plight of the Welsh language and changed the stance of central government to such issues as Welsh-medium education and bi-lingual signage, both of which are now a common feature across Wales.

Following the Conservative government's announcement, in 1979, that it would not keep its election promise to establish a separate Welsh-language television channel, in 1980, Gwynfor Evans, former Plaid Cymru president and MP for Carmarthen, threatened to starve himself to death if the UK government refused to provide a Welsh-language TV service. Cabinet papers released thirty years after the event reveal that the hunger strike was a key factor in the Thatcher government's decision to set up S4C as a television channel devoted exclusively to Welsh-language broadcasting.[9] Probably the best known politician to emerge from the world of direct action in the past twenty years was the late Brynlee Williams AM, Conservative regional member for North Wales. Williams, a dairy farmer from Cilcain near Mold, rose to prominence in 2000 when he led the fuel protests in north Wales and set up a blockade outside the Stanlow Oil Refinery in Cheshire. As vice chairman of the

Farmers' Union of Wales, he had earlier been instrumental in organising mass demonstrations at Holyhead, Anglesey over cheap Irish beef imports.[10]

Violent direct action

Wales has had its fair share of violent direct action over the years, most recently with the organisation Meibion Glyndwr (Sons of Glyndwr) (see Box 8.5). Historically, the Chartists and suffragettes are the best-known groups seen in Wales, although both were very much a part of wider UK movements. Radical Welsh nationalism was first seen in 1936 when the UK government decided to establish an RAF training camp and aerodrome, or 'bombing school', at Penyberth on the Llŷn Peninsula. The facility was set on fire in September 1936, and in the investigations that followed Saunders Lewis, Lewis Valentine and D. J. Williams, all leading members of Plaid Genedlaethol Cymru as Plaid Cymru was then known, claimed responsibility. The initial trial at Caernarfon failed to provide a verdict, so the case was sent for re-trial to the Old Bailey in London. The 'Penyberth Three' were each sentenced to nine months in prison. Subsequently, they were widely seen as martyrs for the cause of the Welsh language and, on their release, received enthusiastic support from over 15,000 people at an event in Caernarfon.

Radical nationalism raised its head again in 1963 when the reservoir at Tryweryn was under construction. This saw the village of Capel Celyn in Merionethshire drowned to provide water for Liverpool. Three young men, members of a group called Mudiad Amddiffyn Cymru (Movement for the Defence of Wales), travelled to the construction site and planted a 5-lb (2.3-kg) bomb at the electricity facility powering the project. These actions merely delayed the construction of the reservoir, which was opened in October 1965.[11] Similar destructive tactics were utilised by another organisation calling itself Meibion Gyndwr in the 1980s and 1990s (Box 8.5).

Box 8.5 What was Meibion Glyndwr?

Meibion Glyndwr, or the Sons of Glyndwr, were a radical Welsh nationalist group active between the late 1970s and the early 1990s. They used *violent direction action*, specifically arson, to hit out at holiday homes and estate agents in north Wales. Their campaign of burning properties began in December 1979 and persisted until the mid-1990s when it finally petered out. This was in protest against rural homes being sold as holiday cottages to people from England. At the height of their campaign the group struck at more than 200 homes, caravans and cars in Wales. The police conviction rate for the crimes was unimpressive with only one man, Sion Aubrey Roberts, convicted in 1993 of posting letter bombs. Most cases linked to the group remain unsolved.[12]

With the arrival of devolution and the establishment of the National Assembly for Wales, the use of violent direct action in the Welsh political arena appears to be a thing of the past on domestic policy. With respect to political issues elsewhere, however, this has not stopped several individuals with their homes in Wales from involvement in violent activities in support of radical Islam elsewhere in the world.

Professional lobbying, or public affairs, organisations

Public affairs and lobbying (see Box 8.6) in Wales has developed alongside devolution, and both activities have grown with the evolution and enhancement of the powers of both the National Assembly and Welsh government. This sector has its own representative organisation called Public Affairs Cymru (PAC) (see Box 8.7).

Box 8.6 Is public affairs just about lobbying?

Public affairs is a branch of the public relations industry concerned with 'an organisation's relationship with stakeholders'. Lobbying politicians and civil servants is really just a small aspect of what public affairs companies do. Public affairs practitioners engage stakeholders, who might be politicians, civil servants, customers and local communities, clients, shareholders, trade associations, think tanks, business groups, charities, unions and the media, in order to explain organisational policies and views on public policy issues, assisting policy-makers and legislators in amending or laying down better policy and legislation. So public affairs is not just about lobbying, but when it is required public affairs firms lobby on issues that could impact upon a client's ability to operate successfully.[13]

By 2017 there were four specialist public affairs organisations operating in Cardiff Bay and a number of smaller ones. Of the four larger public affairs organisations, Grayling, a London-based marketing, public relations and public affairs consultancy, is the only one that is part of a wider UK structure. 'The Bay', founded in 2004 by Mark Hinge, is the oldest Cardiff-based company specialising in public affairs. Positif Politics, established in 2006 by Daran Hill, is probably the most prominent provider of communications advice, knowledge, intelligence and support to the business, voluntary and public sectors. Lastly, Deryn, very much the new kid on the block, was established in 2011 by Cathy Owens, previously a Special Adviser at the Welsh government, and Nerys Evans, a former Plaid Cymru AM (2007–11).

Box 8.7 What is Public Affairs Cymru (PAC)?

PAC is the representative body for the public affairs industry. It is a membership organisation, established in October 2006, for public affairs professionals in Wales and currently has a membership of around 200 individuals. It aims to raise awareness of the public affairs industry in Wales and to promote good practice among professionals via the code of conduct to promote good practice among public affairs professionals via their code of conduct.

The public affairs community in Wales is small and people tend to know one another, but PAC also provides networking opportunities, such as the PAC Gala Dinner which is one of the key events in the Cardiff Bay Village (see Box 8.11). Matthew Francis. who as a public affairs professional for Cardiff University, goes to the Gala Dinner notes that 'there will be people there I have never met before. It always reminds me that the sector is a lot wider than it initially appears to be.'[14]

Why are there so few public affairs firms but lots of 'liaison' or 'policy' officers?

As Wales has a small political arena there fewer specialist public affairs consultancies than there are both Scotland and England. However, in addition to those specialist firms mentioned above, there is usually an 'in-house' liaison or policy person within organisations, although this be just a small element of their broader work remit as few organisations can justify having a full-time individual to work on public affairs. Furthermore, it is not uncommon to find independent consultants, working in discrete policy areas, who may have just one or two major clients. If a politician loses his or her seat they will often become a consultant. This is commonplace in Westminster, whereas in Wales it is still unusual. It is also against the code of ethics of PAC (see Box 8.10) to have full access to the Assembly.[15]

Box 8.8 What do National Assembly/Welsh government liaison officers do?

The role of liaison officers is to 'establish and maintain good communications' between their organisation and the two branches of devolved government in Wales: the National Assembly and the Welsh government.

They need to demonstrate that their organisations' activities are of value and in line with government priorities in Wales. If their organisation receives government funding, it is also the responsibility of the officer to demonstrate 'value for money services, and that their delivery is beneficial to stakeholders'.

In addition, officers will want to show that their organisation has access to knowledge, expertise and resources that can assist government in 'carrying out its strategic and legislative responsibilities'.

Depending on their organisation they may also have the role of liaising with the political parties and attending party conferences, the management of relations with the media, and keeping the organisation's own staff up to speed by making them aware of the activities of the organisation and important sectorial changes taking place.[16]

Some organisations, such as the Association of British Insurers, may have a single person responsible for liaison with all devolved bodies in the United Kingdom.

Think tanks in Wales

Think tanks are usually independent organisations that specialise in the research and development of public policy. In Wales a number of think tanks have seen the light of day. Some, such as the Institute of Welsh Affairs (IWA), have become important and influential contributors to policy debates, while others, such as 'Ideas Wales', have been less apparent. The three best known are the IWA, the oldest and most prominent Welsh think tank; the Bevan Foundation, a valley's based social democratic think tank; and the newest, Gorwel, the Welsh Foundation for Innovation in Public Affairs, established in 2012. All three have active websites that illustrate the extent and nature of their activities and the range of reports/studies they have undertaken.

Box 8.9 In what ways has the Institute of Welsh Affairs been influential?

The IWA has been influential in Wales in a wide range of areas, including:

- building the intellectual case for the devolution of powers to Wales and the creation of the National Assembly and, since its establishment, has continued monitored its development and performance;
- promoting the case for EU Objective 1 status for a large part of Wales, helping to secure hundreds of millions of pounds of additional investment from the EU;
- campaigned successfully for the introduction of a Welsh Baccalaureate for 16–19 year olds and to raise standards and improve educational performance across all age groups;
- made the case for the adoption of the city region concept, now a key part of Welsh government policy;
- promoted the idea of a 'South Wales Metro', an integrated transport system encompassing southeastern Wales. This is now Welsh government policy and is moving forward thorough the electrification of the south Wales rail network.[17]

Compared with London and Scotland there are currently very few think tanks in Wales and critics claim that that this has resulted in a lack of innovative ideas generally. Further to this, some influential ideas originated by think tanks and put into practice by the Welsh government were not properly reviewed afterwards; the Welsh Baccalaureate might be considered an example of this. This situation is not just a consequence of the small political world in Wales, but also due to a lack of financial support from wealthy donors, business, universities and central government. This position appeared to be exacerbated further in 2014 when the Welsh government established its own think tank, the Public Policy Institute for Wales (see Box 8.10), which has further diverted public funding away from the other Welsh think tanks.

In addition, both Cardiff and Aberystwyth universities have specialist research institutes that operate much like think tanks. The Institute of Welsh Politics (IWP) was established within the Department of International Politics at Aberystwyth in 1997, and is internationally recognised as an important research centre on political regionalism and substate nationalism. Cardiff University's Wales Governance Centre is a research unit based on a partnership between the Department of Politics and International Relations and Cardiff Law School. Under the leadership of Professor Richard Wyn Jones, its director since 2009, the Centre has conducted influential research, held high-profile events and promoted various projects in political, constitutional and policy themes in Wales.

Box 8.10 The Public Policy Institute for Wales (PPIW)

The PPIW consists of a team of academics and researchers based at Cardiff University whose purpose is to give Welsh government ministers advice on how to improve Wales' public services. The Institute also allows Welsh government ministers access to independent experts from Wales, the United Kingdom and beyond in their quest to get more from public money. This was launched in January 2014 at a cost of up to £450,000 over three years.

The PPIW offers a wide range of experience and expertise to challenge, inform and provide fresh thinking so that we as a government can better identify priorities, create robust policy and, most importantly, deliver for the people of Wales.[18]

Ministers are able to request the PPIW to consider and provide advice on a wide range of cross-departmental issues. However, the PPIW has been criticised because its advice is only available to Welsh government ministers and civil servants, and it is not open to assist opposition parties in the National Assembly for Wales. In addition, it would seem most of PPIW's funding goes to projects in English, and not Welsh, universities. Critics[19] have also suggested that the PPIW undermines the role of existing think tanks in Wales by diverting funding away from them and also failing to build up research capacity at Welsh universities. In its 2016 report, the PPIW noted that twelve of its nineteen centres of expertise were in either England or Scotland.

Box 8.11 What is the 'Cardiff Bay Village'?

In 2001, the academic Russell Deacon referred to the name given to the policy community that surrounded the former Welsh Office government department as the 'Cathays Parc Village' after its location in the government administrative centre of Cardiff.[20] Those within this community take part, either formally or informally, in governance of Wales, its legislative and policy processes. They often are consulted due to their specific expertise that is not readily available elsewhere. When the Welsh Assembly arrived in 1999 this name was also adapted to cover the new policy community that surrounds the Welsh Assembly in Cardiff Bay. The 'Cardiff Bay Village' consists of a number of identifying factors:

- 'an informal network of individuals involved in public life, policy, academia and communications' whose work focuses in and around the institutions of government in Wales;
- a group of key decision-makers, who are not just elected politicians, political party officials and their staff, civil servants, academics, special advisers, lobbyists, pressure groups and advocates, but also people involved in the press and in the broadcast media;
- this network expresses itself publicly through several Cardiff-based events in the calendar, such as the Welsh Politician of the Year Award, or the Public Affairs Cymru Gala Dinner or civic events at the Welsh Assembly or other bodies based in Cardiff Bay;
- there is a tendency for Welsh government or Welsh Assembly commissions/task groups and public appointments to be drawn from members of this 'Village'.

Critics claim therefore that this world is very small, insular and lacking in new ideas. They state that it gives uneven access to the politicians and that they gain influence over politicians that is neither open nor transparent. Others claim that the 'Village' does not have a monopoly of influence, however, and note that over time this will undoubtedly diminish as the Welsh political scene develops and grows, with many graduates coming into careers in politics and public affairs in Cardiff expanding the pool of expertise available to government

Changes brought by devolution to the civil society of Wales

The premise of this chapter is that devolution has led most UK-based organisations to establish a separate devolved structure in Wales to deal with the new institutions of government, and that this process has been accelerated since the granting of legislative powers to Wales by the Government of Wales Act 2006. We will now examine a small unpublished survey of pressure groups in Wales (2009)[21] to determine whether Professor Paul Chaney was accurate when he stated that 'devolution has led some, or most organisations to rethink, restructure and develop more devolved structures in Wales', and that 'the arrival of the National Assembly for Wales presented an opportunity for a resurgence of civil society in Wales'.[22]

The evolution of pressure groups in Wales under devolution: Southall study

During summer 2009, Rob Southall undertook a small semi-structured survey of pressure groups. The premise of the study was that devolution had acted as a stimulus to the growth of group activity in Wales and that this had resulted in the emergence of a distinctly Welsh civil society. A total of twenty-four groups were surveyed, with all falling into the sectional/cause typology. Just five of the groups were classified as 'a Welsh organisation', that is, those organisations that only exist in Wales and are not a regional representation of a larger body. Only one organisation described itself as a 'UK body with no Welsh organisation', that is, a group with no regional structure or Wales representative. Based upon these figures, it may be reasonable to assume that UK organisations were aware of variations of policy between Wales and England, but that these differences were not considered sufficient to treat Wales separately from the regions of England. This, and the subsequent sections, in this chapter draw on the findings of this Southall study.

Most of the organisations had already established a distinct presence in Wales prior to the arrival of devolution in 1999. Stonewall, Barnardo's and the National Union of Farmers (NFU) all responded positively to the establishment of the new National Assembly by creating a distinct national presence in Wales. The largest bodies in terms of persons employed were those organisations involved in providing services for the public, for children, the elderly and the homeless, or in providing advice and training at a local level, such as Groundwork or WCVA. The largest cause group active in Wales is RSPB Cymru with over 50,000 members. The largest sectional groups are public sector trade unions, with Unison, which represents 96,000 members, being the largest in terms of membership. Wales TUC, which represents Unison, in addition to around fifty affiliated trade unions, speaks for approximately half a million people in Wales, making it both influential and politically important, all the more so because of its close historical links to the Labour Party, both in Wales and the wider United Kingdom.

What are the effects of devolution on the work of the group or organisation?

The Southall study asked groups what they saw as the main effects of devolution for their work and what they saw as being the main positive and negative aspects of this. Summarised below is a small sample of the pros and cons highlighted by the survey.

The positive effects for organisations in the post-devolution period?

The positive effects of devolution for organisations include:

1. increased number of access points to policy-makers and improved accessibility to decision-makers, allowing for greater influence and also the Welsh government's better procedures for formally feeding into and responding to policies;
2. the ability to fashion policy and practice that more accurately reflects the needs of Wales and its communities. Welsh solutions to Welsh problems;
3. devolved government in Wales has an open approach to the third sector and to equalities work in particular; and
4. opportunities to explore more radical policy options with individual UK governments that would be difficult to take forward on a UK-wide basis. The Welsh government, although constrained in its powers, is willing to consider different approaches and to push boundaries.

The negative effects of devolution for organisations

The negative effects of devolution for organisations include:

1. the higher workload and increased pressures on staff without significant help from head office research facilities. This may have led to some lost opportunities through a lack of funding to increase the number of staff in Wales. The escalation in lobbying work stretches finite resources, particularly for small organisations;
2. the amount of government consultation can be overwhelming for small organisations;

3. generally too much policy with too little an emphasis on effective delivery and implementation; and
4. lack of capacity to deliver within the Welsh government – the lack of resources such as specialist staff and finance within certain government directorates.

In summary, most organisations said that there had been both advantages and disadvantages to their organisation, but that the benefits generally outweighed the negative effects. Five organisations said they felt that there had been no negative consequences at all on their work and only one said that the negatives outweighed the positives.

The main resources and methods employed by pressure groups in Wales to achieve their aims

It is important to appreciate that individual pressure groups differ enormously in the range of resources available to them. Their success in getting their message across is often determined by how effectively they can draw on their resources at any particular time. Those who are not the branch of a UK- or London-based body also suffer more greatly from a lack of resources. The particular situation they are trying to affect will often determine which resources are required, and the skill of the lobbyist is often to determine the most appropriate use of resources to effect change, the most effective method for proposing change and the point at which these resources and methods need to be deployed.

The most important pressure group resources are considered to be:

- *Specialist knowledge*: some groups such as the BMA Wales, which represents doctors, and Community Housing Cymru, which represents housing associations, have a high degree of specialist knowledge that government needs to draw upon for successful policy formulation and implementation.
- *Legal resource*: the ability to challenge Welsh government policy or laws through judicial challenge (judicial review) or through shaping or drafting new Welsh laws amending old ones. In 2015, for instance, Friends of the Earth sought an unsuccessful judicial review of the Welsh government's plans for an M4 relief road. In contrast, the pro-cycling body, Sutrans, was more successful in shaping the Welsh

Assembly legislation, the Active Travel (Wales) Act 2013, to fulfil its own policy agenda.

- *High Status*: groups that attract higher prestige generally command greater attention from government, for example, BDA Wales, which represents most dentists practising in Wales.
- *Membership*: the number of members often does not usually influence success, but where the organisation represents a significant proportion of professional or economic groups, for example, FUW and NFU Cymru represent most farmers in Wales, while NUT Wales and NASUWT Wales represent most primary and secondary school teachers.
- *Staffing*: groups that can afford to employ more staff, particularly in specialist areas, might be considered to be more successful than those who cannot.
- *An ability to build formal coalitions with other groups*: an ability to work with like-minded groups who share a common interest is vital within the more open and inclusive politics of devolution. Many groups now, wholly or partially, manage their relations with government via umbrella organisations, such as Homes for All Cymru, for housing-related matters, or Wales Environment Link (WEL), for environmental issues. Members of these coalitions may well find themselves more involved in the pre-consultation working-party stage of the legislative process.
- *Lobbying (see Box 8.2) and participating in consultations*: these were ranked the most important methods utilised by groups, while the complementary activity of 'advising on policy' was placed second. Attending stakeholder meetings where policy is discussed with partner organisations, ministers and civil servants, was seen as a key aspect of the lobbying process. One organisation summarised it neatly: 'We tend to use Government relationships and channels in the first instance over campaigning.'

Who are the key targets of lobbying?

After the implementation of the Government of Wales Act 2006 (GOWA), Welsh ministers with increased powers have become the prime targets for lobbying. They are now seen as significantly more important than either AMs or civil servants. One group noted that if the question had been asked two or more years ago, then AMs would almost certainly rank at the top. They explained that with the 2006 GOWA shifting of power away from the legislature and towards the executive, their organisation had to change its approach and now directs more of its efforts towards ministers and their civil servants rather than towards AMs.

Access points when seeking to influence government policy in Wales

It is clear from the Southall study findings that the earliest stage of policy formation, that is, the pre-consultation stage, is the most important access point for groups seeking to influence government policy. Groups revealed that they seek to influence party policy, including inputting into manifesto preparation, in addition to the obvious focus on influencing civil servants and policy-makers. They also admitted that most campaigns are not about changing legislation, rather, they are about changing policy or changing funding levels. One group even explained that there is even a stage before pre-consultation and that they had been represented at several Assembly-level groups where policy and policy direction were discussed, allowing them to influence how policies and legislation are formed and developed. As a part of this they were asked for suggestions about how to deal with specific issues and to provide ideas for solutions to particular problems. Whether or not it is a feature of a 'new corporatism' remains to be seen and would require a much larger survey of groups to be untaken.

Box 8.12 Case study: lobbying impact on the Welsh policy process

Groups engaged in education saw their influence most clearly with the abolition of SATs and league tables for schools in Wales in 2004, but also over the development of the Foundation Phase curriculum, safer transport to schools, and greater clarity and transparency in funding arrangements for schools.

Environmental groups achieved success in keeping Wales free from GM crops, gaining annual cuts in greenhouse gas emissions, strong support for renewable energy, the carrier bag charge and the 70 per cent recycling target.

Groups representing the elderly lobbied successfully over a range of important sectorial issues, including the development of the Strategy for Older People, the establishment of the Older People's Commissioner for

Wales, health and social care policies, and numerous government strategies including those on anti-bullying, community cohesion, anti-suicide and mental health.

A leading children's charity seconded a manager to undertake a scoping exercise and to re-write the Welsh government's school-based counselling strategy. They also influenced the Welsh government to include children and young people in their definition of domestic abuse and also helped to write a variety of task group reports and guidance.

A more recent example of successful lobbying is the influence of sustainable transport group Sustrans on the Active Travel Wales Act.

The housing sector was seen to be a key area of group influence in Wales. On the issue of homelessness Shelter Cymru said it was 'instrumental in calling for the first National Homelessness Strategy' and that 'this had now led to the Welsh Government's ten year homelessness plan'. Several housing groups also referred to 'Better Homes for People in Wales', which was Wales' first national housing strategy, greater regulation of the housing sector, and the Essex review of Affordable Housing (see Box 8.13) as key policies that had been influenced.

What exactly is meant by the term 'devolution dividend' and how has this affected the work of groups in Wales?

This buzz phrase from 1999 generally referred to the economic benefits for Wales associated with devolution. Has this been the case?

The picture is mixed: Ministers have not shied away from big decisions – gone is the Welsh Development Agency, with economic development now handled in-house by the Welsh government but those targets to close the GDP gap with England, made in the ambitious early days of devolution, have been abandoned. There are benefits though. Bill Davies of the think-tank IPPR North said: 'On a per head basis, the Welsh population gets a lot more spent on economic development by the Welsh government than the UK government does in the North East.' However, Professor Karel Williams, of Manchester Business School, said devolution has been 'something of a non-event' in economic terms with Welsh ministers relying on growth from a trickle-down from a booming southeast of England. He believes rather than the issue of powers, Wales has been lacking in imaginative policy ideas and needs to experiment. 'Some risk is justified because the mainstream orthodoxy of the last 30 years isn't working, it's time for a bit of boldness and imagination,' he said.[23]

The question of the 'devolution dividend' challenged the survey respondents to identify what they consider to be the cherry-on-the cake. Surprisingly, these responses were varied and diverse, and might be considered as a pot of small cherries rather than a single large one. For them the dividend means:

1. *Joint working on public services*: an ability to develop partnership with the Welsh government beyond what could have been achieved with the Welsh Office no matter how much executive autonomy was delegated to it.
2. *Openness of government*: the Welsh government is more open in allowing closer access to decision-making and greater influence on policy-makers – quicker, easier and more regular access to ministers, civil servants and AMs.
3. *A chance to trial innovative policies*: getting policies that move ahead of the rest of the United Kingdom, thinking in a more open way and a willingness to do things differently. The Welsh government, although constrained in its powers, is willing to consider different approaches and to push boundaries.
4. *A centre left government* with strong commitments to progressive politics: had devolution delivered a right-wing government, groups would not have been able to achieve many of the things they have, 'so the dividend can be overstated in terms of constitutional change if you don't take politics into account'.[24]

Box 8.13 Case study: the Essex Review of Affordable Housing

In 2007, on behalf of the One Wales Coalition, the Welsh Deputy Minister for Housing, Jocelyn Davies AM, commissioned former Welsh minister, Sue Essex, to review affordable housing delivery in Wales and to make suggestions for improvement. This Review took place between September 2007 and June 2008. Rather than simply focusing on how the Welsh government could achieve its targets on delivering affordable housing, the Review recommended a raft of changes causing a seismic shift by completely overhauling the regulatory regime for the housing sector in Wales. The Review's forty-three recommendations included:

- overhauling regulations and inspections and implementing a relaxed regulatory regime;
- ensuring the social housing grant is used more effectively in areas of highest need;
- more tenant involvement on boards via the establishment of community mutual housing associations;
- increasing sources of affordable housing funding;
- delivering more financial freedom for housing associations;
- reviewing housing association rents; and
- encouraging all councils to maximise affordable housing opportunities.

Rather than following up the Review with the usual consultations, the recommendations were taken forward by four work streams made up of housing sector stakeholders and civil servants looking at how best they could be implemented.[25]

The review and its implementation provides an example of successful lobbying by one pressure group: Community Housing Cymru. As the former Deputy Minister for Housing said 'CHC requested it, lobbied for it and when it was not in the One Wales agreement they had a meeting with me and they put forward that that was the number one thing and I was persuaded of it, despite the fact that it was not in One Wales because it sat with everything else we wanted to do in housing in terms of having it as a priority and being able to deliver on the affordable housing targets that we'd set. We invited Sue Essex to carry out the review at their request.'[26]

The work streams were made up of 'Welsh government officials plus stakeholders. It would have been everybody in housing: local authorities, housing associations, representative organisations from the sector plus mortgage lenders, the Principality, The Council of Mortgage Lenders, Association of Housebuilders, landlord's organizations.'[27] However, once again the role of CHC was the instrumental to success, as Jocelyn says 'without Community Housing Cymru not just asking for it, but supporting me to get it, I could have easily given up. They had to steer it, getting everybody on board to cooperate because not all the associations were happy.'[28] Then, of course, the recession hit and it looked like the Welsh government would not hit its targets of 6,500 extra affordable homes in the five years of the One Wales Coalition government. However, by this time CHC had ensured that the housing sector were fully on board, as Jocelyn expands 'so when the recession hit and it didn't look like we were going to meet our affordable housing targets because by now having the sector saying if you do this for us we're going to help you meet your targets and we did'.[29]

Not only that, but as Jocelyn admits 'what I decided to do then was have a special adviser, a specialist adviser, not a normal political adviser but a housing specialist and this was Chris O'Meara. She was not the Chair of Community Housing Cymru by this time she was the chief executive of Cadwyn Housing Association in Cardiff. She became my specialist adviser so she was seconded two days a week and her job was to make sure it was all happening.'[30]

Has there been a 'devolution dividend'?

The 'devolution dividend' has not been significant in economic terms, but there has certainly been a 'democratic dividend' associated with devolution and the Essex Review (Box 8.13) perhaps best illustrates this. The establishment of the National Assembly in 1999, and the increased ability of Welsh government since then to develop its own distinctive policies has been a major stimulus for the growth of its own discrete civil society in Wales. What remains to be seen is whether the process of building civil society capacity is able to keep pace with the demands placed on it by institutions of government.

Implications of the survey findings for civil society in Wales

It may be true to say that the relative strengths and weaknesses of civil society in Wales, that is, small size, relative intimacy and limited capacity, are common features of small country governance. However, in essence, this evaluation reflects different sides of the same argument. One of the key advantages of a smaller theatre of operations is that it is a very small policy community within areas such as housing or healthcare. In many cases there are just a handful of individuals working within the relevant organisations, sometimes just a single individual, and, as a consequence, the policy community is very familiar to each other. Furthermore, the smaller size of the policy community in Wales means that it is easy to gather all the key stakeholders in a room together; whether that is about groups coming together for a consultation or as an advocacy coalition to try to proactively sway the direction of government in a certain direction.

This is a very advantageous side of the system because it makes politics work quite easily and it speeds things up.

However, the downside of the small size and limited capacity, is that the small cohort of organisations who can and do work together are not necessarily representative of stakeholders at large.

It may be the case that decisions taken by government are just reflecting those organisations who are switched on enough or, more importantly, have the resources, to work regularly with government in Wales. This is a major weakness as there are many organisations who work on a UK-basis whose voice is missing because they do not have the resources to put in in order to become one of the Welsh government's insider groups. This situation is a particular problem for charitable organisations who rely on donations and cannot fund full-time staff. Further to this, if Wales does develop a culture of 'go-to' organisations is it excluding people by default because others are automatically seen as the voice of the sector?

There is a great danger that relationships can become institutionalised as once relationships between government and groups become established they demonstrate increasing returns and it becomes very difficult to break out of that mould sometimes. That does not mean there is a lack of due diligence on the part of anyone, but just a consequence of small size and limited capacity not just on the part of civil society but also the limited capacity of the Welsh government's Civil Service which is reliant on groups to write and implement specific policy. For example, in the housing sector, these groups are often the same ones who are reliant on Welsh government funding

All of this makes it very difficult for 'new' organisations who do want to develop their presence in Wales to break into the bubble, as it is hard for them to differentiate themselves from other similar, but better established, organisations. If this is this case, then those with this problem can turn to public affairs consultancies who are very familiar with the political landscape and are well placed to offer advice on the best way to get introductions to policy or decision-makers.[31]

Box 8.14 Regulation of lobbying in Wales

Currently, there are no formal rules regarding lobbying and lobbyists in their relationship with either the Welsh government or the National Assembly. Instead, lobbyists in Wales sign up to a voluntary code of conduct adopted in October 2010 by Public Affairs Cymru. However, in November 2016 Plaid Cymru AMs called for the establishment of an official register for lobbyists in Wales along similar lines to those created in Scotland and at a UK level. However, the outgoing Standards Commissioner, Gerard Elias, speaking to AMs on the Standards Committee, said he had not received any complaints about lobbying in Wales. Mr Elias, who has since been replaced by Sir Roderick Evans, also told the committee that setting up a statutory register of lobbyists would 'undoubtedly' have 'significant resource implications'. Standards Committee members recently agreed to hold a written consultation on the issue, but it seems changes are unlikely for the time being as lobbyists in Wales do not have access to Welsh ministers, and Wales has not suffered the scandals involving lobbyists that have been seen in Westminster.[32]

In a twist to this issue, Daran Hill of Public Affairs Cymru, speaking in February 2017 to the Assembly Standards Committee's inquiry on lobbying, said some of its members had faced 'pressure' from the government and that 'sometimes lobbyists are lobbied too, be it by officials, special advisers or politicians'. Further to this, PAC written evidence to the same inquiry added that in recent years examples had occurred where lobbyists and campaigners have been asked to reconsider standpoints or not to say certain things with which the Welsh government is not in agreement.

Responding to these comments, the Welsh government said that it always acts properly with organisations and groups to ensure that the development of policy and legislation is of the highest quality.[33]

Local government in Wales

Welsh local government is broadly the same in its operation as in England with a few notable exceptions. There are no elected mayors or city regions in Wales, although both may be possible in the future. Wales has community councils and not parish ones, and all Welsh county, county borough or city councils are unitary authorities. There are currently twenty-two unitary authorities with 1,264 elected councillors, and 735 community and town councils with around 8,000 community councillors. In addition, there is one remnant of earlier times at Laugharne in Carmarthenshire where, in addition to its town council and representation on the county council, the town retains its medieval corporation with a portreeve, aldermen, a grand jury of twenty men and the body of 460 burgesses.

Box 8.15 The structure of local government from 1974 onwards

County and districts, 1974–96: the Local Government Act 1972 abolished the administrative counties, county boroughs, boroughs and urban and rural districts which had been in existence since the 1890s and replaced them with eight counties which would form the upper tier of a new two-tier system of counties and districts, composing the lower tier of the new arrangement. These were: Clwyd: Alyn and Deeside, Colwyn, Delyn, Glyndwr, Rhuddlan, Wrexham Maelor; Dyfed: Carmarthen, Ceredigion, Dinefwr, Llanelli, Preseli Pembrokeshire, South Pembrokeshire; Gwent: Blaenau Gwent, Islwyn, Monmouth, Newport, Torfaen; Gwynedd: Aberconwy, Arfon, Dwyfor, Meirionnydd, Anglesey; Mid Glamorgan: ynon Valley, Ogwr, Merthyr Tydfil, Rhondda, Rhymney Valley, Taff-Ely; Powys: Brecknock, Montgomery, Radnor; South Glamorgan: Cardiff, Vale of Glamorgan; West Glamorgan: Lliw Valley, Neath, Port Talbot, Swansea.[34]

Unitary authorities, from 1996: Blaenau Gwent; Bridgend (Pen-y-bont ar Ogwr); Caerphilly (Caerffili); Cardiff (Caerdydd); Carmarthenshire (Sir Gaerfyrddin); Ceredigion; Conwy; Denbighshire (Sir Ddinbych); Flintshire (Sir y Fflint); Gwynedd, Isle of Anglesey (Ynys Môn); Merthyr Tydfil (Merthyr Tudful); Monmouthshire (Sir Fynwy); Neath Port Talbot (Castell-nedd Port Talbot); Newport (Casnewydd); Pembrokeshire (Sir Benfro); Powys; Rhondda Cynon Taf (RCT); Swansea (Abertawe); Torfaen; Vale of Glamorgan (Bro Morgannwg); and Wrexham (Wrecsam).

City regions, 2017–: in 2015, the Welsh government also announced plans to establish two city regions: Swansea Bay City Region and the Cardiff City Region/Cardiff Capital Region. These both combine the local authorities within their 'metropolitan area'. They are currently run by an appointed chair who heads a regional board representing the local authorities, academia, business, trade unions and the Welsh government. The central role of these city regions is to maximise economic develop, communications, energy supply, and health and wellbeing within them. They are funded by the UK Treasury and Welsh government through the City Deal.

Elected mayors, ??: a number of unitary authorities and city regions in England have established elected mayors. The most famous is London, where the elected mayors Ken Livingstone and Boris Johnson became nation and international figures. Others include Bristol, which sits just over the Bristol Channel from Newport and Cardiff. An elected mayor has considerable powers available to them to govern their constituency and among to other things stimulate economic growth. This has lead to people in Wales to call for elected mayors in areas such as Cardiff and Newport and for the new city regions in order to repeat the economic success demonstrated elsewhere. Such a move requires a referendum, which has not so far seen significant grassroots support to enable it to be successful. In May 2004, voters in Ceredgion voted 3:1 against having an elected mayor. No other unitary authority has held a referendum since.

Unitary authorities

On 1 April 1996 the eight counties and thirty-seven districts (see Box 8.15) were abolished and replaced by twenty-two unitary authorities or principal areas. These unitary authorities were established by the Local Government (Wales) Act 1994 on 1 April 1996. Eleven are named as counties – this includes the Cities and Counties of Cardiff and Swansea – and ten are styled as county boroughs. Newport in Gwent which was granted city status in 2002, was a county borough but is now referred to as the 'City of Newport'. Collectively, these are perhaps best all thought of as unitary authorities and are the most important tier of local government in Wales. While there was some satisfaction in rural Wales with the return of such ancient counties as Monmouthshire, Pembrokeshire and Ceredigion, there was a widespread belief that many of these new authorities were too small to efficiently provide strategic services for their areas.

In addition to unitary authorities there are also over 735 community and town councils throughout Wales. Some represent populations of fewer than 200 people, others populations of over 45,000 people. Community and town councils can deliver many services, depending on the size of the community they represent and their budget.[35]

Box 8.16 Welsh Local Government Association (WLGA)

The Welsh Local Government Association was established in 1996 primarily as a policy development and representative body. It has since developed into an organisation that represents the interests of the twenty-two local authorities in Wales, and the three fire and rescue authorities and three national park authorities are associate members.

The WGLA also leads on improvement and development, procurement, employment issues, promotes local democracy in Wales, and hosts a range of partner bodies supporting local government. It regularly holds consultations with and responds on consultations held by the Welsh government. The WLGA's leader in 2017 was Councillor Bob Wellington, the leader of Torfaen County Borough Council, and its chief executive is Steve Roberts CBE. The WLGA remains a constituent part of the LGA in the United Kingdom, ensuring that the interests of Welsh local government are represented to the UK government.[36] We should also note that One Voice Wales is the equivalent body that represents town and community councils in Wales.

Party representation in Welsh unitary authorities

The Labour Party has dominated local government in Wales for the past 100 years. This may be seen largely as the legacy of the heavy industries such as coal mining and steel working that once dominated the Welsh economy. The majority of councils have been controlled by the Labour Party for long periods of time and in some case this has resulted in dominant control, for example, Torfaen has been controlled by Labour since its inception. Outside the coastal areas there is little multi-party competition. Most councils are two-party systems, for example, Caerphilly and Rhondda Cynon Taff alternate between Labour and Plaid, and many councils alternate between Labour and independent control. Women have tended to be rare as both leaders and chief executives, although things are beginning to change with both Newport and, briefly, Cardiff having female leaders in recent years.

In 2017, the largest political party in Wales in terms of representation on unitary authorities is Labour with 472, followed by Plaid Cymru with 202, the Conservative Party with 184, and the Lib-Dems with 62. There are also 322 independent councillors, and Gwynedd is unique in Wales in having its own political party, Llais Gwynedd, or Voice of Gwynedd, which in 2017 has six of the authority's seventy-four councillors. As of the 2017 election, Plaid Cymru is now the majority party with forty-one councillors and forms the executive. The independents, as the second largest group with twenty-six councillors, lead the official opposition.[37]

In terms of overall control of councils, the Labour Party is clearly not having it all its own way, with Labour controlling just ten of Wales' twenty-two unitary authorities. Of the remainder, ten are controlled by groupings of independents and another ten currently have no overall control (NOC).

In addition to encouraging local democracy and participation in the decision-making process, local councils in Wales play a vital and essential role which largely corresponds with those of the combined functions of district and county councils in England, ensuring the provision of a wide range of public services in their area. Unitary authorities are responsible for primary and secondary education, main and local roads, transport, planning, social services, environmental health, refuse collection and disposal, trading standards, social housing, libraries and leisure. Most local authorities are also involved promoting the arts and sport.

Town and community councils

In 1922, the Church of England was disestablished in Wales, meaning the link between the state and church was cut. This had been a long-standing desire of the mainly nonconformist (chapel-going) Welsh Christians. The long-term effect of this was that parish councils were renamed community councils, which was restated by section 27 of the Local Government Act 1972. Today there are over 730 town and community councils in Wales with over 8,000 councillors sitting on them. They do not cover all areas of Wales, however, but new ones can be established if there is sufficient local demand. They go by the name of either community or town council. Town councils have a mayor and community councils a chair as the principal figure.

These councils are Wales' smallest layers of democratic governance, although most elections outside the urban areas for these councils go uncontested. They can range in size from those covering a few hundred people to Barry Town Council in the Vale of Glamorgan that covers a population of around 50,000 and has an income of £1.1 million (2016/17). Community councils in Wales typically provide a more limited range of functions, such as public information signs and notice boards, public seating and bus shelters, war memorials, community centres and indoor recreation facilities.[38] The principal administrator in each council is known as the clerk.

Where central and local government conflict

Because the majority of councils in Wales tend to be run by the Labour Party and the Welsh government has also been led by the Labour Party since devolution overt signs of conflict tend to be limited. This does not mean that conflict does not occur, however. The two main points of conflict between central and local government in Wales are funding and the number of authorities, and at present both are major bones of contention with central government reducing the finance available to local authorities while at the same time seeking to reduce the number of unitary authorities. Both of these issues will now be considered.

Funding local government

The twenty-two unitary authorities in Wales are financed in two ways: via funding for revenue expenditure and funding for capital expenditure. The local authorities receive around 80 per cent of their funding in the form of a revenue grant from the Welsh government known as the Revenue Support Grant (RSG). The RSG is the main component of the local government revenue settlement, which comprises RSG and non-domestic rate income, which together are known as Aggregate External Finance. This is distributed on the basis of a needs-based formula. Other local authority funding is raised locally in the form of council tax, which is set by each authority as part of its annual budget-setting process. In addition, local authorities are able to apply for additional funding through Welsh government grant programmes. This is short-term funding and its effect is temporary, that is, the benefit is received immediately within the accounting year and it is a regular requirement.

Is local government funding in Wales in crisis?

Following the global financial crisis and the subsequent UK government policy of austerity, local government in Wales has found itself stretched to the limits with many councils forced to abandon, outsource or privatise local services. In response to this challenge a number of innovative approaches to service provision have been developed. One of these approaches has been asset transfer, where some specific local service has been outsourced via transfer to third sector organisations. For example:

- Torfaen County Borough Council transferred its housing stock to Bron Afon Community Housing, a new community-based mutual housing association;
- Blaenau Gwent County Borough Council transferred ownership of its leisure, learning and cultural services, that is, libraries, heritage and community education services, country parks, sports centres and sports development team, to Aneurin Leisure, a registered charity and not-for-profit company.

The size of spending cuts has varied considerably across local authorities, which reflect differences in the size of cuts to grants. The percentage cuts to spending on services by local authorities in East Wales (8.4 per cent per person) exceed those in West Wales and the Valleys (7.8 per cent), with the biggest reduction taking place in Newport (16.5 per cent) and the smallest in Carmarthenshire (2.9 per cent). The size of these spending cuts also differs significantly between services. Spending on regulation and safety services received the largest cuts between 2009/10 and 2012/13 (24.6 per cent per person), followed by planning and development (22.9 per cent) and housing (20.6 per cent). Significantly, spending on social services in Wales has been relatively protected (falling by 3.8 per cent), which may reflect government targets to protect spending in this area. Spending on environmental and refuse services and education have also been relatively protected, falling by 4.8 per cent and 7.3 per cent per person, respectively.[39]

So is local authority spending in crisis? It obviously depends upon the particular service as funding to certain services, such as social services, is safeguarded more than others such as environmental health, housing and libraries, and this appears to be a direct result of Welsh government priorities at any one time. The biggest threat to local government capital funding is almost certainly going to be the United Kingdom's exit from the EU, and at the time of writing it is uncertain what the full implications of this will be.

Reducing the number of unitary authorities in Wales

The Welsh government has concluded that there have been a number of major problems with the twenty-two authority structure since it was created by the UK government in 1996. The financial situation following the global financial crisis of 2007/8 and the subsequent period of UK government enforced austerity only served to exacerbate the problems. Since then there have been a number of attempts at altering local government structures in Wales (Box 8.17).

Box 8.17 The case for local government reform in Wales

Leighton Andrews, as the Welsh government's Public Services Minister (2014–16), was a strong advocate of the reform of Welsh local government, including the merger of Welsh councils. Rhys Iorwerth in his 2011 study of Welsh local government highlighted a number of significant arguments for reform, later taken up by Andrews. The foremost were:

- There are too many authorities delivering and duplicating the same services and many are too small to achieve any significant efficiencies.
- Collaboration, as advocated by past Welsh ministers, is not a solution. It needs initial funding and time, and is merely a means of avoiding the fact that reorganisation is required. The collapse of the South East Wales Shared Service project in 2010 – which aimed to bring ten local authorities together to share back-office functions – showed the difficulties of collaborating successfully.
- Although the Beecham Review, published in July 2006, did not support reorganisation at that time, it said that councils had to make considerable progress on joint working by 2011 or reorganisation would be back on the agenda. Many would contest whether progress has been made; and in the longer term reorganisation is the only way of securing efficiencies.[40]

There is also an additional argument connected with Welsh local government elections. Under the FPTP electoral system Welsh local government elections outside the coastal cities frequently lack full multi-party competition, or any competition at all. They give a large advantage to incumbent councillors, who can hold the same seat for decades so councils can resemble one-party states on occasions.

In response to these conclusions (Box 8.18) a commitment was made by the Welsh government that local government in Wales should undergo a period of major reform. This was moved forward in April 2013 when a Commission on Public Service Governance and Delivery, chaired by Sir Paul Williams, was established. The Williams Commission reported its findings in January 2014, proposing options for ten, eleven or twelve local authorities, instead of twenty-two. The Welsh government broadly accepted the Report's findings and recommendations, and in July 2014 the Welsh government published its White Paper *Devolution, Democracy and Delivery: Improving Public Services for People in Wales*, setting out its strategic reform agenda for local government and the delivery of other public services in Wales.

Discussions were held during the summer and autumn of 2014 by a number of neighbouring local authorities on whether to merge voluntarily, and ahead of a Welsh government deadline of 28 November 2014 within which to make their formal expressions of interest and by the deadline six local authorities had agreed to work together. However, in January 2015 Leighton Andrews, the Public Services Minister driving the reforms, announced that he had rejected the voluntary council mergers put forward by six local authorities and in the same month he introduced the Local Government (Wales) Bill, the first legislative step towards reforming local government. Six months later, the Welsh government published its long-awaited map outlining the replacement of Wales' twenty-two local authorities with eight 'super' authorities. No changes occurred prior to the 2016 Welsh Assembly elections, and subsequently Leighton Andrews lost his Rhondda constituency seat to Plaid Cymru leader Leanne Wood. Following the election, the new Local Government Secretary, Mark Drakeford, said the plan to cut the twenty-two councils to eight or nine was no longer a priority. Further to this, in October 2016, Mark Drakeford announced that the twenty-two councils would remain as the democratic tier of local government, but there would be an expectation of 'concerted collaboration' and Welsh councils would be expected to deliver key public services under a system of 'mandatory regional working'.[41]

In January 2017, the Welsh government published a Local Government Reform White Paper that, among other things, proposed lowering the voting age to sixteen and changing the way councillors in Wales are elected from FPTP to a system of proportional representation, possibly STV. This would also help to address some of the electoral problems noted in Box 8.18. The White Paper also explains how councils will have to work together to deliver services. Under this scheme, councils will be grouped into three regions – southeast Wales, southwest and central Wales, and north Wales – to work together on developing the economy and on transport, and decisions will be taken by joint committees of councillors, with the authorities pooling their budgets. In justifying the changes, Mark Drakeford stated that: 'Local government reform is essential if we're to make these services stronger and more resilient to cope with the demands of the future.'[42]

Box 8.18 The Public Service Ombudsman for Wales (PSOW)

The Public Services Ombudsman for Wales has legal powers, granted by the Welsh government and National Assembly, to look into complaints about public services and independent care providers in Wales. The PSOW, whose services are free and impartial, can investigate complaints that local authority members have broken their authority's code of conduct. The PSOW is independent of the Welsh government and has a team of staff who help to consider and investigate complaints. Since April 2014, Nick Bennett has been the Public Service Ombudsman for Wales. He is a former Liberal Democrat special adviser, public affairs consultant (lobbyist) and latterly Chief Executive of Community Housing Cymru (CHC), which represents housing associations in Wales.

What can the PSOW do?

The PSOW can deal with complaints of maladministration in public services in Wales. These include services provided by the following organisations:

- local authorities;
- joint boards of local authorities;
- police and fire authorities (not complaints about individual police officers);
- National Assembly for Wales;
- Welsh government;
- local health boards;
- NHS trusts;
- GP services;
- community health councils;
- housing provided by housing associations and by local authorities;
- national park authorities;
- education appeal panels;
- Natural Resources Wales;
- school governing bodies (admission matters only).[43]

The PSOW can only look into complaints of maladministration that cause injustice, suffering or hardship. This means that they can only take up complaints about the way an organisation has done something or not done something it should have done. They cannot investigate complaints about specific things such as teaching and management in schools and colleges or rent and service charges set by a social landlord. In addition, they are not able to provide a quick solution to complex problems.

Conclusion

The establishment of devolution in Wales has had a huge influence over, and brought great change to, pressure group activity, civil society and local government in Wales. However, it should be recognised that much of this change occurred after 1964, rather than after 1999, as a consequence of the establishment of administrative devolution via the Welsh Office. Furthermore, it is true to say that the coming of devolution via the establishment of the National Assembly and the subsequent increase in the powers of the Welsh government has greatly expanded both the scope and reach of representative organisations in Wales. Importantly, it has also greatly increased the potential for the Welsh government itself to generate and sponsor innovation, particularly with regard to public service delivery. Certainly, the evidence suggests that devolved government is more inclusive, representative and responsive to the needs of the Welsh people than government in Westminster could ever be. However, there are dangers due to the small and undeveloped nature of civil society in Wales, the predominance of the Labour Party and the limited capacity and finance of the Welsh government. All of these things could result in exclusive, overly reliant, overbearing and uncritical relationships developing between government ministers, civil servants and key pressure groups in the small and intimate environment of the Cardiff Bay Village. Only time will tell if this is the case.

The Welsh government also faces great challenges if it is to improve its relationship with local government. The recession, and the subsequent need to limit public spending, followed by the drive to restructure and modernise local government under former minister Leighton Andrews, have not fostered good relations between the two levels of government. At the beginning of fifth term of the National Assembly, First Minister Carwyn Jones appears conciliatory on the subject of local government reform and it now seems there will be no reduction in the number of Welsh local authorities. However, interested parties should certainly 'watch this space' to see how things proceed over the next few years.

Questions for discussion

1. Is it true to say that there is a distinctive Welsh civil society?
2. To what extent has Welsh devolution been of benefit to pressure groups?
3. Consider the strengths and weaknesses of pressure group activity in relation to the National Assembly and the Welsh government. Do pressure groups enhance or hinder democratic government in Wales?

Case study: working together to exert influence[44]

Read the text in the case studies in Boxes 8.3 and 8.4 and answer the following questions:

1. Explain why membership of policy networks, policy communities and issue networks might be beneficial to (a) ministers, civil servants and AMs; and (b) pressure groups and lobbyists.
2. Identify and describe the disadvantages for pressure groups working in formal coalitions, partnerships and networks.

Case study: the advantages and disadvantages of pressure group influence in Wales[45]

Read the text in Boxes 8.12 and 8.13 and answer the following questions:

1. Identify and describe three examples of Welsh government policy areas where group influence has taken place?
2. Drawing on examples from the sources explain why pressure groups have been influential on the development of Welsh government policy.
3. Explain why Community Housing Cymru was so important to the One Welsh coalition's strategy for delivering affordable housing.
4. Using both sources draw a two-column table to identify the advantages and disadvantages of pressure group influence on government in Wales.

9

Summary: Future Directions

Russell Deacon

This short final section makes a few comments on the likely changes to Welsh politics over the next few years. It also covers those related to an increase in powers in a bit more detail. Unfortunately, the restrictions in the size of the book and the continuing changes in the political scene mean that these can only be briefly noted.

Changes

Observers of British and Welsh politics will be well aware that British politics has entered a turbulent time due to Brexit and the political ramifications this is having, which at the time of writing are still not known. Indeed, it may be some years before they are likely to be fully understood with respect to Welsh government and politics. With this in mind, therefore, what are some of the central issues likely to affect Welsh politics?

Brexit

It is likely that Brexit will mean far more prominence in UK politics for the First Minister and the Welsh government as Wales seeks to ensure that it is neither disadvantaged nor forgotten in negotiations. It may also mean that the United Kingdom develops a more formal federal arrangement of government, which will strengthen Wales' role and status with the United Kingdom. Such a wish has already been expressed by Carwyn Jones and he is likely to push this further.[1]

Changes in voter choice

At the same time, Welsh politics may itself be evolving. Welsh Labour's hegemony has been challenged both by the rise of UKIP in its traditional heartland and by divisions within its own ranks over the leadership of Jeremy Corbyn. At the same time, its vote share has been in continual decline. All of these factors may impact on Labour's long dominance of Welsh politics.

Welsh political institutions are evolving

There are moves to change the name of the Welsh Assembly to Parliament. At the same time, the Assembly is changing to become a more mature legislature. This is likely not only to bring law-making and tax-raising powers, but also to see a rise in the number of AMs from sixty to eighty. This expansion will also alter the nature of the Welsh Assembly/government with an increasing shift in power from Whitehall to Cardiff Bay. This point on new powers needs a bit more explanation.

New powers for the Welsh Assembly

When the Welsh Assembly was established in 1999, those powers it had were defined in statute (the Government of Wales Act 1998). This was known as the conferred powers model. The main problem with this type of power was that it was not always clear whether it was the Welsh Assembly or the Westminster Parliament that had the power. This led to three Welsh Bills being referred to the Supreme Court for judgment as to whether or not they were within the powers of the Welsh Assembly to legislate on (*ultra vires*) (Box 9.1).[2] Academic[3] and political opinion, together with the recommendations of a Commission chaired by Sir Paul Silk[4] on devolution, supported a change to the reserved legislative powers model of government.

Box 9.1 Case study: what is the deferred powers model, and how and why does the Supreme Court block Welsh legislation?

In Scotland and Northern Ireland all the powers given to them are devolved to them unless expressly 'reserved' to the UK Parliament. The Welsh Assembly, however, under the Government of Wales Act 2006 uses a conferred powers model. This means that the Assembly can legislate only on those subjects itemised in the Act. Since 2011, it is these subjects that have been set out in Schedule 7 of the Act. Thus, the Attorney General can argue that the Assembly is exceeding its competence and refer the matter to the UK's Supreme Court under Sections 112 or 114 of the Government of Wales Act 2006. This they have done on a number of occasions and it has the immediate effect of delaying the implementation of the legislation. The Agricultural Sector (Wales) 2014 Act, for instance, was delayed for almost a year because of this process.[5]

Sometimes the Bill can suffer worse than delay. On 9 February 2015, the Supreme Court handed down its judgment regarding the Recovery of Medical Costs for Asbestos Diseases (Wales) Bill. It found that the Assembly does not have the legislative competence to enact the Bill in its present form under its 'conferred powers'. The Bill had been referred to the Supreme Court not by the Westminster government, but by the Welsh government's own counsel general. He had done so in order to prevent future challenges by insurances companies. The result was something of a 'home goal' for the Welsh government as a majority decision by the Supreme Court was that they did not have the fiscal powers to levy charges for Welsh NHS services.[6]

On 27 February 2015, the then Prime Minister David Cameron and Deputy Prime Minister Nick Clegg, announced at the Millennium Stadium in Cardiff a new draft of new powers to the Welsh Assembly. These included guaranteed minimum funding for the Welsh government, control of fracking and larger energy projects. Known as the St David's Day Agreement, it proposed a legislative framework to introduce many of the recommendations from the two national commissions on devolution held by Sir Paul Silk over the previous years. Aside from those already mentioned they also included:

1. transport powers, such as the setting of road speed limits;
2. more power over the Assembly's running of its own affairs, including the voting age for its elections, and the power to call itself a parliament.

In 2016, an attempt to bring in a new Welsh Bill to radically alter the way that laws were made, which taxes could be raised, how elections were undertaken, and the powers and remit of the Welsh Assembly failed to come into law. The Welsh government and Assembly had rejected it because at the heart of the new law they felt it gave the Westminster government an effective veto over the passing of laws at the Welsh Assembly.[7] Negotiations between the Welsh and Westminster governments continued in order to try to reassure the Welsh government that Westminster would not unduly influence the Welsh Assembly's law-making powers. These included powers for the first time over water from Wales going to England,[8] the ability to borrow up to £1 billion for infrastructure projects and enshrining the convention that Westminster will not pass laws on devolved matters without the Assembly's approval. On Friday, 31 January 2017, the latest Wales Act gained Royal Assent and came into force two months later. Welsh Secretary, Alun Cairns, described the new Act as allowing the Welsh Assembly to mature into a fully-fledged parliament for the first time, while others said it still left too much power with Westminster.[9] The arguments concerning whether politics needed more devolution or already had enough remained as topical as when the arguments had first been raised in the nineteenth century.

Conclusion

Throughout this book readers will have become aware that Wales does indeed have its own distinct form of government and politics. Whereas in the twentieth century it was true to state that aside from the Welsh language there were few differences between England and Wales politically, this is not true today. These differences continue to develop. Events, however, are moving at a rapid pace and will continue to do so. Therefore, readers need to be aware that whereas the contents of this book were as correct as possible when it was written some areas may have evolved since. So ensure that you keep abreast of Welsh current political affairs in order to update yourself.

Questions for discussion

1. What are the major changes that are likely to impact on Welsh government and politics in the next five years?
2. In what ways has Wales finally evolved a model of modern parliamentary democracy?

Case study: the deferred powers model[10]

Read the case study in Box 9.1 on the deferred powers model and the surrounding text. You will also need to undertake some of your own research. Then answer the questions below:

1. What is the difference between the reserved and conferred power models?
2. How can the Westminster government block a new Welsh law?
3. Through your own research see how powers for Wales may increase in the post-Brexit period?

Suggested answer points are provided in the Welsh Government and Politics online resource for both the questions and the case study. The web link for these answer points is given at the front of the book.

Glossary of Key Terms[1]

Act of Wales: The final process of a Bill, which after Royal Assent becomes legally binding and enforceable. Most Acts come from the Welsh government, although they may also come from AMs directly (Private Members' Bills), Assembly committees and the Assembly Commission. Welsh Acts are also distinguished from UK legislation by having the word 'Wales' inserted in them in brackets.

Additional Member System (AMS): The AMS system is a hybrid electoral system using FPTP elections for forty Welsh constituencies and then having a second election for a regional list member (the proportional element). There are twenty regional list members spread across five regions, with four members allocated per region.

administrative devolution: The devolving of power over the implementation of government policy to a regional level.

advocacy: In the context of the Welsh Assembly, it means that an AM is paid or expects some other reward either now or in the future for working on behalf of another person, business or organisation in order to pursue their interests in the Welsh Assembly.

annual budget: The annual budget process and budget motion in the Assembly is passed in the Assembly's plenary session. The budget determines the amount of financial resources to be allocated to specified services and purposes for individual financial years. The National Assembly is responsible for approving budget motions and supplementary budget motions proposed by Welsh ministers. Without this approval the Welsh government cannot function.

appropriate (supply) motions: The mechanism by which the government puts forward its plans to spend and raise money. This is normally through a majority vote on a motion within the Welsh Assembly.

Assembly committees: There are twelve committees named after the area of government policy that they cover. They are chaired by a non-government AM and include representatives from all the political parties. Their central aim is to scrutinise government policy or examine a new topic and come up with options for future policy direction or new laws. Committee chairs are appointed by secret ballot.

Assembly measures: The name given to a type of lower primary legislation resulting from Assembly Legislative Competence Orders (LCO) (see below). It was deemed as being lower because it did not contain a large bulk of powers, which occurs in Westminster legislation. The LCO transferred power to legislate from the Westminster Parliament to the Welsh Assembly to a 'Matter' in one of the 'Fields' provided under Schedule 5 of the Government of Wales Act 2006.

Assembly Member (AM): The name given to the legislator who is elected, salaried and represents a geographical area of Wales.

Attorney-General (for England and Wales): The Attorney-General is the UK government's most senior law officer. The post is a member of the government and is held by an MP who is also a barrister. They are responsible for examining Welsh legislation to see whether the Assembly has the competence to legislate in that area. If they believe it does not they will refer it to the Supreme Court for a decision. In Wales, this role is also partially undertaken by the **Counsel General**.

Bill: The name given to an Act prior to it gaining Royal Assent. When the Act is a Bill it can still be amended and reshaped during stages 1–4 of the Welsh law-making process.

by-election: A single election in a seat where a vacancy has arisen between all-Wales elections, if the SV or FPTP electoral system has been used. This is usually as the result of a death or resignation, and like other elections is held on a Thursday.

Cardiff Bay Village: The informal network of individuals and organisations involved in public life, policy, academia and communications whose work focuses in and around the institutions of government in Wales.

centre: The part of the political spectrum that seeks a clear middle way between capitalism and socialism, or follows a different ideology that is not readily applicable to the political spectrum, such as Liberalism. In Wales, they are represented by the Welsh Liberal Democrats, although this party is also seen sometimes as centre left ideologically.

city region: A city region is a concept that has been in use since the 1950s and refers to a metropolitan area and hinterland. This consists of a core city, conurbation or network of urban communities, sharing resources such as a central business area, labour market and transport network. City regions in Wales are combinations of local authorities that have (or will have) a shared administration with over-arching functions, such as transport and economic development. Examples in Wales are Cardiff Capital Region and Swansea Bay City Region.

civil law: This is the body of law that deals with the statutory regulation, establishment and restructuring of public bodies, regulation of business and dealing with non-criminal disputes between individuals, organisations and other bodies. It is also the mechanism by which the Welsh government and AMs give legal status to their policy ideals. Normally, the penalty for breaking civil law is monetary (a fine) or suing for legal redress. The Welsh Assembly has the power to create civil laws, but not those relating to criminal law.

civil society: This involves the activities of individuals and groups operating outside formal governmental structures. Wales operates a pluralistic democracy whereby a multitude of representative organisations, pressure groups, trade unions, religious groups and charities seek to influence government in their making and implementation of policy.

class alignment: The voting theory that supports the view that people vote for a political party according to their social class. Traditionally, this has been mainly working-class support for the Labour Party and middle-class support for the Conservative Party.

closed party list system: The closed party list allows voters to have a single vote for a political party rather than one or more candidates. Seats are then allocated in turn on the largest shares of the votes through a mathematical formula known as d'Hondt, and is the same one used in the Welsh Assembly elections.

Clwyd West question: This question was posed after Labour's Alun Pugh won Clwyd West constituency in the 2003 Welsh General Election. Pugh's three losing opponents where all subsequently elected as members of the regional list. This posed the question of 'how is it fair that candidates' who are beaten in one election can still get elected to the Assembly through another method (backdoor). It was the principal argument that Labour then used to disallow candidates from standing in both constituency and list elections between 2007 and 2011 before the bar was removed by the Westminster coalition government in 2014.

coalition government: A formal arrangement between political parties in order to govern for a set period either in British or Welsh government. For both types of government, the junior (smaller) political party gets the deputy prime minister/first minister portfolio, as well as a number of other secretary/minister portfolios. Coalition normally occurs after both parties have agreed a manifesto for government, which is published as a joint document. The United Kingdom has had only one coalition government since 1945, that of 2010–15. The Welsh Assembly has had two coalition governments, in 2000–3 and 2007–11. It has also currently has a smaller type of coalition arrangement, called a partnership, with the one Welsh Liberal Democrat AM, 2016–21. The object of the coalition is to have enough elected members to form a majority government.

collective responsibility or collective ministerial/Cabinet responsibility. This is a constitutional convention that binds all government ministers into publicly supporting government policy and decision-making. In Wales, this has also been applied to government appointments such as committee chairs. If the minister or chair publicly disagrees with their own government they must normally resign or face dismissal.

community council: The most grassroots form of democracy in Wales, community councils cover villages and the urban areas of some towns and cities. They have limited powers, but are able to set their own taxes through the precept. They are run by an elected chair and an unelected clerk.

conferred powers: These are areas where the UK Parliament has specified subject areas in which it has granted the Welsh Assembly law-making powers. Under Schedule 7 of the Government of Wales Act 2006, there are twenty of these areas, ranging from local housing and tourism to water and flood defences. The Welsh Assembly cannot make laws outside these conferred powers.

confidence vote: A vote of confidence is given when a minister or government is deemed to have failed on one or a range of issues. If the government loses the vote then it should resign. In 2000, the threat of a no-confidence vote forced First Secretary Alun Michael to resign as leader of the Welsh government.

constituency Assembly Member (AM): Forty of the sixty members of the National Assembly for Wales are elected to represent a relatively small single-member constituency rather than a region. The constituencies used are the same as those for General Elections to the Westminster Parliament. These representatives are elected by the FPTP system at the same time as regional AMs.

constitutional convention: This is an action or procedure that occurs because it has normally evolved as such rather than there being a specific Act or rule stating so. Examples are the fact that the UK government does not legislate on matters devolved to Wales or that the monarch will accept and act on any advice given to him or her by the First Minister

core executive: The core executive is the name given to that part of the Welsh government that implements policy and is responsible for running devolved services in Wales. This covers the First Minister, the Cabinet and Deputy Ministers, the Cabinet committees, the Welsh government departments, special advisers (SPADs) and the senior civil servants responsible for supporting the Welsh government.

councillor (member): These are the democratically elected members of local councils, unitary authorities and community councils in Wales.

Councillors are currently elected to represent single or multi-member wards by the FPTP electoral system.

d'Hondt electoral system: This type of voting uses a highest averages method for allocating seats in party list proportional representation. In Wales, this is either used in the party list system for European elections or the regional lists in the Welsh Assembly elections. It is named after the Belgian mathematician Victor d'Hondt who came up with his calculation for allocating seats proportionally in 1878.

devolution: The process of transferring (devolving) power from central government.

dominant party state: A state in which one political party has become the dominant party in the political process and gains the largest number of elected representatives over a long period. In Wales, the Labour Party have gained the largest number of MPs since 1922 and AMs since 1999. It is not the same as 'a one-party state' because other political parties are also represented. It is, however, sometimes mistakenly referred to as such.

dominant party system: The name given to a political system in which one political party dominates politics over a period of time. In Wales, this party is the Labour Party; prior to 1922 it was the Liberal Party.

ethics: These can be seen as a system of moral principles. In politics they follow what are called the seven Nolan Principles of conduct in public life. If an AM is found to have breached these ethical principles, they can face a series of sanctions.

ethnoregionalism: A political party that represents a distinct group within a nation. Therefore, Plaid Cymru could be said to represent the interests of the Welsh in Wales and in Westminster, and are therefore an ethnoregionalist rather than what it often termed as a nationalist party.

executive devolution: The devolving of power over the implementation of executive functions to a regional level.

executive: The executive is the body of the government with the authority and responsibility for administration of the state on a daily basis.

federal party system: A political party system in which state/regional parties are given full autonomy in certain areas, such as party name, devolved policy creation, leadership election, candidate selection and state constitutional rules. At the same time, they are part of a federal party structure upon which they have representation but that remains autonomous of the state party in Wales. The Liberal Democrats and their predecessors the Welsh Liberals have operated using this structure since 1966.

financial resolution: This is the name given to the authorisation by the Assembly for Welsh ministers to spend money on a new service, or for a new purpose, or to increase spending on an existing service or purpose, as a consequence of a Bill. The Presiding Officer determines whether such a resolution is necessary. It is the Welsh government through a minister, however, who moves the motion, even if it is a Private Members' Bill. The resolution must then be voted on and passed by the Welsh Assembly. The same procedure is also used if the Welsh government needs to provide additional funding for a new policy area that requires legislation.

First Minister: The Head of the Welsh government and chair of the Welsh government Cabinet. They are also an elected party leader and AM and act as the Crown's official representative in Wales.

First-Past-The-Post electoral system (FPTP): The system of elections in Wales currently used for Westminster and local government elections. Candidates are successful if they gain a simple majority (one vote) over the next placed candidate. The system is favoured because it enables the top placed party to gain dominance more easily (strong government). It is, however, often non-proportional and penalises smaller political parties.

Home Rule: The term given to political devolution in the nineteenth and early twentieth centuries.

Joint Ministerial Committees (JMC): Joint Ministerial Committees involve ministers from the UK government and the devolved administrations meeting to formulate specific policy or discuss issues of policy and government.

jurisdiction: This is the authority to interpret and apply the law within a specified geographical area. This is recognised nationally and internationally by accepting that the nation has the sovereignty to do so. It is normally granted to a formal body such as a court. Wales shares its jurisdiction with England and it is centred on the UK Parliament rather than the Welsh Assembly.

left wing: The part of the political spectrum that represents those ideologies that emphasise the importance of the role of the state in society and public ownership or control of key sectors of the economy and welfare system. Their ideology is influenced by Socialism or Marxism. In Wales they include Plaid Cymru and the Labour Party.

legal sovereignty: This is the power to make law and these laws are then regarded as final and recognised by the courts and enforced by the executive (e.g., police/government). Westminster has ceded this sovereignty to the Welsh Assembly for conferred areas.

legislative body: The name given to an elected body that can create new laws – the Welsh Assembly or the Houses of Parliament (Westminster) in the context of this book.

Legislative Competence Orders (LCOs): The name given to a piece of constitutional legislation in the form of an Order in Council. An LCO had to go through both Westminster and the Welsh Assembly and was a lengthy process. Fifteen LCOs were passed between 2007 and 2011. The process ended in 2011 after the referendum on primary powers made the LCO process redundant.

list member: *see regional Assembly Member*

lobbyist: Lobbyists are the employees of organisations who try to influence policy decisions, especially in the executive and legislative branches of government.

majoritarian electoral system: To win a candidate needs just one more vote than the candidate who came second. The votes cast for losing candidates (and those over the number the winning candidate needed to win) are effectively wasted, and do not count.

manifesto: The programme for office drawn up by a political party prior to an election being held. Each political party has a different way of compiling their manifestos. They also act as the guidelines for civil servants and local government officials in implementing a programme of government. Over time they have become more detailed and specific to devolved matters in Wales. Manifestos are now often costed with respect to how much they will cost to implement.

marginal seat: A marginal seat is a FPTP constituency seat in which the sitting member has only a small majority over his or her opponent(s). This is typically under 2 per cent. As these seats are the most likely to change hands at elections, political parties target their resources and campaigning on these seats between and during elections.

Member of European Parliament (MEP): A legislator elected to the European Parliament for the all-Wales constituency, using the party list system. There are four MEPs elected for Wales. They normally serve a period of five years in office before seeking re-election. An MEP represents and is selected by a political party. They cannot not form part of the European executive (Commission) as in the UK and Welsh electoral systems due to the separation of separation of powers within the EU system of government.

Member of Parliament (MP): A legislator elected to the Westminster Parliament for a single constituency, using the FPTP electoral system. They normally serve a period of five years in office before seeking re-election. An MP represents and is selected by a political party. They may also form part of the executive by serving in a ministerial post in government. There are currently forty MPs elected for Wales.

ministerial responsibility: The constitutional convention that a minister and not their civil servants must take personal responsibility for the running of his or her department. This means that the minister must take responsibility for significant mistakes or errors, which may result in their own resignation.

monarchy: The name given to the ruling royal dynasty (the Windsors). It can also be referred to as the Crown.

National Assembly for Wales (Welsh Assembly): The body that legislates new laws and scrutinises the Welsh government's spending, laws and policies. Not to be confused with the Welsh government (the executive). The two bodies are wholly separate. The Welsh Assembly is based in the Senedd building in Cardiff Bay.

nationalist party: The political term given to a political party or movement that is normally on the right or far right of the political spectrum. Nationalist parties are normally distinguished by displaying extreme loyalty to their nation-state/ethnic group, including its cultural symbols, language, a belief that their nation is superior to others ethnically and morally, led by a charismatic and popular leader and anti-immigrant. Plaid Cymru is not a nationalist party in respect of most of these points, but is often referred to as being one. UKIP has or has had a number of these characteristics as have elements of the Conservative Party. *See also ethnoregionalism.*

open and closed party list systems: Open lists allow voters to vote for candidates on lists decided by a party. Closed lists allow voters to vote for a party, not the individual candidates, on that party's list. The party list system used for the National Assembly of Wales elections and the European Parliament elections is a closed system using the d'Hondt method of electoral calculation.

partnership government: *see coalition government*

party list: The former proportional electoral system used for the election of Wales' four MEPs. The political parties put forward a closed list of candidates for voters to elect from. Electors vote from one list and the winners are determined by their percentage of the overall vote.

plenary: The full meetings of Welsh AMs. The plenary is held twice weekly when the Assembly is in session. It discusses issues related to the governance of Wales, legislation or various constituency issues. If there is an emergency, the Assembly can be recalled during any recess.

political devolution: The devolving of power over the implementation of political functions to a regional level – this involves the election of representatives for the devolved body. The devolved political body will have policy-making powers and possibly law-making and tax-raising powers. It may have devolved sovereignty, although ultimate sovereignty remains at Westminster.

political spectrum: The name given to the measuring gauge used to determine where a political party lies in respect to their ideologies. Communism is normally at the extreme left and Fascism at the extreme right. In Wales, most political parties are either centre left or centre right.

political/parliamentary sovereignty: This is a principle that the Westminster Parliament, through the mandate of the people's vote at elections, retains supreme legal authority in the United Kingdom. This means that it can create or end any law, no court can overrule its legislation and no Parliament can bind future Parliaments with its laws. It is a central part of the UK's uncodified constitution.

'pork barrel' politics: A term derived from politics in the United States. In the Welsh context, it normally means offering government spending in a constituency for a project or activity that will persuade the elected member to endorse Welsh government policy or laws.

Presiding Officer (Llywydd): The AM elected by their fellow AMs to chair plenary sessions. Like the speaker of the House of Commons, they seek to maintain a neutral or non-controversial position while in office. They also maintain order among members in the Assembly chamber. There is also a Deputy Presiding Officer.

pressure group: These are also sometimes called interest groups, are organised groups who seek to influence the policies and actions of government in modern representative democracies. Examples include Community Housing Cymru, Stonewall Cymru and Unison Cymru Wales.

primary legislation: Is the type of legislative power that enables the Welsh Assembly to pass its own Acts within the need to have these passed through the UK Parliament. The UK Parliament cedes legal sovereignty to the Welsh Assembly to make laws over specified areas, but retains parliamentary sovereignty, that is, the right to govern Wales within international law.

private office: The office of the First Minister or other minister headed by a Private Secretary, and also including an assistant private secretary and diary secretary.

Private Secretary (Chief of Staff): The senior civil servant who runs each Secretary of State's private office. They are the middle management-level civil servant whose responsibility it is to ensure that the Secretary's are briefed on relevant issues and that Secretary's/ministers' decisions are actioned by the wider Civil Service. They also act as a gatekeeper to those seeking a meeting with the Secretary/minister, and they may also accompany the minister on many of their formal duties.

proportional electoral system: A system that seeks to accurately reflect the percentage of votes cast in the percentage of seats gained by redistributing votes cast for losing candidates. Few votes are wasted.

public affairs: This is a branch of the public relations industry concerned with 'an organisation's relationship with stakeholders'. Public affairs practitioners engage stakeholders, who might be politicians, civil servants, business groups, charities, unions and the media, in order to explain organisational policies and views on public policy issues and legislation.

QUANGO: An abbreviation for quasi-autonomous non-governmental organisation. *See also WGSB*

referendum: A vote given to the people on a set question, for example, do they wish to see the UK leave the EU? It is a form of direct democracy.

regional Assembly Member (AM): Twenty of the sixty members of the National Assembly for Wales are elected to represent one of the five large, multi-member regions rather than a single constituency. They are elected by the party list system using the d'Hondt method of electoral calculation.

reserved powers: This refers to the reserved powers model for creating legislation. In this model, the UK Government makes it clear which powers are reserved for it, which only it can make laws on, for example, to create and maintain an army. Anything not reserved would be devolved, and the National Assembly for Wales would be able to pass laws in those areas. This is already the case in Scotland and Northern Ireland.

right wing: The part of the political spectrum that represents those ideologies that emphasise the rights of the individual over the group, private enterprise and a weaker role for the state. In Wales they include the Conservative Party and UKIP.

safe seat: These are seats that tend to be won comfortably by the incumbent party and have not changed party allegiance for a number of elections successively. They are also associated with little active political campaigning between and during elections.

secondary legislation: This comes from original (primary) Acts of the Westminster Parliament. It is through secondary legislation (Statutory Instruments) that an Act is enacted, developed or applied to particular Welsh circumstances. In essence, it is filling in the detail about how the Act will be made into law (enacted). Most secondary legislation is signed off directly by the relevant minister without ever going through a scrutiny process.

Sewel motion: Also known as a Legislative Consent Motion. It is a motion passed by the Welsh Assembly enabling the UK Parliament (Westminster) to pass legislation on a devolved issue. It is normally used when Westminster is passing legislation that is relevant to Wales. To accept this UK Parliament legislation would avoid the Welsh Assembly having to duplicate this legislation again in Assembly. It is named after Lord Sewel, who as a Scottish Office Minister announced this policy in 1998. A Sewel motion also applies to legislation in Scotland and Northern Ireland if their respective legislatures agree to it.

Silk Commission: A Commission established by the Welsh Secretary to examine the future direction of devolution in Wales with respect to law-making and tax-raising powers. It was published in two parts in 2012 and 2014. Its recommendations were taken on board in the 2015 St David's Day declaration by the Westminster coalition government. The move to a 'reserved powers' model was a key recommendation in the Silk Commission 2014 (Silk II).

single transferable vote (STV): Regarded as the most proportional of electoral systems, but also one of the most complex to understand. It allows voters multiple preferences enabling them to vote for candidates individually rather than from party lists. From 2021 Welsh local authorities can hold STV elections if they wish.

sovereignty: The supreme power of the political institution with respect to its legitimate legal authority.

special advisers (SPADS): SPADs are political civil servants, who are appointed directly by ministers in order to help them in their political role as ministers.

Standing Orders: These are the rules that state how the Welsh Assembly should be run. They must be followed as breaches of these can cause serious problems for members.

supplementary vote: The electoral system used for Wales Police and Crime Commissioners. It involves voters having to vote on a first and second preference basis. After the first preferences are counted, the top two candidates go through to the next round. In this second round the second preferences of all those eliminated candidates are re-apportioned to the two top placed candidates and the winner is the one with the most first and second preferences combined.

tactical voting: Tactical voting is where a voter's preferred candidate stands little chance of being elected and the voter votes instead for the candidate most likely to keep out the candidate the voter most dislikes. This occurs more frequently in the AMS regional list elections in which Labour voters, for instance, realise that their party is not likely to gain list seats and so vote instead for a potential coalition partner for the their own party.

Territorial Secretary: also known as the Welsh Secretary.

think tank: These are usually independent organisations that specialise in the research and development of public policy. Examples in Wales include the IWA, PPIW, Bevan Foundation and Gorwel.

third sector: This is the 'not for profit' or voluntary sector of the economy. The Wales Council for Voluntary Action (WCVA) is the peak organisation for the third sector in Wales and represents thousands of national, regional and local voluntary organisations.

'Three Wales Model': A political model designed by Dr Denis Balsom that splits Wales into three politically distinctive geographical areas.

Developed in the 1980s, the model determines voting patterns and is still used today.

town council: The most grassroots form of democracy in Wales. Town councils cover small towns of up to 50,000 people. They have limited powers, but are able to set their own taxes through the precept. They are run by an elected leader, have the position of mayor for civic duties and are administered by clerk. Three town councils in Wales also use the title city council: Bangor, St Asaph and St David's.

Union, the: The name given to the 'union of nations' that makes up the United Kingdom of Great Britain and Northern Ireland (England, Northern Ireland, Scotland and Wales).

unitary authority: The single effective tier of local government in Wales combining the functions of district and county councils. There are currently twenty-two unitary authorities, also termed principal areas, which were established by the Local Government (Wales) Act 1994, on 1 April 1996. Examples include Neath–Port Talbot, Rhondda Cynon Taff (RCT) and Ynys Môn (Isle of Anglesey) County Council.

Wales Office: This is a Civil Service department that supports the Westminster government in its monitoring and working relationship with the Welsh government on a daily basis. It sits within the Ministry of Justice.

Welsh government sponsored bodies (WGSBs): These are bodies directly funded by the Welsh government. Although they are not directly part of the Civil Service, their internal structures are based on the Civil Service. Before the Government of Wales Act 2006, they were also known as Assembly Sponsored Public Bodies (ASPBs). They are also known as quangos, and in England they are referred to as non-government department bodies. Examples include Qualifications Wales, Cadw, the National Library of Wales and the National Museum of Wales.

Welsh Consolidated Fund: This acts as a pot in which the money voted by the UK Parliament for Wales is held; it is similar to a bank account for governments. The Fund provides the money for the Welsh government's budget, the expenditures for each of the Assembly Commission, the Auditor General for Wales and the Public Services Ombudsman for Wales.

Welsh General Election: On this day an election of all forty Welsh constituencies and twenty regional list members occurs. This election day is fixed and occurs on the first Thursday in May every five years. The election can be varied by up to one month depending on prevailing circumstances.

Welsh government: *see core executive*

Welsh Secretary (Secretary of State for Wales): This is the post in the UK Cabinet for the person who is central to the liaison between the UK and Welsh governments. Historically, this post was also responsible for the running of the government department in Wales known as the Welsh Office; today it is a much smaller department called the Wales Office.

Westminster: The location of the British Houses of Parliament in London, and the generic name often used to refer to the British Parliament or government.

Whip: The AM(s) who is responsible for ensuring party discipline. Specifically when it comes to voting in the Assembly or committees. The term derives from an old hunting name related to the member of the hunt responsible for ensuring that the hounds remained in the hunting pack chasing their quarry (the whipper-in).

Whitehall: The location of the head office of most Westminster government's departments. It also includes the official residence of the Prime Minister, 10 Downing Street and the Cabinet offices.

'Yes Minister': Fictional TV series of the 1980s which portrayed government ministers as frequently being manipulated on policy direction by powerful civil servants.

Notes

Chapter 1

1. Ron Davies, 'Devolution: A Process and Not An Event', Institute of Welsh Affairs, 1999.
2. John Graham Jones, *The History of Wales*, University of Wales Press, 2014.
3. Kenneth Morgan, *Wales in British Politics 1868–1922*, University of Wales Press, 1980, p. 121.
4. Russell Deacon, *The Welsh Office and the Policy Process*, Welsh Academic Press, 2002.
5. The *Curriculum Cymreig* is designed to reflect the history, geography and culture of Wales.
6. 'International Body Grants Wales Country Status after Principality Error', *Western Mail*, 1 August 2011.
7. 'Welsh Devolution, the Reluctant Dragon', *The Economist*, 24 November 2012.
8. Information from the High Sheriffs' Association of England and Wales, available at: http://www.highsheriffs.com.
9. 'Welsh History Month: When Welsh Politics meant Business', Professor Russell Deacon, *Western Mail* 14 October 2015.
10. This case study covers the WJEC AS Government and Politics Specification Element 2.3.1 Political Parties and Participation in Politics – Leadership.

Chapter 2

1. Denis Balsom, 'The Three Wales Model', in John Osmond (ed.), *The National Question Again*, Gomer, 1985.
2. Gwyn A. Williams, *When was Wales: A History of the Welsh*, Black Raven Press, 1985.
3. John Osmond, 'The Lie of the Land', discussion paper for the Arts Council of Wales, 2009.

4. Roger Scully and Richard Wyn Jones, 'Still Three Wales? Social Location and Electoral Behaviour in Contemporary Wales', Wales Governance Centre, 2012.
5. See at: http://www.bbc.co.uk/news/election-2016-wales-36207410, last accessed 4 August 2017.
6. Roger Scully, 'Is Labour Dominance of Welsh Politics under Threat?' 2016, available at: blogs.lse.ac.uk.
7. Open University, 'Contemporary Wales', course notes, 2016.
8. Richard Wyn Jones, 'How Welsh Labour became the UK's most Invincible Electoral Machine', *The Guardian*, 6 May 2016.
9. Roger Scully, 'Labour in Wales: Perhaps the Biggest Polling Movement in Recent UK History that Almost No-one has Heard Of', 2015, blogs.lse.ac.uk, last accessed 4 August 2017.
10. David Jones (former Welsh Secretary (2012–14), 'A Minister Reflects', Institute for Government, interview Jen Gold and Nicola Hughes, 15 September 2015.
11. See Wales Factfile, 'Welsh Language', Institute of Welsh Affairs, 2003, available at: www.iwa.wales/click/wales-factfile.
12. Russell Deacon, *The Welsh Liberals: The History of the Welsh Liberal and Liberal Democratic Parties in Wales*, Welsh Academic Press, 2014, p. 111.
13. Nicholas Edwards, *Westminster Wales and Water*, University of Wales Press, 1999, p. 62.
14. Russell Deacon, *The Welsh Office and the Policy Process*, Welsh Academic Press, 2002, p. 127.
15. 'S4C Budget Cuts Threaten Jobs and Programmes', BBC News, 4 August 2015.
16. 'Just 3 per cent back Welsh Independence', *The Guardian*, 24 September 2014.
17. 'English parliament unworkable', BBC News, 17 January 2007.
18. Ibid.
19. Bill Jones and Phillip Norton, *Politics UK*, 8th edn, Routledge, 2014.
20. Russell Deacon, *The Welsh Liberals: The History of the Liberal and Liberal Democratic Parties in Wales*, Welsh Academic Press, 2014.
21. Laura McAllister, *Plaid Cymru: The Emergence of a Political Party*, Seren, 2001.
22. Duncan Tanner, Chris Williams and Deian Hopkin, *Labour Party in Wales 1900–2000*, University of Wales Press, 2000.
23. Information supplied by Welsh political parties to author, July 2016.
24. 'Nigel Farage Disowns UKIP's Entire 2010 Election Manifesto', *The Guardian*, 24 January 2010.
25. This case study covers the WJEC AS Government and Politics Specification Element 2.3.1 Political Parties and Participation in Politics – Differing Party Ideologies.

Chapter 3

1. David Melding, 'Will Britain Survive Beyond 2020?' Institute for Welsh Affairs, 2009, p. 85.
2. Russell Deacon, *The Governance of Wales: The Welsh Office and the Police Process 1964–99*, Welsh Academic Press, 2002.
3. *Hansard*, col. 1107, 6 March 2014.
4. Helen Catt and Michael Murphy, *Sub-State Nationalism: A Comparative Analysis of Institutional Design*, Routledge, 2003, p. 34.
5. Q&A: Police and Crime Commissioners, 12 November 2013, BBC News.
6. Westminster Parliament, Welsh Affairs Committee role, 2015, website at: http://www.parliament.uk/business/committees/committees-a-z/commons-select/welsh-affairs-committee.
7. David Williamson, 'Rolling Together the Welsh and Scottish Select Committees in the Wake of the SNP Victory would be "Unconstitutional"', *Western Mail*, 19 May 2015.
8. Russell Deacon, *The Welsh Liberals: The History of the Liberal and Liberal Democratic Parties in Wales*, Welsh Academic Press, 2014, p. 73.
9. 'Welsh Parliamentary Party Revived by Plan to Cut MPs', BBC Wales News, 10 November 2012.
10. Wayne David, 'The Job of Being a Government Whip', *Western Mail*, 9 August 2007.
11. Information on the Lords provided through an interview with Lord German, 28 March 2016.
12. Russell Deacon, *Devolution in the United Kingdom*, 2nd edn, Edinburgh University Press, 2012, p. 139.
13. David Jones, 'A Minister Reflects', Institute for Government, interviewed by Jen Gold and Nicola Hughes, 15 September 2015.
14. Definition of the role of the Welsh Secretary from Gov.UK website, June 2015.
15. David Jones, 'A Minister Reflects'.
16. Localism concerns the transfer of power, authority and resources from central government to local government and other local public agencies/devolved bodies with the intention of devolving it further into local communities (also called empowerment).
17. David Jones, 'A Minister Reflects'.
18. Wales Office, 30 June 2015, available at: https://www.gov.uk/government/organisations/office-of-the-secretary-of-state-for-wales.
19. Baroness Randerson, former Minister at the Wales Office, to author, April 2015.
20. 'Wales Office "hard to justify" says Plaid Cymru leader', *Western Mail*, 7 March 2011, p. 3.

21. British Institute for International and Comparative Law, 'A Constitutional Crossroads: Ways Forward for the United Kingdom, May 2015.

22. Memorandum of Understanding and Supplementary Agreements, Between the United Kingdom Government, the Scottish Ministers, the Welsh Ministers, and the Northern Ireland Executive Committee, September 2012.

23. 'Sturgeon and Welsh First Minister Carwyn Jones in Joint Call Over EU vote', *The Herald*, 3 June 2015.

24. Alun Davies to author, March 2015.

25. David Cornock, 'Cheryl Gillan Bids to Revive the Welsh Grand Committee', BBC News, 11 November 2013.

26. Memorandum of Understanding and Supplementary Agreements, Between the United Kingdom Government, the Scottish Ministers, the Welsh Ministers, and the Northern Ireland Executive Committee, September 2012, p. 24.

27. Kenneth O. Morgan, *Revolution to Devolution: Reflections on Welsh Democracy*, University of Wales Press, 2014, p. 272.

28. You Gov/Cardiff University Poll, 22 March 2016.

29. Alun Davies to author, March 2015.

30. Wales and the European Union, Welsh government website at: http://gov.wales/topics/international/europeanaffairs/?lang=en, last accessed 17 February 2016.

31. This case study covers the WJEC AS Government and Politics Specification Element 1.3.1 How the Government Works in Wales – Collective and Ministerial Responsibility.

Chapter 4

1. Russell Deacon, *Devolution in Great Britain Today*, Manchester University Press, 2006, p.72.

2. Russell Deacon, *Devolution in the United Kingdom*, 2nd edn, University of Edinburgh Press, 2012, p. 142.

3. Deacon, *Devolution in the United Kingdom*, p. 142.

4. Russell Deacon, 'Going into Labour: The Welsh Liberal Democrat Coalition Experience 2000–2003', *Journal of Liberal History*, Liberal Democrat History Group, 83 (2014): 22.

5. Martin Shipton, *Poor Man's Parliament: Ten Years of the Welsh Assembly*, Seren, 2011, p. 27.

6. Deacon, *Devolution in the United Kingdom*.

7. Alun Davies AM to author, March 2015.

8. Alun Davies AM to author, March 2015.

9. In June 2016, Welsh UKIP leader Neil Hamilton chastised Nathan Gill AM for breaking 'collective responsibility' with respect to his party's position on

the new M4 motorway in southeast Wales. 'UKIP's Nathan Gill should not "double job", says Hamilton', *BBC News*, 9 June 2016.

10. Peter Lynch and Paul Fairclough, *AS UK Government and Politics*, 4th edn, Phillip Allan, 2013.
11. David Deans, 'Carwyn Jones Defends Sacking Rebellious AM Jenny Rathbone over M4 Relief Road Criticised', *Western Mail*, 14 October 2015.
12. 'Secret Ballot for Assembly Committee Chairs, Presiding Officer Announces', *BBC News*, 17 June 2016.
13. 'Education Minister Leighton Andrews Resigns in Schools Row', *BBC News*, 25 June 2013.
14. Jeff Jones, 'The REAL Scandal Behind Last Week's Resignation of Environment Minister Alun Davies', *Western Mail*, 13 July 2014.
15. 'Cigar Blunder Minister Quits Job', *Western Mail*, 19 July 2008.
16. Alan Lawton and Aidan Rose, *Organisation and Management in the Public Sector*, Pitman, 1994, p. 84.
17. 'Ex-councillor Named Deputy Police and Crime Commissioner for South Wales', *South Wales Echo*, 7 February 2013.
18. Written Statement: Special Advisers, Welsh Government, 1 August 2012.
19. House of Commons, Civil Service Statistics No. 2224, 9 November 2015, p. 8,
20. Civil Service Statistics, SN/SG/2224, 13 March 2013, and also 8 October 2015m Civil Service Statistics, House of Commons, Civil Service Statistics No. 2224, 9 November 2015.
21. Russell Deacon, *The Governance of Wales: The Welsh Office and the Policy Process 1964–99*, Welsh Academic Press, 2002, p. 235.
22. Anna Nicholl, *The Capacity of the Civil Service in Wales*, Institute of Welsh Affairs, Click on Wales, 2012. Anna provides a clear account of the need to increase the size and scope of the Welsh government's Civil Service.
23. This case study covers the WJEC AS Government and Politics Specification Element 1.3.1 How the Government Works in Wales – Collective and Ministerial Responsibility.

Chapter 5

1. Tom Jackson, Clerk to the Assembly, to author, June 2016.
2. 'E-cigarette Law Fails after "Cheap Date" Jibe at Plaid Cymru', *BBC News*, 16 March 2016.
3. Information across the chapter has been supplied by various clerks' offices in the National Assembly for Wales.
4. There have so far been no 'independent' Welsh AMs that were not previously a member of a larger political party. Of the six 'independent' AMs in the Assembly's history John Marek, was formerly a Labour AM who left the party and then stood against Labour over issues concerning his reselection,

as were both Paul and Trish Law; Rod Richards had been suspended from the Conservative Party, where he had been leader and therefore became an 'independent'; and there were similar, but not identical, cases with Lord Elis Thomas (Plaid Cymru) and Nathan Gill (UKIP).

5. Alexander Phillips-Graylings, former head of office to an AM.
6. Russell Deacon, *Devolution in the United Kingdom*, 2nd edn, Edinburgh University Press, 2012, p. 73.
7. Martin Shipton, 'Revealed: One Third of Assembly's 60 AMs have Employed their Own Relatives, *Western Mail*, 9 June 2014.
8. 'UKIP's Neil Hamilton "Had No Part" in Employing Wife', BBC News, 2 November 2016.
9. Welsh Assembly, Code of Conduct, section 3, as at 18 June 20 June 2015.
10. Standards Commissioner Annual Report, 1 April 2013–31 March 2014.
11. Welsh Assembly Code of Conduct for Members, no date.
12. Alun Davies AM to author, March 2015.
13. 'Secret Ballot for Assembly Committee Chairs, Presiding Officer Announces', BBC News, 17 June 2016.
14. Peter Black, 'A Budget Caste in Partnership', Click on Wales, 9 December 2015.
15. This case study covers the WJEC AS Government and Politics Specification Element 1.3.2 How the National Assembly of Wales Works – The Role and Influence of AMs.

Chapter 6

1. Wales Act 2017.
2. The bulk of the development of the law-making process has been provided by the Assembly Communication Team Publications, with some additional material from Martin Shipton, *Poor Man's Parliament: Ten Years of the Welsh Assembly*, Seren, 2011.
3. David Melding, *Will Britain Survive Beyond 2020?*, Institute of Welsh Affairs, 2009, p. 160.
4. British Institute for International and Comparative Law,, *A Constitutional Crossroads: Ways Forward for the United Kingdom*, Bingham Centre for the Rule of Law, May 2015, p. 6.
5. Summary extracts of the Silk Commission, British Institute for International and Comparative Law, *A Constitutional Crossroads: Ways Forward for the United Kingdom*, Bingham Centre for the Rule of Law, May 2015, pp. 6–7, and Commission on Devolution in Wales (Silk II), *Empowerment and Responsibility: Legislative Powers to Strengthen Wales*, March 2014.
6. Secretary of State for Wales, *Powers for a Purpose: Towards a Lasting Devolution Settlement for Wales*, Wales Office, Cm 9020, 2015, p. 8.

7. Silk II, *Empowerment and Responsibility*, p. 9.
8. Welsh government, *A Separate Legal Jurisdiction for Wales*, 2013, p. 2.
9. Welsh government, *A Separate Legal Jurisdiction for Wales*, 2013, p. 2.
10. Russell Deacon, *Devolution in the United Kingdom*, 2nd edn, Edinburgh University Press, 2012, p. 139.
11. National Assembly for Wales, Assembly Commission, Corporate Performance Report of the Assembly Commission, April 2014–March 2015.
12. Finance Committee, *Consideration of Powers: Public Service Ombudsman for Wales*, Report, May 2015.
13. Tom Jackson, Clerk to Welsh Assembly, to author.
14. David Melding AM, Deputy Presiding Officer, to author, 20 July 2015.
15. National Assembly for Wales, *Guide to the Member Bill Process*, March 2011.
16. There are a number of technical ways a Bill could run out of time, but not in exactly the same way as Westminster. For instance, if a Bill (1) requires a financial resolution, and the Welsh government does not move such a resolution within six months of the completion of stage 1, it will fall; (2) has not been passed or approved by the Assembly before the end of the Assembly in which it was introduced, it will fall. For clarity, Royal Assent can occur after dissolution, but the Assembly itself has to have passed and approved the Bill; and (3) was passed and approved by the Assembly, but was then referred to the Supreme Court, which produced a judgment after the end of the fourth Assembly that the Bill was wholly or partly outside the Assembly's competence, there would be no opportunity for a reconsideration stage (because the fourth Assembly had ended), and the Bill would fall. So a Member could potentially elongate the process of a Bill being considered by tabling and speaking to a huge number of amendments. Depending on when a Bill was introduced, this could potentially put it at risk of not being passed before the end of the Assembly (perhaps more so for Private Members' Bills as the dates for stage 3 consideration are determined by the Business Committee). But in reality this did not occur in the fourth Assembly (information supplied by Welsh Assembly Scrutiny Support Team).
17. This case study covers the WJEC AS Government and Politics Specification Element 1.3.2 How the National Assembly of Wales Works – The Legislative Process.

Chapter 7

1. In 2015 the figure was 2,181,800. The median total parliamentary electorate across constituencies in 2015 was about 54,300 in Wales, 66,700 in

Scotland, 68,200 in Northern Ireland and 70,100 in England. Figures are from the Office for National Statistics, Electoral Statistics for the UK, 2015.

2. Ceredigion held a referendum on the issue of a establishing a directly elected mayor in May 2004. The proposal was rejected by over 70 per cent of those who voted.

3. Although the system is called FPTP, confusingly it does not involve the candidate passing a threshold, a 'post'. It simply means that they gain a majority of one vote over the next placed candidate(s).

4. Those wanting to explore the pros and cons of each voting system in greater detail should visit the website of the Electoral Reform Society at: https://www.electoral-reform.org.uk.

5. Russell Deacon, The Welsh Liberals: The History of the Liberal and Liberal Democratic Parties in Wales, Welsh Academic Press, 2014, p. 67.

6. Boundary Commission for Wales, '2018 Review of Parliamentary Constituencies', Initial Report, 2016, p. 2.

7. Richard Wyn Jones, 'How Welsh Labour became the UK's most Invincible Electoral Machine', The Guardian, 6 May 2016.

8. Russell Deacon, Devolution in the United Kingdom, 2nd edn, Edinburgh University Press, 2012.

9. 'Wales Offered Income Tax Powers Without Referendum', BBC News, 25 November 2015.

10. David Moon, 'Welsh Labour in Power: "One Wales" vs. "One Nation"?' Renewal: A Journal of Social Democracy 21(1) (2015): 2013.

11. Anwen Elias, Policy-making Capacities of Political Parties in Wales, Institute of Welsh Affairs, 2012.

12. Russell Deacon, 'Going into Labour: The Welsh Liberal Democrat Coalition Experience 2000–2003', Journal of Liberal History, Liberal Democrat History Group, 83 (Summer 2014).

13. Rosanne Palmer, Stephen Thornton and Mark Crowley, 'Government Formation in the National Assembly for Wales', in Alex Brazier and Susanna Kalitowski (eds), No Overall Control? The Impact of a 'Hung Parliament' on British Politics, Hansard Society, 2008.

14. This case study covers the WJEC AS Government and Politics Specification Element 2.2.2 Electoral Systems in the UK.

Chapter 8

1. Duncan Watts, AQA AS Government and Politics, Nelson Thornes, 2008, p. 123.

2. Adapted from http://legal dictionary.thefreedictionary.com/Lobbying.

3. Wyn Grant, Pressure Groups, Politics and Democracy in Britain, Philip Allen, 1989.

4. Andrew Heywood, *Politics*, 3rd edn, Palgrave Foundations Series, Palgrave Macmillan, 2007, p. 432.
5. Watts, *AQA AS Government and Politics*, p. 137.
6. See at: http://www.tpascymru.org.uk/partnerships-2/homes-for-all-cymru.
7. See at: http://www.disabilitywales.org/projects.
8. See at: http://www.waleslink.org/about.
9. 'New Papers Reveal Hunger Strike Secret of S4C's Birth', BBC Wales News, 30 December 2010.
10. 'The Welsh Farmer Behind the Protest', BBC Wales News, 14 September 2000.
11. 'Tryweryn: 50 Years Since Bombing of Reservoir Dam', BBC Wales News, 10 February 2013.
12. Helen Carter, 'Police take Fresh Look at Sons of Glyndwr', *The Guardian*, 11 March 2004.
13. Adapted from http://www.publicaffairsnetworking.com/what-is-public-affairs.php.
14. Matthew Francis to author, August 2015.
15. Matthew Francis to author, August 2015.
16. IWA Agenda, summer 2009, p. 29.
17. See at: http://www.iwa.wales/about-us/history.
18. 'Public Policy Institute for Wales Set Up to Improve Public Services', BBC Wales News, 27 January 2014.
19. Interview sources to author.
20. Russell Deacon, *The Welsh Office and the Policy Process*, Welsh Academic Press, 2001.
21. Robert Southall, 'The Effects of Devolution on Pressure Groups in Wales', unpublished survey, 2009.
22. Paul Chaney, Tom Hall and Bella Dicks, 'Inclusive Governance', *Contemporary Wales* 13 (2000): 218.
23. Sarah Dickins, 'Measuring Devolution: What Impact on the Economy?' BBC Wales News, 10 June 2014.
24. Cathy Owens, Amnesty International UK, in Southall, 'The Effects of Devolution on Pressure Groups in Wales.
25. Beena Nadeem, 'Inside Housing, The Welsh Revolution',, 20 February 2009.
26. Jocelyn Davies to author, June 2016.
27. Jocelyn Davies to author, June 2016.
28. Jocelyn Davies to author, June 2016.
29. Jocelyn Davies to author, June 2016.
30. Jocelyn Davies to author, June 2016.
31. Matthew Francis to author, August 2015.
32. See at: http://www.bbc.co.uk/news/uk-wales-politics-37949267.

33. See at: http://www.bbc.co.uk/news/uk-wales-politics-38842771.
34. See at: http://www.clickonwales.org/wp-content/uploads/13_Factfile_ Democracy_6.pdf.
35. See at: http://gov.wales/topics/localgovernment/communitytowncouncils/ faqs/?lang=en.
36. Adapted from http://www.wlga.gov.uk/about-us.
37. See at: http://www.gwydir.demon.co.uk/uklocalgov/makeup.htm.
38. See at: http://gov.wales/topics/localgovernment/communitytowncouncils/ faqs/?lang=en.
39. See at: http://apse.org.uk/apse/index.cfm/members-area/briefings/2011/ 11-06-devolved-settlementsdocpdf.
40. Rhys Iorwerth, 'Local Government in Wales: Time for a Change?', in Owain Roberts (ed.), *Key Issues for the Fourth Assembly*, National Assembly Research Service, National Assembly for Wales Commission, 2011, pp. 50–2.
41. See at: http://www.bbc.co.uk/news/uk-wales-politics-37540192.
42. See at: http://www.bbc.co.uk/news/uk-wales-politics-38802658.
43. See at: https://www.citizensadvice.org.uk/wales/law-and-rights/civil-rights/ complaints/how-to-use-an-ombudsman-in-wales-w/#h-what-type-of-complaint-can-the-ombudsman-investigate.
44. This case study covers the WJEC AS Government and Politics Specification Element 2.3.2 Pressure Groups and Participation in Politics. It relates to the ways in which groups combine to influence government in Wales.
45. This case study covers the WJEC AS Government and Politics Specification Element 2.3.2 Pressure Groups and Participation in Politics. This case study examines the benefits and drawbacks of the relationship between pressure groups and government in Wales.

Chapter 9

1. Magnus Gardham, 'Federalism is to the Fore as the Constitutional Debate Re-opens', *The Herald*, 6 June 2015.
2. Stephan Boyce, 'The Draft Wales Bill and the Reserved Powers Model', National Assembly for Wales Research Service, 2015.
3. 'Delivering a Reserved Powers Model of Devolution for Wales', Wales Governance Centre, 2015.
4. The Commission on Devolution in Wales (also known as the Silk Commission), two parts, 2012 and 2014.
5. Ann Sherlock, 'Supreme Court Ruling on Welsh Legislation', UK Constitutional Law Blog, 30 July 2014.
6. George Manon, 'The Supreme Court: A Threat to Devolution', *The Welsh Agenda*, Institute of Welsh Affairs, 54 (spring/summer 2015): 38.

7. 'Draft Wales Bill "English Veto on Welsh Laws", says Jones', BBC News, 20 November 2015.
8. The political dispute over the flooding of the Welsh-speaking village of Capel Celyn to create the Tryweryn reservoir in 1965, despite protests from almost all Welsh politicians, was one of the central focus points of the political campaign for Welsh devolution in the modern era. Welsh politicians were powerless to stop its construction, and in 2017 the Welsh Assembly was given the powers to prevent any such repeat of this in the future.
9. 'Welsh Assembly now Fully-fledged Parliament, Alun Cairns Says', BBC News, 31 March 2017.
10. This case study covers the WJEC AS Government and Politics Specification Element 1.3.2 How the National Assembly of Wales Works – The Power of the National Assembly.

Glossary

1. Some information has been supplied for the definitions directly from the National Assembly's Policy and Legislative Affairs Service.

Bibliography: Suggested Further Reading

Andrews, Leighton, *Wales Says Yes*, Seren, 1999.

Barry Jones, John and Denis Balsom, *The Road to the National Assembly*, University of Wales Press, 2000.

Catt, Helen and Michael Murphy, *Sub-State Nationalism: A Comparative Analysis of Institutional Design*, Routledge, 2003.

Chaney, Paul, *New Governance: New Democracy? Post-Devolution Wales*, University of Wales Press, 2001.

Chaney, Paul, Tom Hall and Bella Dicks, 'Inclusive Governance', *Contemporary Wales* 13 (2000): 203–29.

Deacon, Russell, *The Governance of Wales: The Welsh Office and the Police Process 1964–99*, Welsh Academic Press, 2002.

Deacon, Russell, *Devolution in the United Kingdom*, 2nd edn, University of Edinburgh Press, 2012.

Deacon, Russell, *The Welsh Liberals: The History of the Welsh Liberal and Liberal Democratic Parties in Wales*, Welsh Academic Press, 2014.

Euroscepticism, Information Guide, European Sources Online, Cardiff University, 2013.

Graham Jones, John, *The History of Wales*, Welsh University Press, 2014.

Heywood, Andrew, *Politics*, Palgrave Foundations Series, 3rd edn, Palgrave Macmillan, 2007.

Jones, Bill and Phillip Norton, *Politics UK*, 8th edn, Routledge, 2013.

Lynch, Peter and Paul Fairclough, *AS UK Government and Politics*, 4th edn, Phillip Allan, 2013.

McAllister, Laura, *Plaid Cymru: The Emergence of a Political Party*, Seren, 2001.

Melding, David, *Will Britain Survive Beyond 2020?* Institute for Welsh Affairs, 2009.

Morgan, Kenneth, *Rebirth of a Nation: Wales 1880–1980*, Oxford University Press, 1980.

Morgan, Kenneth, *Wales in British Politics 1868–1922*, University of Wales Press, 1980.

Morgan, Kenneth, *Revolution to Devolution: Reflections on Welsh Democracy*, University of Wales Press, 2014.

Royles, Elin, *Revitalizing Democracy? Devolution and Civil Society in Wales*, University of Wales Press, 2007.

Shipton, Martin, *Poor Man's Parliament: Ten Years of the Welsh Assembly*, Seren, 2011.

Tanner, Duncan, Chris Williams and Deian Hopkin, *The Labour Party in Wales 1900–2000*, University of Wales Press, 2000.

Watts, Duncan, *AQA AS Government and Politics*, Nelson Thornes, 2008.

Index